P9-AQL-786

REREADING CAMARA LAYE

Rereading Camara Laye

ADELE KING

University of Nebraska Press

LINCOLN AND LONDON

Manufactured in the United States of America

Library of Congress Cataloging-in-Publication Data

King, Adele.

Rereading Camara Laye / Adele King.

p.   cm.

Includes bibliographical references and index.

ISBN 0-8032-2752-3 (cloth : alk. paper)

1. Camara, Laye—Criticism and interpretation. I. Title.

PQ3989 .C27 Z728 2002

843'.914—dc21

2002003616

Designed by Jeff Clark at

Wilsted & Taylor Publishing Services

This book is dedicated to my doctors,

John Eliades, Charles Routh, and Nicki Turner,

without whose care it would never have been written

Camara Laye talks a lot about totems and things you could find in ethnology books. I never heard people talking about totems in my own ethnic group. In Camara Laye's book [L'Enfant noir] *the mention of totems is done in such an artificial manner that it is not believable. You have the impression that someone suggested it to him.*

MONGO BETI, *MONGO BETI PARLE*

CONTENTS

ILLUSTRATIONS

ACKNOWLEDGMENTS

For their help with my research, I would like to give special thanks to Lilyan Kesteloot, Simon Njami, and Martin Conway and to librarians in France and in Belgium. Many others have been willing to respond to my inquiries, although some of those listed here would not agree with the conclusions I have reached.

In Belgium: Paula Cheter, Alain Colignon, Jean-Marie Delaunois, Bernard Delcord, L. De Vidts (of L'Auditorat Général près la Cour Militaire), Albert Gérard (†), Franz de Haes, Pierre Halen, Luc Huyse, Marc Laudelout, Bénédicte Ledent, Dirk Martin, Count Ivan du Monceau de Bergendael, Liliane Schraüwen, Jean Stengers, Marie-Linde Tarzia, Fernand Toussaint (†), Pol Vandromme, Chantal Zabus. Also L'Auditorat Général près la Cour Militaire, la Bibliotheque Royale, le Centre de Recherche et d'Études historiques de la Seconde Guerre mondiale.

In Cameroon: Mongo Beti (†), Jeanne Dingomé

In Canada: Ambroise Kom, David Lewis

In Côte d'Ivoire: Alexandre Agbomi

In England: Dorothy Blair (†), Martin Conway, Nicholas Hewitt, James Kirkup, Gerald Moore, Clive Wake

In France: Pascale About, Philippe Pierre Adolphe, Louis Amigues, Pierre Assouline, Georges Barboteu, Leone Barboteu, Raymond Barboteu, Francis Bébey, Anne Blancard, Françoise Bouteiller, Nicolas Buat, Aïcha Camara, Mady Camara, Reine Carducci, Denis Castaing, Tirthankar Chanda, Jacques Chevrier, David Coad, Marcelle Colardelle, André Derval, Madame Alioune Diop, Guy Dupré, F. Durand-Evrard, Liliane Elsen, Michel

Fabre, Bernadette Fournier, Philippe Gaillard, Camille Galic, Guy Georgy, Michel-Claude Jallard, Paulin Joachim, Marie-Louise Joncour, Ibrahima Kaké (†), Madame Ibrahima Kaké, Laminé Kamara, Vanfing Nfaff Doré Koné, Malon Keita Kouyaté, Koffi Kwahulé, José André Lacour, Fanny Lalande, F. Lavinal, D. Letouzey, Cynthia Liebow of Editions Denoël, Henri Lopes, Herbert Lottman, Bernard Mouralis, Henri Mouton (†), Blaise N'Djehoya, Michael Neal, Simon Njami, Chantal Nourrit, Isabelle Palacio, Delphine Parmenter, Jean-Luc Pidoux-Payot, André and Anise Postel-Vinay, Denis Pryen, Elisabeth Rabut, Alain Ricard, René Richard, Robert Sabatier, Pierre Silvain, Thierry Sinda, Jacqueline Sorel, Sami Tchak, Henri Tissen, Olivier Todd, Jacques Tournier, Jean-Jacques Tourteau, Anne Trevarthan, Claude Wauthier, Chantal Weill. Also les Archives de la France d'Outre-Mer at Aix-en-Provence, les Archives de l'Assemblée Nationale, les Archives Départementales de Paris, les Archives du Ministère des Affaires Etrangères, les Archives Nationales du Ministère de la Coopération, la Bibliothèque Administrative de la Ville de Paris, la Bibliothèque Nationale de France, la Bibliothèque Public d'Information, la Caisse Française de Développement, l'Ecole des Hautes Etudes en Sciences Sociales, la Librairie Plon, Peugeot Poissy, la Préfecture de Police de Paris, le Service des Archives du Rectorat de Paris.

In Germany: Ulli Beier, Hans Dieter Klee of Deutsche Welle, Cornelie Kunze, Jacqueline Leiner, Reiner Müller, János Riesz, Katharina Städtler
In Guinea: Cheick Oumar Camara, Mohamed Salif Keita, Marie Lorifo
In Italy: Luisa Benatti
In New Zealand: Patricia Duffy
In Nigeria: Wole Soyinka
In Norway: Ingse Skattum
In Poland: Janusz Krzywicki
In Senegal: Lilyan Kesteloot
In Sierra Leone: Eustace Palmer
In the United States: Irene d'Almeida, Evelyn Barish, Douglas and Linda Jane Barnette, Simon Battestini, Brenda Bertrand, Richard Bjornson (†), Jacques Bourgeacq, Eloïse Brière, Hildegund Calvert, Claire Dehon, Olivier Delers, Latif Diallo, David Dorsey, Jean-François Duclos, Michael Echeruo,

Alain Fresco, Bertram Gordon, Karin Hall, Tony Judt, Lansiné Kaba, Karen Keim, Abdoulaye Keita, Charles Larson, Sonia Lee, Christiane Makward, Karen Offen, P. Rygiel, Eric Sellin, Helen Solanum, Louise Staman, Michael Stevenson, Steven Ungar. Also the Ball State University Office of Academic Research, the Hoover Institution at Stanford University.

Introduction

After the Second World War the French attitude toward their colonial empire began to change. While exploitation of Africans and violent repression of uprisings in Africa continued, increasingly the government and the general public realized that the colonies must be treated more fairly. The Rights of Man should be extended to all. At least in theory there must be parliamentary representation in the colonies and citizenship for all in a French Union (l'Union Française).[1] In this new atmosphere, African writers and intellectuals who advocated assimilation rather than nationalism and favored the ideal of uniting France and its colonial territories in a Greater France, were welcomed and often given support by the Ministère de la France d'Outre-Mer (Ministry of France Overseas).

It was at this propitious moment that Laye Camara, a young student of automotive mechanics who had received only technical education in Guinea, arrived in France. Encouraged by a member of the Assemblée de l'Union Française (Assembly of the French Union) and other members of the government and with help from a young woman interested in African culture, he became one of the earliest modern African novelists, the author of two of the seminal works of African fiction in French and two other less praised books written years later. His first novel, *L'Enfant noir* (1953), holds a position in Francophone African literature similar to that of Chinua Achebe's *Things Fall Apart* (1958) in English; it is a portrait of a classic traditional culture. Unlike Achebe, however, in showing the strength of traditional cultures Laye did not criticize colonization or the continued association of the African territories with France.

L'Enfant noir is a part of African literature courses in many countries and is taught in French schools. It was translated into English in 1955 as *The Dark Child*, later *The African Child*. Laurent Chevallier, who made the novel into a film in 1995, wrote: "The novel, written in 1953, is nowadays a pillar of African culture. Every child in French-speaking Africa has read it, as have many French students since it's part of the programme in schools."[2]

One year after the publication of his first novel, Laye published *Le Regard du roi*, a story of a white man's salvation in Africa. The book was published in English as *The Radiance of the King* in 1956. Many critics considered it one of the greatest works of African literature, a novel that showed African fiction could have a complexity similar to the best modern European writing. Others, however, have found it distant from the usual concerns of African literature. Many remarked on how different it was from *L'Enfant noir*.

When I published the first book about Laye, *The Writings of Camara Laye* (1980), I knew about rumors that he had not written the two famous novels attributed to him, particularly *Le Regard du roi*. I assumed that like most authors he had had editorial help, perhaps more help than others. I regarded such rumors as racial prejudice, as they seemed to assume that Africans were incapable of writing as well as Europeans. Having lived in Nigeria in the presence of Wole Soyinka, Achebe, Christopher Okigbo, and other writers, I had no doubts about the authenticity of the new African literature that was then surprising the world with its quality and originality. Besides, when I met him in 1978, Laye was an exile from the horrors of Ahmed Sékou Touré's Guinea, and he was ill, in need of money for operations; it would have been more than ill-mannered to discuss such rumors with him. We had exchanged letters, and I had been invited to lunch with him and had invited him to a party and to my apartment for dinner. I believed what he told me about his life in Paris during the early 1950s and about the writing of his novels, although I realized that he did not give much specific information. A Nigerian student from Ahmadu Bello University whom I taught had, while studying in Senegal, met Laye; Laye had confided to him that *L'Enfant noir* was written by a white woman. I assumed that Laye meant a girlfriend had helped him revise the manuscript.

After Laye's death in 1980, the situation changed radically. In 1981 Lilyan Kesteloot, in a footnote in an anthology, claimed that Laye told her that a white man had written *Le Regard du roi*.[3] Kesteloot is one of the founders of the study of Francophonic African literature, an authority in the field who teaches most of the year in Africa. I met her, listened to her, and set out to disprove her. I asked, as have others, Who could have written such a good book and not taken credit for it? I wrote to many scholars and friends, including Soyinka, who replied that Kesteloot was a very responsible scholar but that Laye had a mischievous sense of humor.[4] I wanted to believe that Kesteloot had misunderstood.

After I spoke with a number of people, some of whom knew Laye during his years in Paris, and especially after I interviewed Simon Njami in 1994, I realized that Kesteloot was right. Laye had confided the story of *L'Enfant noir* and *Le Regard du roi* to Njami's father, Dr. Simon Bolivar Njami, who had been a professor at the University of Lausanne, Switzerland, from 1955 to 1970. Laye had visited Dr. Njami in Switzerland and told him how the two books were written, speaking of a collaboration among himself and four other people in the writing and publication of *L'Enfant noir*. There was, technically, no one named Camara Laye; Laye used it as his pen name, an inversion of his birth name, Laye Camara.[5] The author "Camara Laye" was a creation of Laye and these four people. Laye also told Dr. Njami that *Le Regard du roi* was not his own work.

Dr. Njami is apparently in possession of all or part of the manuscript of *Le Regard du roi*, but he regards any research into this question as damaging to the validity of African literature. Some younger African writers, however, such as Koffi Kwahulé and Sami Tchak, are aware that the Africa portrayed in *Le Regard du roi* is "mythical."[6]

After nine years, many letters and interviews, and research in available files, I now feel confident that Laye was helped in the composition and writing of *L'Enfant noir* and was given a manuscript of *Le Regard du roi* to which he contributed little. I do not, however, have a smoking gun, and there are gaps where I would like to be able to fill in the details. There were no manuscripts of either *L'Enfant noir* or *Le Regard du roi* to be found. When I met him, Laye was in need of funds, and I suggested that the University of Texas might like to buy his manuscripts. He wanted to sell them the manuscript of his last work, but he did not mention manuscripts for the first two books. While his publisher, Plon, had a file of readers' reports and other documents, Hélène Bourgeois, Laye's editor in the 1970s, told me that Laye's manuscripts had been destroyed in a flood.

In 1978 I did have, without realizing it at the time, several pieces of information about this story. The readers' reports and other official Plon documents showed that Laye had been sponsored by the Ministry of France Overseas even before he had submitted the manuscript of *L'Enfant noir* to the publisher. I had also met André Postel-Vinay, who had arranged a job for Laye with the Central Funding Office of the Ministry of France Overseas in 1954. Postel-Vinay told me that he met Laye because he was a good writer and employed him because he needed help. Later that explanation seemed unlikely, especially after I learned that Postel-Vinay's sister, Marie-Hélène Lefaucheux, was active in the Assembly of the French Union and was one of the four persons Laye had identified to Dr. Njami as involved in the creation and publication of *L'Enfant noir*.

Two others whom Laye had identified to Dr. Njami were Belgians. In August 1992, before I met Dr. Njami's son, I had interviewed Baba Ibrahima Kaké, a noted historian from Guinea who had lived in Paris since 1960. Kaké told me about Francis Soulié, a wealthy Belgian homosexual allied to surrealist literary circles before the Second World War, who befriended Laye in the 1950s and with whom Laye and his first wife, Marie, had lodged. There was, according to Kaké, some influence of Soulié in Laye's writing style. Laye had never mentioned Soulié to me or to any other interviewers.[7] Later I realized that Soulié's address was also the address Laye gave when he submitted the manuscript of *L'Enfant noir* to Plon. The reader at Plon was Robert Poulet. Like Soulié, whom he had known in Belgium in the 1930s, Poulet had escaped to France after being condemned to death for his collaboration as a journalist with the Nazi occupiers.

The fourth person whom Laye mentioned to Dr. Njami, and who visited Njami in Lausanne with Laye in the 1950s, was a young woman. Laye said that she helped him write his memoirs, which became *L'Enfant noir*. I have been told that her name was Aude Joncourt but have little information about her.

The story of *L'Enfant noir* has two related themes: the support the French government, specifically the Ministry of France Overseas, gave to Laye's literary career and to those of others who supported French policy on the overseas territories in the period after the Second World War; and the role of the four persons Laye mentioned to Dr. Njami. Two groups were involved in the publication of this novel: two French women interested in the publication of a book that would present a favorable view of the French Union, on the one hand, and on the other, two Belgians who acted as literary advisors, helping prepare the manuscript for publication. To what extent, if any, these two groups were in contact with each other is not clear.

The story of *Le Regard du roi* differs. The novel is primarily the work of Soulié, a Belgian with a passion for Africa and an unsuccessful literary career. Another Belgian, Poulet, who had a reputation as an excellent literary critic and stylist who would help authors revise their manuscripts, gave advice on the manuscript.

After I started to find the truth I also discovered that some African writers and intellectuals knew or suspected parts of the truth but for various reasons had remained silent or had alluded only vaguely in print to what they knew. It became obvious that the project that had started as perhaps an academic article about the authorship of two novels would require a book, and that book would have the ingredients for a detective novel and scandal.

I did not want a scandal. I knew that some of the information could not be proved. Most of the people directly involved were dead by the time I began my research, and even when I knew manuscripts existed, I could not gain access to them. Still, the story should be told, even if it necessarily will be incomplete in places. It brings to light some extraordinary but formerly little known individuals and examines the French government's involvement in the creation and promotion of areas of modern African culture, showing the extent to which a pliable young African could be encouraged to support the official policy of creating a French Union rather than to advocate African independence. The story also helps to clarify the canon of modern African literature, and it raises questions about the way interpretation and evaluation are shaped by assumptions, in this case by the belief that Laye wrote his first two books without substantial help.

Le Regard du roi, often a highly praised work of African literature, might not have been judged so highly if it had been published anonymously or if it was known to be the work of a European. There have been many, varied interpretations of the meaning of the novel and especially of the final scene, readings that might be different if they were not at least partly based on suppositions about the author. Interpretations of *L'Enfant noir* and *Le Regard du roi* have been influenced by assumptions about the author but also by critics' search for an essential African nature in the two novels, their need to define a "myth" of the continent. The questions of authorship and ethnicity raise many other issues of common sense and theory. As a work of literature, however, *Le Regard du roi* is not less good if written by a European. It is a coincidence, but an illuminating one, that Paul de Man, who, like Soulié, wrote for Belgian newspapers supporting collaboration with the Nazis during the war, was a deconstructive reader who subverted traditional assumptions concerning authorship. Both authors had reasons to hide their past. After the war de Man denied the autobiographical. After the war Soulié wrote under the name of one African and later tried to write under the name of another, Kelefa Keita, whom he adopted.

Some of the story may at first seem improbable. A seminal work of African literature can now be seen as a product of a collaboration of several Europeans with the backing of the French government. A woman known for her work in the French Resistance and two Belgians who had been sentenced to death for collaboration with the Germans were all involved in the literary and political career of the same African.

This book, which began as an attempt to disprove Kesteloot's allegations, has become in part the story of how the French tried to retain control of Africa. It is also the story of an unknown Belgian whose activities during the Second World War were odious but who found through his interest in Africa a way of going far beyond his earlier creative writing.

1

A Historical Context for *L'Enfant noir*

THE FRENCH COLONIAL EMPIRE

At least since the division of Africa in the late nineteenth century, French policy toward its colonies and attitudes about the importance of promoting French culture and continuing ties between the colonies and France were reflected in many areas, including literature. Before almost any literature was written by West Africans in French, there had been a colonial literature, with a moral and political purpose. One periodical, *Outre-Mer*, published in France from 1929 to 1937 and devoted to writing by Frenchmen and Frenchwomen living in the colonies, had a program of advancing the "mission civilisatrice." Having conquered the colonies and brought peace and order, this mission held that it was necessary to "conquer the souls" of the indigenous people. The periodical stressed "[the] necessity for representatives of the race that has reached a higher level of civilization to apply themselves to the study of the characteristics of the less evolved races . . . to understand . . . the native soul."[1] Roland Lebel, in *L'Afrique occidentale dans la littérature française* (1925) and *Histoire de la littérature coloniale en France* (1931), said that colonial literature was not exotic but was based on "scientific" study of the economy, sociology, and ethnography of the colonies. Lebel felt that such literature would usually be written by a Frenchman or Frenchwoman born in the colonies or one who had long lived there, but it could be written by "one of our native subjects, who expresses himself in French of course."[2]

The first black writer outside of metropolitan France to gain a reputation in French literature was René Maran. Neither African nor French, Maran was from the colony of French Guiana and served as an administrative officer in French Equatorial Africa. His novel *Batouala*, which was critical of the effects of colonialism, won the Prix Goncourt in 1921 but was not well received by the colonial services.

Some texts by Africans were incorporated into "colonial" literature soon thereafter, several of which were written in the 1920s and 1930s and published by commercial publishers in Paris. Usually they were not politically radical and thus were accepted by the French public. Neither Bakary Diallo's *Force Bonté* (1926), the autobiographical story of a Senegalese herdsman with a limited education, nor Ousmane Socé Diop's *Karim* (1935) criticize French colonialism. Paul Hazoumé's *Doguicimi*, a historical novel of considerable power published in 1938, ends with a soliloquy on the merits of different European nations. As Dorothy Blair has commented, "This is a period when an African intellectual who has had some success in France would be prepared to whitewash the image of the colonists and present them as having brought a measure of salvation to a primitive people."[3] Other Africans who gained some stature in France before the Second World War include Léopold Sedar Senghor, the first African to earn the *agrégation* (in 1935), and Maximilien Quenum, a professor of philosophy who wrote about the confrontation of traditional and European values.

In addition to writers, there were Africans within the political structure in France before the Second World War, including Senegalese in the Assemblée Nationale (National Assembly). Blaise Diagne was a deputy from the four communes in Senegal as early as 1914. He sponsored a law requiring French citizens in these communes to do military service as did all metropolitan Frenchmen, thus working toward an assimilation of France and Africa. He was supported by Georges Clemenceau, who put him in charge of recruitment in Africa in 1918.[4]

Between the wars the policies of the French government varied, being somewhat more liberal toward Africa during the period of the Popular Front in 1936. Commercial interests often overrode republican principles. Before the Second World War the few "assimilated" West Africans who were part of the French system were not in any way radical; more radical students, however, were already beginning to make political demands, writing of nationalism rather than assimilation.

During the war, after Charles de Gaulle went to London and was condemned for treason by the Vichy government, the first French territory in which the Free French were accepted was Chad, under the orders of the only black governor in the colonies, Félix Eboué, who came from Cayenne, in the colony of French Guiana. De Gaulle recognized the value of having the endorsement of the French empire, even though initially it was only French Equatorial Africa and Cameroon. After the Allied invasion of North Africa in November 1942, the colonies of French West Africa deserted Vichy for de Gaulle and the Allies. In 1940 the capital of Free France moved from Brazzaville to Algiers.

In 1944 de Gaulle opened the Conference of Brazzaville. In its recommendations, the conference representatives insisted on holding together the French empire and dismissed any idea of self-government of the colonies. There was, however, to be administrative decentralization. In spite of contradictions within the recommendations of the conference, it was the first step toward decolonization.[5]

The war effort created some hardships for the African farmers. The French also relied on Africans to fight; more than half of the Free French forces during the first two years of the war were African natives. Soldiers from the colonies were essential to France's role during the war, a contribution that has not always been recognized. De Gaulle sent many of the African troops home in the summer of 1944, so that metropolitan soldiers and Resistance fighters would be given more prominence.[6]

After the war the French continued to enforce administrative rule in West

Africa. Sergeant André Grenard (known as "Matswa"), who had fought for
the French in the Rif War and in 1940 and had been wounded, advocated an African voice in the administration of the empire. He was condemned to forced
labor for life and died in prison in the Congo. Another incident, later the subject of works of post-independence literature, was the massacre at Thiaroye,
Senegal, in 1944 of some "tirailleurs sénégalais" [Senegalese infantrymen]
who had fought for France and were demanding their back salaries.[7]

THE CONSTITUTION AND COLONIAL POLICIES OF THE FOURTH REPUBLIC

The history of the adoption of the Fourth Republic's constitution after the Second World War is complicated and reflects the divisions in French opinion
about what to do with the colonies. The debates in the Premiére Assemblée
Constituante (First Constituent Assembly), convened in Paris, show the atmosphere in France a year before Laye's arrival in Paris, an atmosphere that
partly explains why Laye's pro-France opinions would help him gain support.
In this assembly many of the delegates were products of the Resistance movement; the Communist Party was the largest bloc. Six Africans were among the
sixty-four overseas delegates (divided between white colonists and natives of
the colonies). The debate over the empire was one of the more contentious.
In 1946, according to an American observer, Gordon Wright, "Most educated
Frenchmen possessed some academic knowledge of the size and complexity of
the empire, and were deeply imbued with the conviction that the colonial peoples at heart loved and respected France."[8] Yet the need to convert the empire
into some form of commonwealth was evident, especially to de Gaulle. The
hope that France could retain the status of a major power seemed to depend
upon it having a large base, the "hundred million Frenchmen" of the metropolis, the colonies, and the associated territories.

The Comité Constitutionnel de l'Assemblée (Constitutional Committee of
the Assembly) adopted the phrase "French Union," with a plan for each overseas area to have its own legislature and to be part of the union by "free consent." The overseas areas would, however, continue to send deputies to the
legislature in Paris, a supranational assembly rather than one equal to the colonial legislatures. "The French Union structure which finally emerged from

Committee was a pretty nebulous affair, marred by gaps even more than by inconsistencies."[9] The proposed constitution did include considerable reforms. All inhabitants of the French Union were to have the same rights, the franchise was to be wide, if not universal, and there were to be no seats reserved for European settlers.

On April 19, 1946, the First Constituent Assembly approved this proposed constitution for the Fourth Republic by a vote of 309 to 249. (Senghor and Félix Houphouët-Boigny, who were among the small group of Africans in the assembly, voted for this constitution.) The constitution, however, was rejected by the electorate in May 1946, with 10 million against to 9 million in favor; this was the first referendum ever to be rejected by French voters. (Natives of the colonies, however, voted to approve the constitution.) Rejection was based at least in part on the constitution's demand for a weak executive and a monocameral legislature with strong powers, which many voters feared would give the Communist Party too much strength. There were also, however, fears that the equality of representation would mean that the Civil Code could be decided by polygamous Africans forming a majority.[10]

The Second Constituent Assembly, elected June 2, 1946, was dominated by the Mouvement Républicain Populaire (MRP, a left-wing Christian party newly formed after the war), which had the votes of many of the white colonists. Before this assembly convened, de Gaulle, who had retired as president, gave a speech at Bayeux on June 16, in which he proposed his ideas for a Grand Conseil de l'Union Française to deliberate problems of the union in the areas of budgets, foreign affairs, defense, and the economy, with a president who would also be president of France. While the Communists and Socialists wanted to build a federal French union from below, the MRP, with ideas similar to those of de Gaulle, felt that positive imperial bonds should be created at once from the top.

The constitution written by the Second Constituent Assembly gave much less power to the overseas colonies and territories than had the earlier one. The franchise for the colonies was smaller, and the electoral roll was arranged so that the African majority would be narrow. The native peoples of the colonies were to be "citizens of the French Union," not full-fledged French citizens. Decrees did, however, abolish forced labor and recognize freedom of the press and the right to form trade unions. In addition, the colonies were to receive

funds from the metropolis. This constitution was accepted by the electorate in October 1946, although by a minority of the population, as there were many abstentions. (White colonists tended to vote no; natives of the colonies voted yes, believing they could not do better at the time.) African representatives in the National Assembly after 1946, only a small percentage of whom were African natives, included 83 deputies to represent 62 million people; there were 544 deputies for the 50 million citizens of metropolitan France.

The preamble to the constitution of the Fourth Republic states, "France forms with the populations overseas a Union based on equality of rights and duties, without distinction of race or religion."[11] The French Union included metropolitan France, the overseas departments and territories, and associated territories and states (this latter category included Tunisia, Morocco, and, of particular importance, Indochina). The constitution also established the Assembly of the French Union, composed half of representatives from France and half of representatives from overseas. The Assembly of the French Union considered proposals to transmit to the National Assembly, but it had no real power. According to some historians, it served as an outlet for candidates who did not win election to the National Assembly. Even among the delegates from the associated states and the colonies, some were not indigenous to the countries they represented. Delegates from Guinea in 1957, for example, included two white Frenchmen as well as two deputies born in Guinea. African politicians, like the French, preferred to sit in the National Assembly.

After the war, the Ministère des Colonies (Ministry of the Colonies) became the Ministry of France Overseas, a name change that did not reflect any policy change on the part of the government, which still wanted to retain the colonies. Independence movements were beginning to make claims, however, in Africa and particularly in French Indochina. Among students from French West Africa and Cameroon were some, such as Mongo Beti, who criticized French colonial policy and already advocated independence. Laye was not one, nor were many African intellectuals at the time; they saw the advantages of remaining within the French Union. Bernard Dadié, the Ivoirian writer, in an undated document of this period, wrote: "Far be it from us to underestimate all the contradictions and faults of the French Union. . . . But that doesn't contradict the fundamental principle of the alliance of the proletariat and the masses in the colonies resulting from capitalist imperialism, and the possibility of effecting such an alliance within the framework of the French Union."[12]

With the war in Indochina, and especially after the French defeat at Dien Bien Phu in 1954, the end of the French Union was already in sight. Even earlier, the union had no chance. It was suspect to many conservative leaders, especially when movements toward independence were supported by the Communist Party during the Cold War. In contrast to many rank-and-file militants, moderate leaders among the Socialists and MRP leaders were less than enthusiastic about moves toward independence. It was a firm supporter of the French Union, Marie-Hélène Lefaucheux, who played an essential role in the publication of *L'Enfant noir*.

In 1956, the year that the war in Algeria became increasingly a war of parties within France, Gaston Defferre, minister of France overseas, promulgated a *loi cadre*, which created local legislatures in sub-Saharan Africa, and "conseils de gouvernement," in which the governor was French but the vice president was African. France was trying to prevent wars of independence in sub-Saharan Africa, trying to preserve the French Union.

AFRICAN LITERATURE IN THE 1940S AND 1950S

After the war, literature in French from the colonies slowly began to prosper. Many French liberals and intellectuals were interested in Africa at this time. The first Francophone African poets published in France were well received. Senghor published two volumes with the prestigious Editions du Seuil in the 1940s (*Chants d'ombre*, 1945, and *Hosties noires*, 1948). His influential *Anthologie de la nouvelle poésie nègre et malgache*, with a preface by Jean-Paul Sartre, appeared in 1948. Dadié (*Afrique debout*) and Keita Fodeba (*Poèmes africains*) published volumes of poetry with Seghers in 1950. Both Senghor and Dadié later held important positions in West African governments, positions for which, to some extent at least, they were being prepared by the French colonial authorities. French interest in black culture is also evident in the reception given to Richard Wright's *Black Boy* in 1948 and to the popularity of American jazz.

Five years before the appearance of *L'Enfant noir*, Corrêa published *Je suis*

Martiniquaise, a book by Mayotte Capécia, a Martinican mulatto woman. The book became popular because of French interest in exotic culture. Interestingly, Capécia, who was at best semiliterate when she arrived in France in 1946, gave explanations for her work similar to those Laye was later to offer. In *Je suis Martiniquaise*, Capécia wrote that the winter weather in France gave her a nostalgia for her island and the desire to write her memories of her childhood.[13] In an interview she added, "I had about enough to live on for a month or two. I was desperately (and with no success) looking for a job when, one day, while walking in the Luxembourg, I had the idea to . . . tell my life in a book." This quote was included in a review of Capécia's second book, *La Négresse blanche*, which the reviewer introduced with words similar to those Laye used in talking about *Le Regard du roi*. The reviewer believed that Capécia wanted to prove that she was not the author of a single autobiographical book but a real writer.[14]

Apart from poetry, not much creative writing by Africans was published before *L'Enfant noir*. Published prose included folk tales by Quenum (*Trois légendes africaines*, 1946) and by Birago Diop, whose *Contes d'Amadou Koumba* shared the Grand Prix Littéraire de l'Afrique Occidentale Française in 1947. Concerned with traditional culture, these works would not have seemed threatening to the French political establishment.

Présence Africaine was founded in Paris in 1947 to promote African culture. The group's journal, *Présence africaine*, did not publish many novels during its early years, although its first issue included a segment of *Nini*, a novel by the Senegalese writer Abdoulaye Sadji about the life of a young mulatto girl in Saint-Louis. In 1954 *Présence africaine* published a special issue titled "Trois écrivains noirs," which included the complete *Nini* and another work from an older generation, Jean Malonga's *Coeur d'aryenne*, as well as Beti's *Ville cruelle*. Malonga was a member of the National Assembly from 1946 to 1951. His novel is perhaps the earliest of the novels protesting against colonialism. Beti's novel is a dark picture of oppression in Cameroon. The *Présence africaine* issue was less favorably received than was *L'Enfant noir*.

After the publication of *L'Enfant noir* in 1953, several African authors published with mainstream French publishers. Ferdinand Oyono's *Une Vie de boy* and *Le Vieux Nègre et la médaille* both appeared with Julliard in 1956, the same year that Beti's *Le Pauvre Christ de Bomba* was published with Robert Laffont and Dadié's *Climbié* appeared with Seghers.

Claude Wauthier, the distinguished French writer and journalist, told me that the French encouraged African writers, because writing books was seen as proof of the success of the colonial system of education. The interest the French government displayed toward Laye was part of a long policy within the French government of promoting Africans who would believe in the French Union and not seek political independence.

The French often had a feeling of competition with Britain. The idea of the French Union seems somewhat modeled on the British Commonwealth. In the Assembly of the French Union in 1949, a representative said that if the United Kingdom could establish a university in Nigeria, France should do so in Cameroon. The earliest West African novel in English published by a major London publisher was Amos Tutuola's *The Palm Wine Drinkard*, which appeared in 1952, a year before *L'Enfant noir*.

FRANCE'S CONTINUED ROLE IN AFRICA

During the period between 1950 and 1960 (and continuing after "independence" in 1960), the Ministry of France Overseas had several areas for technical and cultural cooperation, including education, literacy programs, training of professional staff, and schoolbooks. The Bureau pour l'Enseignement de la Langue et de la Civilisation Française à l'Étranger (BELC) was one of the instruments for promoting French language and culture.[15]

French schoolchildren were indoctrinated with the mentality of the French Union through such publications as *La Belle Histoire de l'Union Française*. It includes many pictures of exotic scenes, praises Eboué's role during the war, cites Vincent Auriol at the opening of the Maison de la France d'Outre-Mer at the Cité Universitaire in Paris, and concludes, "We have undertaken a moral commitment to our faithful overseas territories during the war; in addition, we had to take into account the deep changes brought by France's activities in the minds and customs of the indigenous peoples, through education and social reforms."[16]

France continued its cultural colonization of Africa well after independence. Files in the archives of the Secrétariat of the Ministry of France Overseas include, for example, many documents concerning theatrical tours and radio programs to be sent to Dahomey between 1960 and 1972. The Office of Coopération Radiophonique (OCORA) produced programs and handled remuneration of French personnel in Dahomey (although Dahomey wanted these funds to be deposited in the national treasury). Even after Guinean independence in 1958 there was an attempted agreement on technical cooperation between France and Guinea in 1963.[17] Guinea was to use OCORA for assistance in its national radio system. OCORA was to provide cultural and educational programs and a studio-school for training personnel. In September, the director of Radio Guinée asked to send five or six apprentices to study with OCORA. Although the minister for cooperation liked the idea, the protocol was never signed. In spite of Sékou Touré's rejection of the French Union, the French were still interested in considering some form of cultural indoctrination. The director of OCORA did add, in a letter to the minister for cooperation, that it would be a good idea to say that France would use Guinean programs, to give the agreement less of a tone of an order.

Among the organizations that received some support, if indirectly, from the French ministry was the Congress of Black and African Writers, which met twice, in Paris in 1956 and in Rome in 1959. The first congress was opened by Alioune Diop, the director of Présence Africaine; the chairman was Dr. Jean Price-Mars, then the rector of the University of Haiti. Speakers included prominent African, Caribbean, and American writers—Senghor, Hazoumé (who was also an advisor for the French Union), Jacques Rabemananjara, Aimé Césaire, and Frantz Fanon. Messages of support were received from such European anthropologists and scholars of African culture as Claude Lévi-Strauss, Father Placide Tempels, and the Reverend Jean Danielou. The second congress included many of the same speakers, as well as Cheikh Anta Diop. Among those who sent messages of support were political leaders of different persuasions—Patrice Lumumba, Sékou Touré, Eric Williams, and François Duvalier as well as Basil Davidson and Arnold Toynbee. Pope John XXIII gave an address. The level of support from centers of power and prestige in Europe for Africans of moderate political aspirations is evident. *Présence africaine* had, among its Comité de Patronage, André Gide and Emmanuel Mounier, as well as Albert Camus, Sartre, Michel Leiris, Hazoumé, and Richard Wright. Among its regular contributors were Georges Balandier and Roger Bastide.

FRANÇOIS MITTERRAND AND AFRICA

The career of François Mitterrand reflects the shifting thoughts of French political figures on the relationship of France to the former colonies. After the war, as a member of the Union Démocratique et Socialiste de la Résistance (UDSR), Mitterrand was strongly anticommunist and believed that African nationalism was a product of Communist Party propaganda. He managed to woo members of the African Rassemblement Démocratique Africain (RDA) from the Communist Party to his own UDSR. He got Houphouët-Boigny, the deputy from the Côte d'Ivoire, to sign a letter committing himself to "French authority."[18] Mitterrand had visited French West Africa in 1949, and from July 1950 to February 1951 he was minister of France overseas in the government of René Pleven. He said later of these months, "It is in effect the major experience of my political life because it began my evolution."[19] He resigned as minister delegated to the Council of Europe in 1953 over the way Georges Bidault, then minister of foreign affairs, handled a crisis in Morocco.

In *Aux Frontières de l'Union Française* (1953), Mitterrand wrote of the "worlds" (he does not use the word "empire") acquired by the European powers as a result of determination and "heroism," although he added that much French "heroism" was misdirected. Africans fighting for France during the Second World War proved, he wrote in 1953, that there was no separation, that the French Union would endure. "Africa loves France and hopes to find from her its unity, balance and ideal." "There is an intelligent young generation which is fond of the lessons of our culture."[20] Mitterrand believed that Black Africa was evolving calmly but also that North Africa was strongly linked to France, an obviously optimistic prediction in 1953.

Mitterrand was not, of course, blind to the independence movements, and he was well aware of the dangers that the war in Indochina posed for the French presence in Africa. (In May 1954, within a year of the publication of *Aux Frontières de l'Union Française*, France suffered military and political de-

feat at Dien Bien Phu.) He suggested that the policy for Africa must be reconsidered, must not repeat the mistakes of Southeast Asia. The French Union that
he envisaged would need to be different from the empire. He advocated a federal solution with internal autonomy and an interdependent economy and with
Paris as the "necessary capital" of the union. The union would be essentially a
military, diplomatic, and economic entity, but there would also be internal autonomy for each of the constituent parts. As minister of the interior under
Pierre Mendès-France in 1954, however, Mitterrand sent paratroopers into Algeria to put down a militant revolt. He said at that time: "Algeria is France.
From Flanders to the Congo, there is one law, one nation." For Mitterrand, but
also for many of the political leaders in Africa for some years, there was to be
a "Euroafrican" France, composed of 85 million inhabitants. Geographically
it was a "colossal mass which, from Lille to Brazzaville and from Abéché to
Dakar, covers seven thousand kilometers in length and three thousand in
width."[21]

Since Mitterrand had been the minister of France overseas in 1950 and minister of the interior under Mendès-France in 1954–55, and since Laye mentioned to me his gratitude to Mitterrand, it is possible that one of the sources
of support for *L'Enfant noir* in the government was the future president of
France. The novel would obviously fit into an aim of giving a favorable picture
of the life of the indigenous people of Guinea, of showing life in French West
Africa in terms of the benefits of colonization. The character Laye in *L'Enfant
noir* was grateful for the help he had received from the colonial administration
in being awarded a scholarship to France. There is no mention in the novel of
forced labor or production quotas during the war. If Laye had not known of
such problems as a young Guinean, he presumably learned more about the history of French colonization while in France. Throughout his life, however, he
remained convinced that the French had brought many good things to West
Africa, that colonization had been beneficial. Yet, because Guinea became independent in 1958, Laye never received the support given to other African
writers in the 1960s.

With the independence of the countries in the former French West Africa
and French Equatorial Africa in 1960, French policy did not change radically.
A paternalistic attitude continues. Not surprisingly, Senghor wrote in 1988,
"since African nations became independent in the 1960s, Francophone African

literature, including that of the Maghreb, is being taught in the schools, even in France. And it will be taught ever more widely *when* the French-speaking countries are recognized as a political reality."[22] As Nicolas Buat, a French civil servant to whom I spoke in 1999, said, "We gave them independence so as not to have to give them French nationality. Otherwise little has changed."

According to both Beti and Guy Dupré, an editor at Plon, those in the conservative political milieus of the 1950s would have approved the opinions Laye expressed. Plon, like the French government, would have been interested in *L'Enfant noir* because it was not an attack on France.[23] The novel offered a portrait of a traditional but mysterious African culture, which was implicitly contrasted with the modern world that Africans would learn from France. It was a portrait of the "African soul" that was acceptable to the French intelligentsia but unacceptable to African militants striving in the 1950s for independence from France.

2

The Life of Laye Camara

Laye Camara was born in Kouroussa, Guinea, to a Malinké family, on January 1, 1928 (the date may be an approximation). He was the eldest of twelve children. His father, a blacksmith, occasionally went on Sufi retreats. Laye did well in the colonial primary school and was sent to the Ecole Georges Poiret, a technical school in Conakry, at the age of fourteen. While in Conakry, he stayed with the family of his uncle, Mamadou Camara. His own parents were illiterate, but this uncle had been educated in the French system. Through his uncle he met Marie Lorifo, whose father was half Corsican and who became his first wife. Laye came first in the final examinations for the Certificat d'Aptitude Professionnelle de Mécanicien in 1947 and was given a scholarship to pursue studies in automotive mechanics in a school in Argenteuil, in the suburbs of Paris.

L'Enfant noir tells the story of Laye's early life. The novel, while basically autobiographical, is highly fictionalized and structured to create a pattern typical of the life of a young boy in Guinea. Many details, particularly about Laye's life in Conakry and his uncle's connections, remain vague. For example, his uncle knew the family of Kelefa Keita from Kankan, whose financial support allowed Laye to go to France, but this is not mentioned in the novel.

There was a small group of students from West Africa in France at the time Laye arrived, probably only a few dozen from Guinea.[1] Unlike other West Africans of his generation, who had received more formal education in Africa and were being trained in French universities for professions, Laye had not earned a higher school diploma in Guinea. After his scholarship year, reluctant to return to Guinea and anxious to continue his studies, he drifted into various jobs over a period of several years. He was employed in the Simca factory in Nanterre from May 15 to July 13, 1951, as an "Ouvrier Spécialisé" in the assembly line of the "Simca Aronde."[2] He also enrolled at the Conservatoire National des Arts et Métiers (National Conservatory of Arts and Crafts). At that time, the conservatory had approximately seven thousand students. The basic courses were in mathematics, physics, and chemistry.

At about the same time Laye met a young woman who helped him compose a manuscript of his memoirs. In an obituary for Laye, Mamadou Traoré Ray Autra, who directed Laye's research in Senegal, wrote that at the Simca factory or in Paris (the obituary is not clear) Laye met "une jeune française [*sic*] professeur de lettres, à qui il raconte l'histoire de sa vie" [a young Frenchwoman, a teacher of literature, to whom he told the story of his life].[3] Laye never mentioned the name of this woman, but I have been told it was Aude Joncourt. Joncourt's father was a high-ranking French civil servant. Dr. Njami met this young woman when she accompanied Laye to Lausanne in the 1950s, sometime after the publication of *L'Enfant noir*. Joncourt had lived in Africa and was highly educated and very rich. She was perhaps a musician.[4]

Before 1955, the few Africans in Paris found considerable hospitality from liberal French men and especially women. Some of the hospitality Laye received came from Marie-Hélène Lefaucheux, who was interested in Africa and in promoting the French Union. She was the sister of André Postel-Vinay, the French civil servant who was later to help Laye in finding a job with the Caisse Centrale de la France d'Outre-Mer, the funding office for the colonies. (Although Laye mentioned Postel-Vinay to me, he did not mention Lefaucheux.) Besides supporting Laye's writing, she undoubtedly helped him obtain the job with Simca in 1951, as her husband was the director of Renault.

Laye told interviewers about the various odd jobs he did to survive in Paris, but he did not talk much about his connections with the French government, particularly the Ministry of France Overseas, in the period before the publication of *L'Enfant noir*. At some point after he came to France, however, Laye met some members of the French colonial administration, probably through Lefaucheux. This part of the story remains rather clouded, but he met her before he got the job at Simca in 1951 and thus before the manuscript was finished, or perhaps even started. Lefaucheux was, if not the first to suggest publication of the manuscript, the person whose interest led to French government support. There are many other indications of the interest that the French government took in Laye, interest that started before he submitted the manuscript of *L'Enfant noir* to Plon.[5]

According to his comments in several interviews, Laye came in contact with two persons who encouraged him to write, whose names he gave as Madame Baraboteur and Monsieur Gally: "We were entrusted to a lady in Paris called Madame Baraboteur. She had an orchestra, she played the piano; I did my work quietly; and later she saw it and read it and said, 'This is interesting, we are going to publish it!' "[6]

It is doubtful that Baraboteur is a real name. The archives of France Overseas informed me there had been no one by the name of Baraboteur with the ministry. It is an unusual name. A member of the family Barboteu (the closest spelling I could find in any archives) who was interested in genealogy had no idea who this Madame Baraboteur could have been. There was a Raymond-Julien Gallet who gave courses at l'Ecole Nationale de la France d'Outre-Mer about 1954.[7]

Laye wrote that he was encouraged by a friend, who read what he had written. Others tell a slightly different story. Tierno Diallo, a friend of Laye's who met him in Paris in the late 1940s, said Laye was encouraged by someone in the ministry and then by his editor at the publishers.[8] Laye eventually submitted a manuscript to Plon. It was published as *L'Enfant noir* in 1953.

According to the contract that Laye signed with Plon on July 9, 1953, he was to receive seventy thousand francs (old francs, of course, not a great sum, the equivalent of seven hundred francs at present) and 10 percent royalties on the first five thousand copies. The novel won the Charles Veillon prize, given in Switzerland, in 1954, worth five thousand Swiss francs.[9]

On July 16, 1953, Laye submitted a publicity form to Plon, giving some biographical information. At that time he was studying at the Ecole Technique d'Aéronautique et de Construction Automobile (Technical School for Aeronautics and Automobile Construction). The form included a request for a photograph, with a suggestion of a photographer to use. This line, which included the photographer's address, was crossed out on the form Laye completed. On a copy of the handwritten form, which was then typed at Plon, someone added on the line for the photographer, "Ministère," another indication of the ministry's interest in Laye. It is also worth noting that the contract was signed only four days after the first reader's report, from Robert Poulet, was submitted.

Poulet mentioned in his report that the Ministry of France Overseas wanted to see this work published. (How Poulet knew this is, of course, another question, to which I will return later.) The ministry's interest stemmed from concerns larger than Laye's possible friendship with two ministry employees, Baraboteur and Gallet. The reasons for this interest are, in hindsight at least, evident. Here was a young African (only twenty-five when the contract for *L'Enfant noir* was signed), by all accounts with a charming and open personality, who was far from a radical demanding quick independence for his country, who rather naively believed in a brotherhood of man to be accomplished through the French Union. He needed financial support to stay in France. Evidence from *Dramouss* suggests that his main contact with those who could provide funds was Lefaucheux, who was a model for Tante Aline in that novel.

When he submitted the manuscript to Plon, Laye gave his address as 15 rue Molière, an apartment belonging to Francis Soulié. When Laye met Soulié can no longer be established with certainty, especially because Soulié's own arrival in France was clandestine, and he later gave various dates to the police. Marie Lorifo, Laye's first wife, told me that she thought Laye met Soulié in the Latin

Quarter, perhaps at a bar. When he moved to Soulié's apartment is never mentioned. Information obtained by Roger Mercier and Monique and Simon Battestini for their 1964 book includes the notation that Laye worked on *L'Enfant noir* in his room in the sixth arrondissement. Laye told me in 1978 that he lived near the Porte d'Orléans, in the fourteenth arrondissement. He perhaps changed addresses several times before moving into Soulié's apartment. Laye never mentioned who owned the "tiny apartment on the rue Molière" where he said he lived until 1955.[10] In a conference paper delivered in Dakar, Senegal, Laye said that he wrote *L'Enfant noir* while living in poverty in a underheated room, trying, under the bare lightbulb in a poor room, to recapture the sun of Guinea. The Senegalese novelist Boubacar Boris Diop parodied this story in *Le Temps de Tamango*, where a narrator says, "Each time I stand at the window of my apartment, I color everything black and I see again my native land."[11] It is doubtful that Soulié, who had considerable funds, would have had an apartment of the sort Laye described. In May 1952 Soulié himself lived in the small apartment at 15 rue Molière, according to police records, or at least that was his official address.

Laye told me and others that he rewrote the manuscript of *L'Enfant noir* seven times. In an interview with Radio France in 1954, he said that he had to adopt a certain tone in the novel, which meant that some of his memories of Guinea could not be used.[12] The Frenchwoman Joncourt helped him by writing down his memories, but he could not use all his memories within the structure they decided upon. He also worked over drafts with the help of others, including both Poulet, whose assistance he mentioned, and Soulié, about whom he never spoke. (Later, Laye's daughter Aïcha told me she remembered typing parts of *Le Maître de la parole* many times as her father revised.)

In February 1954 Laye returned to West Africa for a short visit with his family in Kouroussa, Kankan, and Conakry. In an interview with a reporter for *Paris-Dakar*, February 6, 1954, Laye said he was still studying at the Ecole Aéronautique, that he was going to finish his second book (then titled "Ciel d'Afrique"), and that he was writing a report on his trip to Guinea (never published to my knowledge).[13] During this trip to Africa he was given a special reception by the governor-general of French West Africa in Dakar, Bernard Cornut-Gentille, to whom Laye's second novel would be dedicated.[14] Although there is no record of how Laye obtained the money for this trip, as he was still a student, undoubtedly he was helped by the Ministry of France Overseas.

The contract for Laye's second novel, *Le Regard du roi*, is dated September 8, 1954, and sets the same advance and royalty provisions as for *L'Enfant noir*. The novel was published in November 1954. The initial reviews of *Le Regard du roi* in Europe were very favorable. Several critics commented on the many parallels to the work of Franz Kafka.

On November 8, 1954, a week before the publication of *Le Regard du roi*, Laye was interviewed on Radio France. The interviewer spoke of the great success of *L'Enfant noir*. Laye said that his new book was about "the discovery of Africa by a white man, a response to *L'Enfant noir*." He then read a piece about how he discovered the importance of African sculpture while studying in Paris and visiting the Musée de l'Homme and described his father's work as a sculptor. There is no further mention in the interview of *Le Regard du roi*. Beti, who was a student in Aix-en-Provence in the 1950s, heard Laye on the radio and thought that he expressed himself poorly, reading a prepared text and not replying to questions. In an interview Beti explained, "When you heard Camara Laye talking on the radio about his book [*L'Enfant noir*], you wondered: 'Has he even read his book?' The rumor about Camara Laye seems to be plausible. One might say there was a team of ghost writers who wrote *L'Enfant noir*."[15]

On June 7, 1955, Charles Orengo, the director of Plon, wrote to inquire whether Laye was going to write a documentary report about Africa, as he felt such a book would have large sales. Orengo also mentioned that Plon had given a young French producer, G. Rosetti, an option until October for filming *L'Enfant noir*. Orengo later wrote to Rosetti suggesting that the executive board of Fonds d'Investissement pour le Développement Economique et Social (FIDES) might offer financial support for the film and recommending that Rosetti send his scenario to the director of the Caisse Centrale de la France d'Outre-Mer.[16] Although the name is not mentioned in the letter, this director was André Postel-Vinay, who gave Laye financial support for several years.

At some point during this period Laye was married. Laye told me that he brought Marie Lorifo to Paris before the publication of *L'Enfant noir* in 1953. He was often rather vague about dates, and this is almost certainly an error, since a reporter in Dakar in February 1954 referred to Marie as his fiancée.[17]

They were married in a Muslim ceremony that did not require her presence. Alain Fresco, who interviewed Laye in 1977, gave the date of the marriage as November 10, 1955, when Laye was in Paris. Fresco commented on the "contradictory statements that Camara himself made at various times" about his life in Paris.[18]

Laye's comments about writing while lonely in Paris contradict what Marie later told a friend. Laye, she said, would read a few pages of *L'Enfant noir* to her, and if she seemed unhappy, he would destroy the text. He might rewrite the same paragraph fourteen times. (Marie's comment was quoted to me by a friend of Laye's to prove that he wrote *L'Enfant noir*. The letter is an example of the lack of rigorous examination of the evidence by many critics of African literature.) It is difficult to reconcile this statement with those in which he speaks of his loneliness. It is also, however, impossible that Laye read the manuscript of *L'Enfant noir* to Marie, if, as Laye told Fresco in 1977, she was still in Africa when the book was published. It is possible that Marie was referring to *Dramouss*, as she was living with Laye when that novel was written.

Marie lived with Laye in the studio at 15 rue Molière that belonged to Soulié for, she said, about two years. Soulié also had a residence in Chantilly, Oise, where he lived after Marie's arrival and where Marie and Laye visited him occasionally. Soulié did not give up the studio, according to police reports, until he moved to 50 rue des Francs-Bourgeois in 1957. Laye was then attached to the Ministère de la Jeunesse (Ministry of Youth) until he returned to Guinea in 1956. Laye's work for the Ministry of Youth primarily involved doing radio broadcasts.

Mendès-France was prime minister from June 1954 to February 1955. According to Paul Bernard, it was Mendès-France who asked Laye to work for the Ministry of Youth.[19] Fresco quoted Laye on this work: "I was given this mission by the French Prime Minister. It was during the government of Mendès-France. At that time France had difficulties with Indochina, Morocco, Tunisia, etc. . . . He wanted a man with a cool temperament, a young person who could undertake missions and could if necessary speak of these countries. . . . So, even if I wanted to study, for reasons of state it was necessary to quit my schooling to serve the government, since that government at the time was my government, as Guinea was not independent."[20] This interview is, I believe, the only time Laye mentioned undertaking missions for Mendès-France. I have found no independent verification of this appointment. Laye's interview appears to exaggerate to some extent his importance as a diplomat. He was only twenty-six or twenty-seven at the time, with no formal training beyond automotive mechanics. But it does show that he felt he had a role serving the colonial policy of the French government.

During this same period Laye published an article on being an African in Paris, "Premiers Contacts avec Paris," in *Bingo* (Dakar). It is addressed to Africans who may come to France and begins with a description of the noise and bustle that first greets a visitor from Africa. Soon, however, this visitor is changed by his experience, becomes in a sense a Parisian. "We are influenced, whether we want to be or not, by the prestige of a city which has a long and glorious past and admirable monuments which witness today to that past. . . . It is a great prestige that we should keep within us, which can and must serve, just as science learned at its most authentic source will serve, in the building of our native land."[21] The article suggests that Laye appreciated the culture he found in Paris. It is written in a style similar to Laye's other work of the period, with hesitations such as "j'allais dire" [I was going to say].

Another of Laye's works of this period is "Les Yeux de la statue," a short story with a clear relationship to the spirituality and surrealistic atmosphere evident in *Le Regard du roi*. Published in *Présence africaine* in 1957 but written earlier, the story creates a dreamlike atmosphere with few realistic details.[22] Except that the main character, a woman, is wearing a "pagne" [wrapper], there is nothing to establish the setting as African. The story can be read as a reversal of some elements of *Le Regard du roi*, as the woman feels drawn to visit the ruins of a city, where she looks at a statue of the prince who built the palace. The "regard" [look] of the statue expresses solitude, emptiness, a search. It seems that the statue is looking for her as much as she is looking for the statue. Instead of finding peace, however, she feels her skull being crushed as she is caught by a rising tide of thistles, which she compares to an ocean. Her search leads to death, without fulfillment; the ocean engulfs her. The statue does not present the fragility and love of the king in *Le Regard du roi* but rather is gigantic and without warmth.

Laye never mentioned a second short story, "Le Prince," which was published under his name in 1954 in *La Table ronde*, a right-wing literary magazine published by Plon. The story was not listed in bibliographies of Laye's work and was unknown to critics until Eric Sellin discovered it in 1981.[23] "Le Prince" is told in the first person by a man who, with his friend (but perhaps, he speculates, he and his friend are the same person), meets a young man at a fair on the beach. When they realize that the young man is in fact the prince of the country, who will be crowned ruler in the morning, they try to protect him. Eventually he leaves them, his youth about to vanish under the strain of his responsibilities. The narrator looks across at the mountain—the country of enemies—and worries about the prince's ability to defend his people. He decides that the mountain "ne pourrait plus rien détruire qui ne fût détruit déjà" [could no longer destroy anything that was not already destroyed].[24] The pessimism is similar to that of "Les Yeux de la statue," in contrast to *Le Regard du roi*. Both stories are set in lands only vaguely African. The obsessive concern with royalty in this story, rather like that of *Le Regard du roi*, seems less like Laye's than like that of the two Belgians who helped him, as the position of the Belgian king during the Second World War was used as a justification for collaboration with the Nazi occupiers. The king of Belgium did not defend his people against the Germans but cooperated with them, perhaps realizing how much was "already destroyed."

Both of these stories have the very tentative style—uncertainty indicated by "peut-être" [perhaps], with many questions and repetitions—common to *L'Enfant noir* and especially *Le Regard du roi*. The *imparfait du subjonctive* is used frequently. Both stories, like *Le Regard du roi*, involve the relationship of a rather hesitant, uncertain person with a divine figure—the prince, the statue, the king. In each case this figure is unknowable and is described in part in terms of his eyes. In each of the stories, as well as in *Le Regard du roi*, there is a palace, with corridors that seem unending. Physical movement through a labyrinthian structure symbolizes the spiritual quest of the main character. A reader's report on "Les Yeux de la statue" states that it is not as good as "Le Prince," indicating that both stories were submitted to Plon, probably around the same time.

In 1957 another article was published in *Présence africaine* under the name of Camara Laye. "Et demain?" is about what to retain from Western technology and what to keep of traditional culture; it advocates the necessity of building high-rise apartments in the cities of Africa. While this idea and the description of housing in Conakry may be Laye's, several of the comments cannot be his but must come from the pen of Soulié, the Belgian art critic and victim of the purges after the Second World War:

> ces autres victimes de la mode, pour lesquelles l'art abstrait est soudaine-ment devenu le fin du fin, et qui, se figurant être à la pointe de l'avant-garde, ne se doutent pas un instant qu'elles sont revenues, trente ou trente-cinq ans en arrière, aux premiers balbutiements du cubisme; et encore savons-nous que ces balbutiements, alors, n'étaient pas déraisonnables, mais une bonne médecine pour se débarrasser du flottement impressionniste.[25]
>
> [*these other victims of fashion, for whom abstract art has suddenly become the ultimate end and who, thinking they are at the height of the avant-garde, don't suspect for a moment that they have gone back, thirty or thirty-five years in the past, to the first steps of Cubism; and of course we know that these first steps, then, were not unreasonable but a good remedy to cure Im-pressionist vagueness.*]

It is unlikely that Laye would discuss European art movements about which he had shown no knowledge.

> Serait-ce que ce siècle est plus corrupteur qu'édifiant? Ou serait-ce seule-ment que le monde présent est toujours plongé dans les scènes de cauchemar de la dernière guerre? *Serait-ce simplement que l'esprit de justice, après plus de dix ans, n'a pas pu encore dépasser l'esprit de revanche?* (294–95; my italics)
>
> [*Is it possible that this century is more corrupting than edifying? Or is it only that the present world is still plunged in the nightmare scenes of the last war?* Is it simply that the spirit of justice, after more than ten years, has not yet overtaken the spirit of revenge?]

Rereading this essay today, I wonder how I ever thought it expressed Laye's ideas. I doubt that the editors of *Présence africaine* really thought that a con-cern for justice for those who collaborated during the war was a good subject for their review.

The timing of all this literary productivity seems suspect. As Laye wrote on his publicity form for Plon that he was still studying in July 1953, it is difficult to see how he would have found time to write at least one of the short stories, as well as a second novel, by mid-1954. Those who knew Laye later felt that he could never have written a second book so soon after the first one.

Although Laye also spoke of meeting a number of African students in Paris in the early 1950s, with whom he discussed Negritude, he was not part of the group around Alioune Diop who formed Présence Africaine and was not accepted by the African intelligentsia. According to the Beninois writer Paulin Joachim, the black intelligentsia in Paris felt that Laye did not have the talent to be a writer. Joachim, who met Laye after the publication of *L'Enfant noir*, thought he was crushed by his success and realized that he was not up to the level expected of him.[26]

After the publication of *L'Enfant noir*, Laye was given a position through the Ministry of France Overseas with the Caisse Centrale. After December 15, 1954, he worked for this office, which was attached to several ministries (finance, overseas, etc.) and was directed by Postel-Vinay. Laye did an apprentice term in Marseille at the Crédit Lyonnais in September 1955 and then worked at the Caisse Centrale in Cotonou, Dahomey (now Bénin), from March to November 1956.[27]

THE RETURN TO AFRICA

In 1956, Claude Wauthier met Laye in Cotonou. Wauthier did not publish an interview he conducted at that time with Laye, an interview that suggested Laye at least had substantial help with his novels and that Wauthier described to me:

> Je l'avais interviewé en 1955 ou '56, alors qu'il effectuait un stage à la Banque du Bénin à Cotonou, sur les bruits malveillants selon lesquels il n'était pas l'auteur de ses livres. Voici un résumé des notes que j'avais prises: il m'avait dit que l'un des rewriters de son éditeur (PLON) l'avait aidé, ajoutant qu'il était normal que les Africains, dont le français n'était pas la langue maternelle, soient aidés par leurs amis européens quand ils voulaient écrire. Selon certains Européens de l'endroit qui ne l'aimaient guère, il déclarait à qui voulait l'entendre que les blancs étaient un peuple de techniciens et les noirs un peuple d'imaginatifs. Les premiers devant finalement et fatalement devenir dans un avenir plus ou moins proches les "exécutants," les "instruments" de travail des seconds. Il m'a tenu des propos un peu différents:

"Nous autres Africains, nous avons des idées à revendre, la difficulté est de les coucher sur le papier." Il m'a démenti par ailleurs avoir eu une maîtresse juive qui aurait écrit ses livres pour lui. . . . Il faut bien voir qu'à l'époque, l'apparition d'un écrivain noir de talent bousculait les préjugés racistes (anti-sémitisme compris) du milieu colonial européen.

> [*I interviewed him in 1955 or 1956, when he was doing a training course at the Benin Bank in Cotonou, about the malicious rumors that he was not the author of his books. Here is a resumé of the notes that I took: he told me that one of the editors at his publisher's (Plon) had helped him, adding that it was normal that Africans, whose mother tongue was not French, would be helped by their European friends when they wanted to write. According to certain Europeans there who didn't much like him, he declared to anyone who wanted to listen that Whites were a people of technicians and Blacks a people of imagination. The former should finally, inevitably, become, in the fairly near future, the executors, the instruments of work for the latter. He said something a bit different to me: "We Africans have ideas to sell; the difficulty is to put them on paper." He denied having had a Jewish mistress who had written his books for him. . . . One must realize that at the time the appearance of a black writer of talent shook the racist (and anti-Semitic) prejudices of the European colonial milieu.*][28]

Laye was sent to Crédit de la Guinée in January 1957; he resigned in October 1957.[29] According to Postel-Vinay, Laye lived "dans un rêve poétique" [in a poetic dream] and was quite unsuited to handling requests for loans. Laye later worked for the colony of Guinea, as attaché to the cabinet of the governor, Jean Ramadier. After Guinean independence in 1958 he was given diplomatic posts in Ghana and Liberia. Guinea was the only colony in French West Africa to reject de Gaulle's scheme for association with France, and Ghana was the first country to recognize Guinea after this rejection. It gave considerable financial support to Guinea when other aid was suspended. Laye's appointment as ambassador to Ghana, despite his limited knowledge of English, indicates the respect given to him as one of the first major authors from West Africa. Returning to Guinea, Laye worked as director of the Department of Economic Agreements at the Ministry of Foreign Affairs and then was appointed editor at the news bureau attached to the presidency and associate director of the National Institute of Research and Documentation (formerly the Guinean center of the Institut Français de l'Afrique Noire).

Fanny Lalande, one of the small number of French who stayed in Guinea after its independence, worked in the same building as Laye for a time. He asked her to help him by reading drafts of the novel on which he was then working (*Dramouss*). She realized later that the book would have benefited from the help of a French native with a sense of literary style, although she did not have the time to offer that herself. At about the same time, Anne Blancard, who also stayed in Guinea after independence and worked with Radio Guinée in the 1960s, adapted Laye's oral tales for radio broadcast.[30]

In 1963 Laye presented papers at two conferences on African writing. In Dakar in March he spoke on "L'Ame de l'Afrique dans sa partie guinéenne"; the paper includes a story about the genesis of *L'Enfant noir* and how he wrote it to alleviate his loneliness in a small Paris room: "Living in Paris, far from my native Guinea, far from my parents, and living there for years almost always isolated from others, I was carried back in my thoughts a thousand times to my country, near my loved ones. . . . I lived alone, alone in my poor student's room, and I wrote; I wrote as one dreams. . . . and then sitting at my table, a very small table lighted by only the scanty bulb of a lamp . . . I wrote." Laye wrote that he showed his work to "a friend" who encouraged him to continue and then took it to a reader at a publishing house. He did not identify these persons. He also defended his novel as an attempt to rehabilitate African culture, giving his work a more political message than had been apparent to most critics when it was first published.[31]

At the Fourah Bay College conference in Freetown, Sierra Leone, that same year, Laye's talk, titled "L'Afrique et l'appel des profondeurs," was in part a version of the dream of the Black Lion that he later used in *Dramouss*, where he gave it a more political interpretation. Part of the dream, a segment in which the narrator is menaced by two streams of water that threaten to flood the staircase where he is standing, is a reworking of a passage from "Les Yeux de la statue." Both these conference papers make frequent use of the imperfect subjunctive and thus have a more formal tone at times than would be normal for an oral presentation.

The economic situation in Guinea deteriorated, as there was little foreign aid. Sékou Touré sought scapegoats for problems and invented a number of "plots." Laye became increasingly critical of the suppression of liberties and was more or less under house arrest for several years. After Sékou Touré broke off diplomatic relations with France in 1965, Laye left in June with his family, using his need to get medical attention as a pretense for obtaining an exit permit. During part of his visit he stayed in Paris with Baba Ibrahima Kaké, who lived on the rue Molière, almost next door to the Soulié studio in which Laye had lived ten years earlier. Kaké told me that he thought Laye broke off contact with Soulié because of some argument about homosexuality, but he did not tell me when this break took place.[32] Laye showed Kaké a manuscript of *Dramouss* that he brought to Paris, with annotations by Sékou Touré.

Kaké's first wife was a member of the Keita family, which had given Laye financial aid before he left for France in 1946. In reciprocation Laye had introduced Kaké's brother-in-law, Kelefa Keita, to Soulié, who helped Keita and his two sisters come to France and later adopted Keita. According to Vanfing Koné, the adoption took place about 1957.

The contract for *Dramouss* was signed on June 21, 1965, with an advance of five thousand francs. Laye mentioned that friends in several countries warned him that, because of a resolution of the Organization for African Unity, he could not obtain political asylum if he were considered subversive. He therefore revised the manuscript to "adapt it to the present political situation." Laye sent the manuscript to Plon in December 1965, from Dakar. In a letter confirming the dispatch of the manuscript, he thanked the director of Plon in advance for any corrections or ameliorations that could be made. *Dramouss* was published in 1966.

Laye later made contradictory statements about when he wrote *Dramouss*. Several persons claim to have read the manuscript as early as 1963, and Lalande said Laye was working on the manuscript in 1964. He signed a contract with Plon in 1965, in Paris. He said in a 1977 interview with Fresco, however, that he wrote the novel after his arrival in Dakar and that he composed it in a hurry and with little revision. Fresco considered that, since *Dramouss* had received unfavorable reviews, Laye was "perhaps attempting to justify himself in the light of this negative criticism." In this case Laye was clearly inventing stories about the composition of his work.[33]

Dramouss is partly the autobiographical continuation of *L'Enfant noir*. The narrator, now called Fatoman, tells the story of his life after he left Guinea to study in France. This story is interwoven with the larger story of the problems of Guinea just before and after its independence. Its themes include the demagogy of a developing political system that is moving toward a one-party state, the weakening of the ties with France, and the decline of traditional artistic culture. The narrative is episodic and includes a folk tale told by a griot, a description of a political meeting, and a strange dream in which Fatoman foresees a journey through despair to the future and then to a salvation from the tyranny of a dictatorship, a salvation that is more religious than political. *Dramouss* was received favorably by African critics, who admired its political message. Several European reviewers saw the novel as affirming Franco-African cooperation, promoting Western culture, or showing a lack of racism in the school Laye attended in France.[34] These readers appreciated Laye's belief in some continuation of the policies of the French Union and his praise of France, six years after most West African countries became independent. Many others, however, saw the novel as inferior to the first two books.

By November 1965 Laye had taken up residence in Senegal. After some difficulty being accepted because he had no formal academic qualifications, he was given a position as a research fellow at the Institut Fondamental de l'Afrique Noire (IFAN) in Dakar, where he collected Manding folk tales. Yves Person, the distinguished Africanist professor who knew Laye while he was at IFAN, had "feelings of friendship and respect" for Laye but believed that he drank too much. Laye had proposed writing a doctoral thesis ("troisième cycle"), but Person rejected the proposal because he felt the work Laye was doing (which became *Le Maître de la parole*) did not contain sufficient intellectual analysis. He also felt that there were already many versions of the Soundiata story and that other griot tales should be transcribed and analyzed.[35]

While Laye occasionally traveled to Abidjan and to the United States and his work was increasingly studied in schools and colleges and praised by critics, his life in Dakar was not easy. He was heavily involved with a political battle against Sékou Touré, a dictator who, he felt, controlled Guinea against the will of the people and to the "detriment of the cultural bonds that unite Guinea to France."[36] As he had no regular source of income, he relied on small royalties he received for his work. On June 4, 1970, Marie decided to return to Guinea to see her family. She was seized upon arrival and spent the next seven years in prison. Left to raise their seven children during her absence, Laye married a second wife, Ramatoulaye Camara Kanté, which he was entitled to do under Muslim law.[37] When Marie returned to Senegal, she obtained a divorce. Laye had two children by his second wife.

During this time, Laye wrote two manuscripts, which were ready for typing in December 1970, according to a letter he wrote to Plon at that time. The first, "Le Haut Niger vu à travers la tradition orale," is presumably an early version of *Le Maître de la parole*. The second, "L'Exil," is described in a letter of April 13, 1971, as too politically committed to be published while his wife remained "a prisoner of Sékou Touré." Senghor advised Laye not to publish it.

Dr. Lansiné Kaba, a Guinean professor of history who has taught for many years in the United States, met Laye in 1972 at a Manding Conference in London, where Laye presented a paper, "Le Rêve dans la société traditionnelle malinké." Kaba realized that Laye was not in good health and had suffered from cardiac problems for some time. Kaba spoke to Laye at this conference and again in Dakar in 1973, mostly about the political problems of Guinea and the dictatorship of Sékou Touré. Laye also spoke a great deal about Marie, with whom he was obsessed. The marriage of Laye and Marie seems to have been somewhat stormy but a marriage of love. The divorce weighed heavily on Laye toward the end of his life. Kaba said he was received "royally" by Laye in Dakar in 1973. He also praised Ramatoulaye, Laye's second wife, as being very devoted to Laye. Kaba had arranged a visit by Laye to the United States in 1974 or 1975, but Laye fell sick in London at this time. Kaba was impressed with the growth in Laye's knowledge of and practice of Islam.

WHAT LAYE SAID LATER ABOUT HIS LIFE IN FRANCE

In Laye's essays and in interviews with him, primarily those he gave after he came to Dakar, there are numerous contradictions. In some cases these contradictions may result from slips of memory, but sometimes Laye was purposely misleading or was dodging matters he did not want known, matters that would have brought attention to his relationship with those who had helped him survive in France and who were involved in the writing and publication of his first two novels.

When I wrote to Laye in January 1978, through his editor at Plon, Hélène Bourgeois, asking him who guided and helped him in the 1950s and specifically who the reader was at Plon, he replied in a letter to me from Dakar, dated February 15, 1978:

> Je regrette de ne pas pouvoir vous donner satisfaction, car l'ami en question, qui était déjà un vieux Monsieur, est mort depuis 1960, tout comme l'ancien président directeur général de la librairie Plon, qui était, lui aussi, un grand ami.
>
> [*I'm sorry I can't help you, for the friend in question, who was already an old gentleman, has been dead since 1960, as is the former president of the Librairie Plon, who was also a great friend.*]

Bourgeois told Laye that I must be seeking information about Poulet, who was then still alive. It is possible, although unlikely, that Laye did not know this. The person he mentioned who died in 1960 might have been one of the directors at Plon.

While translating *Le Regard du roi*, James Kirkup, the English poet, wrote to Laye through his publisher, asking for clarification of a few passages, but he did not receive a reply. The interviews that Laye gave show his embarrassment in talking in detail about his work, particularly *Le Regard du roi*. When I interviewed Laye in 1978 he said he had learned about Kafka's work through a German friend named Teuscheur, who worked for the broadcasting corporation Deutsche Welle.[38] Laye never, however, showed any detailed knowledge of Kafka's writing. It is very unlikely that the parallels to Kafka's work in *Le Regard du roi*, evident to anyone familiar with *The Trial* and *The Castle*, came from Laye's reading of Kafka.

Laye claimed rather vaguely that the only influence was Kafka's way of telling a dream. Patricia A. Deduck's careful study of the influence of Kafka on *Le Regard du roi* shows, however, that there is "direct imitation in form, style, theme, and characterization," particularly of *The Castle*, which begins, as does Laye's novel, with a character who has broken with his past and is about to begin life in a new situation.[39] Deduck shows how the ambiguities of Kafka's description of the Castle are reflected in Laye's description of the king's palace, how K's assertion of his "right" to be recognized by the Castle is similar to

Clarence's initial denial that he is asking for favors, and how certain characters, such as the beggar, are modeled on characters in Kafka.

Deduck cites the "swarms of crows circling around" Kafka's tower as the source of Laye's "des vautours tournoyaient dans le ciel" (34) [vultures were hovering in the sky] (34). She compares Kafka's description at the end of the first chapter with Clarence's impression of the palace after the king has left:

> The Castle above them . . . was already beginning to grow dark and retreated again into the distance. (Kafka, in Deduck, 245)

> Puis le donjon même parut s'effacer, devenir on ne sait quoi de vaporeux et anonyme . . . Tout, insensiblement, s'estompait . . . Et le palais même semblait s'être éloigné. (Laye, 36)
> [*Then the tower itself seemed to fade away, obliterated somehow, and becoming a kind of anonymous vapour. . . . Everything was gradually becoming blurred. . . . And the palace itself seemed to have been moving imperceptibly away.*] *(Laye, 37)*

Among other similarities, Kafka's assistants are analogous to Nagoa and Noaga, and the whipping episode in chapter 5 of *The Trial* appears to be a source for the ordeal of the master of ceremonies in Aziana. Deduck concludes that although Kafka is more pessimistic than Laye, Laye got his inspiration from Kafka.

One of the earliest written interviews with Laye, by Irmelin Hossman, was published in 1963 in *Afrique*. Laye is quoted as saying both "Clarence, my hero, is a white man looking for God" and "But Clarence is African and his encounter with God is possible."[40] Various interpretations could be given. Perhaps Laye called Clarence African as a way of suggesting that he had a more direct relationship with the mysterious and the supernatural. It is possible, however, to see this answer as an attempt to say something about Kafka without being too specific. Hossman had asked about Kafka's despair, and Laye replied that this despair was not related to his novel. He used only Kafka's technique. "In Africa there is no despair like this," he claimed. In the interview Laye also quoted the epigraph of the novel, one of the least despairing sentences of Kafka: "Le Seigneur passera dans le couloir, regardera le prisonnier et dira: Celui-ci, il ne faut l'enfermer à nouveau: il vient à moi" [The Lord will pass in the corridor, look at the prisoner, and say: This one must not be shut up again: he comes with me]. The epigraph, which is not included in the English translation, comes from a notebook of aphorisms, not from one of Kafka's well-known works. Laye would not have known this work, or at least he never mentioned it.[41] In hindsight it seems clear that Laye had prepared a few things to say about Kafka without committing himself to any extended discussion.

Laye also told Hossman that he avoided certain expressions when he wrote for Africans, choosing images and expressions suitable for the African context. This is contrary to his actual practice in *L'Enfant noir* and particularly in the short stories and *Le Regard du roi*.

Laye was interviewed by J. Steven Rubin in 1972. Laye's comments on *L'Enfant noir* were, again, much more solid than those on *Le Regard du roi*. Rubin said, "It seems to me that you went much further in it [*Le Regard du roi*], that you approached an entirely new level." Laye replied, "It wasn't a question of a new level, but a normal development of thought. One cannot always be writing about one's own experiences. When I wrote my autobiography, which covers my life from infancy to age 20, I had exhausted the subject for the time being. A year later, when I felt the need to express myself in literature again, my personal life was finished as subject matter, so I had to turn to a pure fiction." He talked about Clarence as being in "a new and totally strange country with a different civilization. He comes to his country with his Cartesian logic and finds that the African mentality is not at all Cartesian. . . . If I had chosen a black man for the role, he would not have had the sense of being completely uprooted."[42]

Similar problems of consistency are apparent in Laye's interview with William Lawson, who spoke with Laye at his office at IFAN in Dakar. Lawson's interview, undated but published in 1975, is translated into English. He quoted Laye as saying about *Le Regard du roi*: "Well, an autobiography gets itself written only once. . . . It [*L'Enfant noir*] concerned my childhood and my adolescence, so then the journals were saying is it possible that Laye could write a novel. Certainly I was reading a lot and I discovered around 1946, since I was reading so much (I also belonged to a literary group) I discovered Kafka, Franz Kafka."[43] The date is clearly wrong, as Laye did not leave for France until 1946 or 1947. To my knowledge, he never again mentioned that he had belonged to a literary group in Conakry or France.

Speaking of Kafka, Laye continued, "I read him. I read of his life" and "It's the technique that's Kafkaesque but the spirit is African."[44] Lawson suggested that Clarence follows the Sufi way of seven steps to God. Laye agreed but did not discuss this in any detail. He replied, "That's it." The spirit is African, but the techniques are universal. Laye then talked about combustion engines and about his father's sculpture of a white man with a large penis. Again Lawson returned to Sufi, and Laye interrupted to say: "Yes, yes, because, myself, I had an experience that was, if you will, mystic—I, personally, because I had a father who was very mystical, who had a good deal of—who was turned toward God. My father lived two years in the bush. That, then, that's the Sufi way. I can say that I was influenced" (86). Then an African editor present at the interview said, "Would you say that in *The Radiance of the King* you were writing of African traditions and spirit that you feared losing?" Laye replied, "It's the scale of values. Its value to him and its value to me and to us [gesturing to the editor] aren't the same. First of all, in Paris, money is time" (88). The whole interview might be interpreted as showing a reluctance on Laye's part to discuss the novel in detail.

In an interview Jacqueline Leiner conducted in Dakar in 1971 and published in 1975, Laye contradicted what he told Rubin and Lawson, saying that he always used his own life as his subject matter. He mentioned the importance of Gustave Flaubert and said that he read "tous les Classiques" in school in Guinea. This is doubtful, as his training after elementary education was in a technical college. Although as usual he spoke mainly about *L'Enfant noir*, he did speak of Kafka, but again in the context of technique: "You will note that people will say about *Le Regard du roi* or *Dramouss* that it is a bit Kafka's technique. Yes and no. I have simply used the technique of a dream. My hero tells his dream."[45] I believe he was referring primarily to *Dramouss*, as the interview was conducted when the English translation, *A Dream of Africa*, appeared. Laye continued: "You see that here we are more surrealist! That's what I really mean. . . . When someone says, for instance, that I copy Kafka . . . No, on the contrary, it is perhaps Kafka who copies us? Kafka copies Africa without knowing it." Again Laye seemed to have no awareness of the many details in *Le Regard du roi* clearly based on Kafka. Even in discussing *L'Enfant noir* Laye occasionally contradicted himself. After replying that he was not obsessed by rhythm, he continued: "At the beginning of *L'Enfant noir* I wrote 'alone.' That is for me a key-word, 'alone.' I want the reader to keep that in mind; I wrote: 'alone', 'alone'. . . . I will later take words that conform to a rhythm." The comment is rather unclear, as there is no use of the word *seul* at the beginning of *L'Enfant noir*. Leiner later told me that she had to make considerable corrections to the recorded interview as she transcribed it. Laye's French was often imprecise.

Jacqueline Sorel interviewed Laye in 1976 for a recording produced in the series "Archives sonores de la littérature noire." The first side of the recording is the interview, the second is readings from *L'Enfant noir*. Sorel told me in 1997 that at the time they did the recording she had heard rumors about the origins of *Le Regard du roi*, but she did not question Laye about it. He was very reticent in talking about his second novel. He told Sorel that he had read Kafka, but she feels sure that he had not done so.

Laye spoke to me about three techniques that enabled him to write *Le Regard du roi*: that of Honoré de Balzac for what he termed the "linéaire" (the linear plot), that of Stendhal for the internal dialogue, and that of Kafka for the techniques of the dream. He spoke often of the importance of dreams, mentioning that two minutes of a dream could give him ten pages of text. In another interview in 1978 Laye told me he chose the name Clarence because it was "joli." (In retrospect this seems a curious answer, especially as the name is unusual in France.) In response to my questions concerning the setting of *Le Regard du roi*, Laye replied that it was not necessarily the forest region of Guinea; it could have been Côte d'Ivoire. The setting was "Africa." In the early 1950s Laye had not traveled, nor is there any evidence that he had much knowledge of African anthropology, art, or history. Perhaps for this reason he had wanted to call *L'Enfant noir* "L'Enfant de Guinée." Yet later he was willing to talk of a universal Africa in *Le Regard du roi*.

In two conversations with Laye in 1978, I broached the subject of his attitude toward the sexual activity of his hero. I wondered what he thought of Ben Obumselu's comment that the flesh is a beginning of the movement toward spiritual regeneration. Laye seemed to agree with this. He said the flesh was nothing, it was the spirit that counted. He added, however, that Clarence should be ashamed but that having a harem of women was what was done in Africa. Later he reiterated that your faith is what counts, not what you do. He even commented that mysteries in Africa were reserved for those over forty, who were too old to commit adultery.

None of Laye's comments can quite be reconciled, I think, with some of the scenes in *Le Regard du roi*, either the physical contact that Samba Baloum seems to enjoy or, conversely, the suggestions that the flesh is beastly, a cause for the shame that Clarence feels when he learns of his nightly sexual activity: "Le chien qui était en lui l'attendait peut-être; mais lui il la craignait, il l'abominait" [The beast inside him was looking forward to it perhaps, but he feared it, despised it] (145, 160).[46] Laye never expressed a horror of the flesh; Senghor was presumably right to say that in Africa flesh is a support of the spiritual. But neither did Laye make the sort of gross jokes about sexuality that are common in *Le Regard du roi*. From my own brief interviews I remember him telling me a traditional story about an unfaithful wife who manages to have a lover even though she is enclosed in a sort of cage, by making an unobtrusive opening in the back of the cage. He was almost embarrassed, however, about telling me the story, and he excused himself by saying that after all I was a married woman of a certain age myself.

BIOGRAPHICAL EVIDENCE FROM *DRAMOUSS*

Laye told Leiner and Kesteloot that he always wrote his own life. *Dramouss* can be read as a fictionalized autobiography, which may offer other indications of Laye's life at the time of the publication of the novels. Initially Fatoman (Laye) returns to Guinea after six years in France and marries Mimie (Marie). This part of the narrative corresponds to Laye's visit to Guinea in 1954. Some of the later action takes place after 1957. *Dramouss* is sometimes incoherent in terms of chronology. For example, after attending an RDA meeting in Kouroussa, in which the speaker refers to events since 1956, Fatoman replies, when asked how long he has been gone, "Je ne sais. Peut-être bien six ans" [I don't know. Perhaps as much as six years] (185, 119). It is unrealistic to think that Fatoman did not remember when he left Guinea. Laye was combining material written at different times, but presumably he realized that the chronology was not always logical. The later sections are primarily concerned with Laye's reaction to Sékou Touré's regime.

The evasiveness of the narrator's relation to his wife-to-be is evident from the opening chapter. In this chapter Fatoman's uncle informs him that the Muslim religious ceremonies for his marriage to Mimie have already taken place in the absence of the couple. Mimie, however, is upset by what she has learned about Fatoman's relationship with a French woman named Françoise. Fatoman is, to say the least, not forthcoming with Mimie about his relationship with Françoise. He admits that Françoise wrote to his parents asking their consent for his marriage (22, 15). Later he admits he told Françoise that "Tout est légalisé dans nos coeurs" [In our two hearts, everything is legal] (94, 61). To Mimie, however, he says that the Frenchwoman was only a friend with whom he exchanged ideas. While it is obvious to the reader that Fatoman is lying to Mimie, the first-person narrator never directly admits what he is doing.[47] The episode shows the lack of introspection in the novel and, indirectly, Laye's refusal at least in fiction to confront his own actions.

The incidents recounted in the chapter "Une nuit blanche" [A Sleepless Night] about Fatoman's life in Paris are of particular interest for the period of *Le Regard du roi*. Laye's narrator seldom explains or analyzes his actions; it is as though Laye were writing about what really happened while omitting certain essential facts. The reader is at a loss to understand Fatoman's actions in terms of the novel's incomplete plot.

In "Une nuit blanche" Fatoman first recounts his arrival in France. The episode shows a naive belief in a brotherhood between French and Africans and even in the need for Africans to imitate the French in order to better themselves. When Fatoman arrives at a police station while looking for directions to his school, the police agent notes that he speaks good French:

> Mais ils sont comme nous! répondit l'agent. Ils sont français. Nous avons bâti là-bas des écoles, des hôpitaux. Dans quelques années, ils seront comme nous. Ils auront des cadres, tous les cadres! (72)
>
> [*"But they are the same as us!" the policeman retorted. "They are French like us. We built schools and hospitals out there. In a few years, they'll be just like us. They'll have their own regiments and everything."*] (47)[48]

The episode with the homosexual in a bar is an example of a scene that must almost certainly be based on Laye's life in Paris but that has very little relevance to most of the novel. Fatoman meets a man in the Bar Pergola who attempts to caress his leg. He is extremely shocked by this behavior, which he tells a friend is unknown in Africa. There are two pages narrating his outrage. It is difficult to reconcile this attitude with the somewhat indirect but comic references to homosexuality in *Le Regard du roi*. If, however, as is likely, Laye himself was approached by homosexuals in Paris and was repulsed by this behavior, the passage is comprehensible if not esthetically justified. Denial of the existence of homosexual behavior in Africa is common.

It is probable that this episode has some bearing on Laye's relationship to Soulié, whom he met, according to Marie, at a bar in the Latin Quarter. Perhaps it was the Bar Pergola, which still exists. When Fatoman returns to his hotel after his encounter with a homosexual, he finds that the hotel manager has taken all his belongings to hold until the rent is paid. It is possible that at this point Laye moved into Soulié's studio on the rue Molière.

One of the most evident examples of obscurity or evasiveness in *Dramouss* is Fatoman's relationship to Tante Aline and how it changes his life. He is studying in a private establishment in Paris, with no scholarship money and owing several months rent, when he decides to go see Tante Aline, who has helped many young Africans. How he initially met her is not explained. She is said to be from Normandy, seventy years of age, and living in the rue Saint Jacques. It is also said that she lived in Siguiri for some time before 1925. Fatoman describes her as "la maman de tous les jeunes Africains" [the mother of all young Africans] (77, 51). She is the grandmother of Françoise, who "aime bien les Africains, elle aussi" [She too is very fond of Africans] (80, 53) and already knows Fatoman well enough to visit him at his hotel. At a second meeting in a cafe, Tante Aline suggests that he find work in Les Halles. He works in Les Halles unloading trucks for a few weeks but then finds work at the Simca factory in Nanterre. How he finds this work is left unexplained, as is the reference to a driver's license as one of the objects he leaves with the hotel owner as a guarantee (93, 60). His life is now centered upon working, reading in the evening, and seeing Tante Aline and Françoise. There is no mention of his studies, which was supposedly the reason he did not return to Guinea when his scholarship allowance was spent. He does, however, mention going out "après le cours de Françoise" [after Françoise's classes] (98, 63). Since there is no other reference to what Françoise does, it is unclear whether she is a student or a teacher. Laye is putting down information that is often, I believe, factually accurate, without incorporating it convincingly in his narrative as fiction.

Suddenly Fatoman's life changes radically:

Grâce à "Tante Aline" et à Françoise, j'eus la joie de me lier avec de nombreuses personnes. Bientôt, je ne m'ennuyai plus dans Paris. Je sortais souvent. . . . Un jour, cependant, des messieurs, parents de "Tante Aline" vinrent me chercher. Je les reçus au bureau de l'hôtel. Quelques minutes plus tard, ces messieurs et moi, nous prîmes place dans une voiture noire, qui nous conduisit rue de Varenne. On me dit:

—Jeune homme, nous désirons votre collaboration.

—Excusez-moi, répondis-je, hésitant, c'est un honneur qu'il m'est bien difficile d'accepter. Je dois achever mes études sur les bancs de l'Ecole.

—Si nous faisons appel à vous, répliqua-t-on, c'est pour consolider l'Union fraternelle franco-africaine. . . .

—Oui, pour une véritable union franco-africaine, je suis prêt à tous les sacrifices.

Les matinées, je les passais rue de Varenne. Les après-midi, je les passais ailleurs, comme stagiaire. Je faisais plusieurs choses à la fois. Souvent, le soir, je participais aussi à des émissions radiophoniques. . . . Bientôt je m'offris une petite voiture. . . . Pendant les vacances, j'allais sur la Côte d'Azur, en Espagne, en Belgique, en Suisse. (104–5)

[*Thanks to Aunt Aline and Françoise, I was lucky to make the acquaintance of many people. Soon I no longer felt bored in Paris. I went out often. . . . However, some gentlemen related to Aunt Aline came to call on me one day. I received them in the office of the hotel. A few minutes later these gentlemen and I had taken our seats in a black limousine which drove to the Rue de Varenne. They had told me:*

"Young man, we should like your assistance."

"Please excuse me," I replied, hesitantly, "this is an honour which I find difficult to accept. I have to attend school and complete my studies."

"We have approached you," they replied, "to help us consolidate our fraternal Franco-African Union.". . .

"Yes, for true Franco-African union, I am prepared to make every sacrifice."

I spent mornings at the Rue de Varenne. The afternoons I spent else-

where, as a probationer. I was engaged in several activities. In the evenings
I also took part in broadcasts. Soon I was able to purchase a small car. . . .
During holidays, I would drive down to the Côte d'Azur, to Spain; or go to
Belgium, to Switzerland.] (67)

I have quoted this passage at length because if read as autobiography, it is
evasive, omitting any mention of literary activity. If read as fiction, it makes no
sense. The careful reader has many questions. Why is this young man suddenly
singled out to work for the French Union and to give radio broadcasts? Why
does he suddenly again refer to his studies, which seemed no part of his life
when he worked at the Simca factory? How would he have had enough money
to buy a car? Another inconsistency occurs when we reread the opening chapters of the novel. When Fatoman's uncle tells him to take Mimie with him on
his return to Paris, as they are already married, he worries about how he will
support her:

Il faudra payer le trousseau, payer la chambre, payer mes études, tout payer,
et avec quoi? Je ne m'attends pas à obtenir une bourse d'études de l'État. Mes
tentatives pour en obtenir une ont été vaines. Là-bas, la vie est dure, oncle.
(32)

[*Clothes will have to be paid for, the room, my college fees, so much has to*
be paid for, and with what? I don't expect to receive a study scholarship from
the State. All my efforts to obtain one have been in vain. Life is hard over
there, uncle.] (21)

Fatoman already had enough to buy a car and travel, but this passage suggests
that he is still a struggling student. Laye himself, of course, at that time had
considerable support from the French government and, as Marie has said, a
place to live thanks to Soulié.

Laye only slightly disguised the truth in describing his contacts with Tante
Aline's family. It was indeed a relative of Tante Aline (Lefaucheux), her
brother (Postel-Vinay), who gave Laye work. It was during this time that Laye
traveled to Switzerland and visited Dr. Njami in Lausanne.

From an ideological perspective there is another perplexity. Immediately
after the passage about his work for a Franco-African Union, Fatoman describes his discussion with Tante Aline about politics in Africa. The arguments
he uses initially would not appeal to those working for Franco-African unity,

as he begins by saying that colonized people are not free. She replies that French colonial governors might be replaced by fascist dictators who are much worse. Any abuses are committed by French colonists in Africa who are only looking for quick profit: "n'oublie jamais que, chez vous, ce qui se passe d'ignoble est bien indépendant de la volonté du peuple de France, le plus souvent aussi de celle de ses gouvernants" [never forget that the ignoble things which have happened in your country have occurred quite independent of the will of the French people, and often of its governments]. She continues: "ce combat qu'il est convenu d'appeler le combat libérateur, n'oublie jamais que l'ennemi n'est pas une race, n'est pas le blanc, mais une bande de profiteurs" [the struggle which it has been agreed should be called the struggle of liberation, never forget that the enemy is not a race, is not the white man, but a gang of profiteers]. He agrees that "le racisme est bête" [racism is idiotic] and accepts her opinion that "les hommes qui mènent là-bas une lutte systématique contre les Blancs sont des animaux" [the men out there who are waging a systematic war against white men are in fact just animals] (107–8, 68–69). If it is only at this point that Fatoman accepts Tante Aline's pro-French arguments, one wonders why he was asked to give radio broadcasts. The discussion with Tante Aline seems to be set up so that Laye can express pro-French views.

Careful reading of *Dramouss* suggests that Laye had been groomed for a role supporting French colonial policy for some time. Exactly how he was discovered was not clear, but the novel suggests it was through one or several women, including an older woman with influential contacts and a young woman who was his lover. It is evident from *Dramouss* that women were important to Laye. Dramouss herself is a woman. He needs a woman to admire and help him.

THE FINAL YEARS IN DAKAR

Rumors about *Le Regard du roi* persisted during Laye's years of exile in Senegal, and he was well aware of them. He asked Marcelle Colardelle, who worked at IFAN from 1971 to 1974, if she thought *Le Regard du roi* was written in his style. Beti first met Laye in Berlin in 1979, at a conference. Laye misunderstood a comment in English from another writer and thought the writer was suggesting that Laye was not the real author of his books. According to Beti, Laye became very defensive.

In 1975, Reine Carducci, the wife of the Italian ambassador to Senegal, raised an appeal for funds to treat Laye, then suffering from the nephritis that eventually killed him. She got support from members of the French Academy and collected sufficient money to bring Laye to France for treatment.[49]

Laye continued to be strongly pro-French. On June 4, 1978, when I interviewed him, he said, "Without colonization we could not have risen to the level we have now." I was with him one day in 1978 when an elderly Frenchwoman joined us at a bus stop and said, "I see you are an African and I wish to apologize for how my country treated you." Laye immediately replied, "But no, Madame, your country brought many good things to my country."

Laye published a story, "Prélude et fin d'un cauchemar," in an Abidjan newspaper, *Fraternité Matin*, in 1976. It is a reworking of part of *Le Regard du roi*. He had been working since 1971 on his final book, *Le Maître de la parole*. The contract, which included an advance of ten thousand francs, was signed July 16, 1977, and the book was published in 1978. It is a fictionalized retelling of the history of Soundiata, the great Manding ruler of the thirteenth century, based on Laye's research in Dakar. Many passages are taken, almost word for word, from *Le Regard du roi*.

By this time Laye was a famous author, and his books sold very well. The paperback (Livre de Poche) edition of *L'Enfant noir* was published in January 1970. Three years later, according to Plon records, 111,394 copies had been sold. There had been a number of translations of all Laye's work and some radio and theatrical adaptations. Laye needed money, however. At the end of his life he was writing a biography of Houphouët-Boigny and working on a book of folk tales for children and a novel, "L'Exil," which was never published. Abiola Irele saw Laye in Dakar on February 1, 1980, only three days before his death. Laye spoke of his work for IFAN and of his desire to write his next book in the Manding language. When he died on February 4, Laye left documents, including the manuscript of "L'Exil," which, according to Laye's eldest son, may still be in a bank in Dakar.

3

Critical Reactions to the Work of Camara Laye

L'ENFANT NOIR

L'Enfant noir begins in Kouroussa, in Upper Guinea, when the child Laye was about five years old (1933). The story is told by a narrator seeking to remember his past. He describes life in his father's compound and his first acquaintance with the black snake, his father's guiding spirit. His world gradually expands. He watches his father working with gold, visits his grandmother in the village of Tindican, and observes with awe how his mother plays a role in the community. He is sent to the colonial school but also initiated into manhood within the tribe. When he is about fifteen, he goes to a technical secondary school in Conakry, where he lives with his uncle Mamadou. During the second year he meets Marie, a young student with whom he falls in love. After scoring at the top of his class in his examinations, he is offered a scholarship to France, which he accepts with mixed feelings. As the story ends, he is on the plane to Paris, fighting back his tears. A major theme is the traditional culture—what it meant to the young child and what it means to the narrator, who believes in the customs of his native culture at the same time that he questions them.

L'Enfant noir was received with considerable acclaim by European critics and continues to be praised for its portrait of a traditional society, whose value does not depend upon any outside cultural influences. African reactions have been more mixed. Beti's well-known attack on the novel in *Présence africaine* in 1955, because it ignored the effects of colonialism, was followed by varied responses from African critics. Lamine Kamara, a novelist and the Guinean ambassador to France in 1995, did not like the novel, believing it was accepted at the time only because it responded to what Europeans wanted. Boubacar Boris Diop seems to mock *L'Enfant noir* when N'Dongo in *Le Temps de Tamango* writes a novel and then burns it: "Don't forget of course that I left the country when I was nineteen. . . . I realized that I was a child setting foot on a strange land. So without hesitating I huddled up against the warm memories of my Africa—Mother—Hen."[1] More recently, Koffi Kwahulé, a younger Ivoirian writer who adapted for the stage the work of Ahmadou Kourouma, which uses a very Africanized French, dismissed Laye: "Earlier, African writing was very nice, Camara Laye and the others, used an over-polished style, to show that they had mastered grammar."[2] Eustace Palmer, a Sierra Leonean professor of literature, was suspicious of passages in *L'Enfant noir* that seemed to him more like a European reminiscing about spring, which is quite different from the harmattan.

READING *L'ENFANT NOIR* THEN AND NOW

When I read, taught, and wrote about *L'Enfant noir* in the 1970s, like many non-African readers I looked for an "African soul." I saw the novel both as an account of life in a traditional village in upper Guinea and also as a work with universal themes. Readers of the novel glean anthropological information about life in an African village hardly touched by the western world but also read of patterns of childhood experience similar throughout the world.

L'Enfant noir begins with the story of a five-year-old child playing with a snake, not realizing the danger until adults come to save him. After the opening episode with the snake, there is a leap of about seven years. The child is about twelve during most of the first seven chapters. The memories of childhood are carefully patterned. Although I found some more personal traits among the typical experiences—particularly the strength of the child's attachment to his mother—I realized that the African child is more a type than a person. Indeed, most of the characters are hardly developed as individuals. I got a clearer sense of Laye's father from some comments he made to me and others in interviews than any reader would gain from reading *L'Enfant noir.* There is, for example, no mention of Sufi retreats, nor of carving statues for Europeans. In the chapters relating the child's experiences in Conakry, there is again little specific detail. Even Marie is more a type than an individual. I attributed the vagueness in the accounts of the relationship between Marie and Laye to a desire to portray a pure and virginal love.

I was aware, as have been many readers, of the highly organized structure of the novel. Each chapter describing life in Kouroussa deals with one aspect of traditional culture, giving anthropological explanations; each is introduced by some reference to a member of Laye's family. There is a series of clear parallels, such as the Kondén Diara ceremony and the circumcision ceremony as traditional initiation into society set against the modern initiation of western schooling. This is a work carefully organized to present parallels between traditional and modern life. Most chapters end with an emotional drop, expressing the nostalgia for a lost paradise.

The episode with the snake vividly catches the reader's attention and establishes the perspective of the young child. Laye's opening also refers to others in the compound, who quickly come to the rescue of the child: an apprentice, a friend of his father's. The story of Laye's life in Kouroussa presents both the feelings of the individual child and the pattern of life of the group. Two major themes are the gradual loss of a childhood paradise of love and warmth and the value of traditional society with its rituals for establishing the solidarity of the community.

It was clear to me when I first read the novel that it was unlike other Francophone African literature written a few years later. I commented that "Laye is closer to Anglophone writers in never querying his identity as an African, in never feeling the need to avoid becoming a 'black Frenchman.' "[3] He seems largely unaware of French culture or the need to defend himself against it. Laye does not criticize the Europeans, and in fact the African child is hardly aware of their presence until he prepares to leave for France. The few contacts with foreigners, such as Laye's father's having worked for the Syrians or Laye serving as a translator for a land surveyor, are very briefly mentioned. So as not to place blame on the colonial regime, the villain in Kouroussa is the Guinean schoolmaster who exploits the children.

Examining final-year students at the University of Ibadan, Nigeria, in 1975, I was shocked to find that they had been taught by their lecturer that the book was too pro-French and did not address the horrors of colonial policy. They repeated this in their written examination. Few found any merits in the work or mentioned the artistic structure. In the oral examinations, however, several said that they enjoyed reading the novel and even that their parents, reading the English version, had found it a good account of life in a small African village, not too different from a village in Nigeria. I did not then consider that the perspective of the lecturer in Ibadan, or that of Beti in his review in *Présence africaine*, might accurately reflect the political atmosphere in which *L'Enfant noir* was conceived. I believed then and still would say that *L'Enfant noir* values traditional culture and cannot be dismissed because it is not also anticolonial. Laye had a right to his own political persuasion.

Nor did I consider when talking with the Ibadan students that the similarities between the novel and life in Nigeria showed to what extent the book is a generic portrait of an African life rather than an individual life. If the Kondén Diara rituals are specific to the Malinké, they are similar to those in other ethnic groups. Circumcision ceremonies and other initiation rites are common to much of West Africa.

The book is less a personal memoir than a description of a culture for the sake of foreigners. The desire to make the story applicable beyond Guinea and to make it readily accessible to European readers also explains why typical incidents are chosen: the child fearing to leave the security of home, the first innocent girlfriend at school, the reticence when the boy meets Marie, the conflict between generations. The suggestion that Laye had some less pure sexual experiences is passed over very quickly.

When I first read *L'Enfant noir*, the episode with the snake reminded me of the opening of James Joyce's *Portrait of the Artist as a Young Man*. Reading *L'Enfant noir* again, I am aware of how it was written by someone with a European sense of literary form. When I asked Laye in 1978 if he had read Joyce, I gathered from his reply that most of his reading of European literature occurred in the years after he returned to Africa. He often cited Flaubert's *Education sentimentale* as a model for his technique, but it is hard to see exactly what the influence would have been. Any parallels to Joyce, or to other autobiographical novels, would not have been Laye's idea.

In 1980 I thought *L'Enfant noir* was written in "simple, concise French," rather formal, with no words that the metropolitan French reader would find particularly difficult.[4] I did not consider the subtle use of tenses that a reviewer for the bulletin *Femmes de l'Union Française* praised so highly, in a review that patronizingly mentions Laye's mastery of French verbs. Now I am aware of how many imperfect subjunctives there are and how at times they seem excessive. Proper use of the imperfect subjunctive was almost an obsession with Poulet, who, Laye said, helped him with his writing.

I did notice the use of some words inappropriate to the Guinean setting, such as "le printemps semble s'unir à l'été" [spring and summer seem inseparable] (57, 57). I found the use of metaphor and descriptions of the landscape, particularly when Laye and Marie look at the sea in Conakry, primarily a way of describing physical passion very discreetly. Now these descriptions seem much too consciously based on European novels and even to some extent too "literary." Similarly, the rhetorical style seems inappropriate, rather inflated. The child goes to see his father and feels troubled as he realizes he will leave the security of his family:

> La lampe-tempête, suspendue à la véranda, l'eclairait crûment. Il me parut soudain comme vieilli.
> —Père! m'écriai-je.
> —Fils . . . dit-il à mi-voix. (21)
> [*The hurricane-lamp hanging on the veranda cast a harsh glare on his face. He suddenly seemed to me an old man.*
> *"Father!" I cried.*
> *"Son . . ." he whispered.*] *(27)*

Or, at the end of the chapter describing the harvest in Tindican:

> Ah! que nous étions heureux, ces jours-là! (67)
> [*Ah !How happy we were in those days!*] *(64)*

The story told in *L'Enfant noir*, although reworked by several people into a form that would appeal to the Western public, is, nonetheless, Laye's story, and it conveys his feelings of uncertainty about how much of the traditional beliefs were true. It remains a story that describes "a personal and cultural dilemma in accents that speak to all mankind."[5]

LE REGARD DU ROI

Le Regard du roi tells the story of Clarence, a white man who goes to an un-named African country, loses his money, and seeks acceptance by the African king of the country. It is a bizarre, often comic story of a misplaced white man in archetypal Africa, and, although narrated in the third person, it is told from the point of view of Clarence. He has fought the waves to cross a reef into Af-rica, into the northern city of Adramé, where he loses all his money gambling. Sent in disgrace from a European hotel, he goes to a cheap African inn. This in-formation is divulged gradually, after the opening scene of Clarence standing on a crowded esplanade, hoping to see the black king and to find a job with him. He is befriended by a disreputable beggar and two impish young boys, Nagoa and Noaga. When the king makes a ceremonial appearance, Clarence is daz-zled by his youthful frailty. Hoping to see the king later, he goes with the three Africans toward the south, journeying through a thick tropical rain forest, feeling lost and drugged by the odors of the lush vegetation. He is taken to the village of Aziana, where the beggar barters him for a woman and a donkey. Al-though he is unaware of it, Clarence is to be a stud for the harem of the local ruler, the naba. Each night he is drugged and sleeps with different women. When he discovers the truth he feels unworthy. He wanders down to the river, where he has a strange dream about being pursued by creatures that are half woman, half fish. Then he visits an old woman surrounded by snakes, who has the ability to give visions of the future. She gives Clarence a vision of the king setting off for Aziana. Clarence is increasingly unsure what has happened, what he has done, and what he has dreamed. On the day of the royal arrival in Aziana he remains in his hut, naked and ashamed. Suddenly he feels the king's eyes upon him. He moves forward and the wall of his hut melts away. The king holds out his arms and envelops Clarence "for ever."

Le Regard du roi is a novel about a quest for spiritual salvation. It is also a novel of social comedy. This comedy, of Clarence as a stud in the naba's harem, Clarence as an outsider unable to adjust to a very different society, Clarence as an outcast who must learn humility, is told in a more linear fashion than the anthropological sections of *L'Enfant noir*.

Le Regard du roi has elicited a much wider spectrum of critical opinion than *L'Enfant noir*. Kesteloot commented in her note about the European author of *Le Regard du roi* that it is primarily European critics who have attempted to see an "African soul" in the novel, which she felt few African scholars would have considered. Many non-African critics, as Simon Njami, the son, commented to me, need to find a "myth" of Africa. We may of course question anyone's need to find a specific soul for an ethnic group in any work of literature. Few Francophone African scholars have found an African vision in Laye's second novel. Mohamadou Kane, whose *Roman africain et traditions* several times mentions *L'Enfant noir* and *Dramouss*, ignores *Le Regard du roi*.[6] Hyacinthe Kakou, in a biographical article for the thirteenth anniversary of Laye's death, stated that African critics read *Le Regard du roi* with astonishment and indignation and would not discuss it.[7] The younger Njami, who reread *Le Regard du roi* after interviews with me, found it gave a false picture of Africa.

In *Myth, Literature and the African World* Soyinka praised the African "world-view" rather than "religion" in *L'Enfant noir*. *Le Regard du roi* "less obviously" portrays this vision. While for Soyinka *Le Regard du roi* is Africa's "earliest imaginative effort towards a modern literary aesthetic," he found parts of the novel too derivative of Kafka and commented on the vagueness: "The territory remains unlocated, anthropological specificities are ignored."[8]

In contrast to these African critics, European and American scholars have often seen the influence of Manding culture and Sufi rituals on the work of Laye. Gerald Moore wrote to me that there was an inner consistency in all Laye's work and that it was clearly the work of one man, whose sensibility was formed by Manding culture, the smith's caste, Sufic Islam, and surviving animism of the Upper Niger region. Clive Wake suggested to me that only a very clever white person would not have given himself away somewhere.

Studies of Sufi rituals, of the traditional tale as a model, and of the surrealistic elements of the novel show the rich field *Le Regard du roi* presents to scholars. For William Lawson, Clarence's drowsy state is an indication of Sufism, in which the sinner is "frequently likened to one who is asleep."[9] A similar analogy of sleeping and being awakened by the love of God could, of course, be found in Christianity or other religions. Kenneth Harrow also gave a Sufi interpretation of the novel, while noting that it is not a "key to unlock the mystery of the symbolism."[10] Clarence is a pilgrim en route, for whom the reef marks the boundary between ordinary existence and a state of transition toward the spiritual. Harrow often, however, referred to Dante, Erasmus, and the *Bhagavad Gita* as well as explanations of Sufism; some of his interpretation could as easily be based on another form of mysticism. Faith in Islam is prevalent in other texts signed Laye, but it is difficult to find in the rather vague mysticism of *Le Regard du roi*.[11]

Eileen Julien, in a reading of *Le Regard du roi* as an African text, began by putting Kafka to the side: "Indeed, much has been made of Laye's heritage from Kafka, although Laye himself suggested that Kafka's influence was not so great."[12] That Laye did not discuss Kafka in any detail in the interview Julien cited does not negate the many direct parallels to Kafka that critics have found; it only shows that Laye did not want to discuss them. Julien compared *Le Regard du roi* to a traditional tale told by Birago Diop, "L'Héritage." She found the tale's narrative structure similar to Laye's novel, as both recount a journey in which the hero progresses from ignorance to understanding. There is also, she said, a similar sequence of "surrealistic" occurrences, which are riddles for the protagonists. Finally, "Laye rejects the illusion of actuality and chronology, hallmarks of the novel, in favor of the boundless, timeless landscape of the tale" (802). This does not prove the novel is African, of course. There is no "illusion of actuality" in the work of Kafka, whose work could be compared to tales common to many cultures. Later, however, Julien commented on how *Le Regard du roi* responds to European texts and "parodies Eurocentric mythologies of Africa," without considering why Laye, in 1954, would have parodied these mythologies.[13]

Another discussion of the controversy, one that defends Laye, is an article by Brenda Bertrand, "Gender and Spirituality: Initiation into the Korè in Camara Laye's *Le Regard du roi*." Bertrand sees a parallel between initiation rites in Guinea and in the novel and suggests that this helps to prove Laye's authorship. Bertrand's main source is ethnographic work by Dominique Zahan, particularly *Sociétés d'initiation Bambara*, which describes a vast network of secret male societies. Bertrand discusses the six initiation societies, especially the

sixth and highest society, the *korè*, in which man adopts a feminine role to become the spouse of God. As part of this initiation into the *korè* there is a rite
called "le vol des bagages," followed by fifteen days in a mysterious forest. The
naba's wives, according to Bertrand, represent a spiritual ladder, the only
means of access to the divine. Sexual unity is an ascension toward union with
God, part of man's role in the unfolding of God's plan. In the last day of the initiation the neophyte abandons his clothing. All these actions are close to what
Clarence experiences, as his clothing is stolen, he wanders in what seems an impenetrable forest, and he comes naked to the king, who embraces him. Laye
never showed any detailed knowledge of such rituals in his interviews. Even if
we were to accept Bertrand's reading, it would not establish that Laye wrote
the text. It could be that Soulié, who studied African culture, had found such
rituals in his reading.[14] Maybe the parallels to ethnographic studies such as
Zahan's merely show that it is possible to impose a plausible interpretation on
any text.

Closer to what is actually in the text are interpretations in terms of surrealism. Sellin found "techniques and philosophies of surrealism" that, he said,
lead the reader to "an eerie feeling that Clarence has never set foot in Africa
and never will; indeed, that Clarence's Africa is nonexistent and his voyage a
fable."[15] Laye himself did not accept this interpretation when I asked him about
it, but the text would support it. In fact, of course, the principal author of *Le
Regard du roi*, Soulié, had "never set foot in Africa" and was writing a "fable."

Steven Ungar warned against reading the novel in a tradition of European
surrealism and gave as an example Clarence's voyage toward the south: "the
will to see this series of associations as a dreamlike narrative should, in fact, be
tempered with the phenomena of ritual initiation and the ceremonial use of
mind-altering substances. . . . inebriation is vital to his [Clarence's] identity in
Aziana."[16] Rather than André Breton's brand of surrealism, Ungar suggested
similarity between the vision of the sacred in *Le Regard du roi* and the doc-
trines of the Collège de Sociologie, a loose collective whose members included
Leiris, Roger Caillois, and Georges Bataille. Between 1937 and 1939 this short-
lived group studied the nature of the sacred, seeking to find "points of coincidence between the fundamental obsessive tendencies of individual psychology
and the directive structures of social organization."[17] Caillois gave a lecture to
the Collège on May 2, 1939, in which he spoke of initiation rites and sexual sac-

rilege and cited such students of "primitive" cultures as Marcel Mauss, Henri Lévy-Bruhl, and Sir James George Frazer. Denis Hollier commented that in the late 1930s myth was in the atmosphere: "Some felt that modern life had lost the secret of it" (294). The Collège de Sociologie manifesto was published in *La Nouvelle Revue française* in 1938 and would have been available to Soulié. He had read Leiris and perhaps Caillois and Bataille, so an influence is possible. In any case, he would have shared the interest in myth and ethnography of the era. The "African soul" in *Le Regard du roi* would be a soul as described by European anthropology, not the soul of an African author.

Janheinz Jahn is perhaps the first scholar who spoke forcefully of an essential African vision in Laye's work, one that was fundamentally difficult for Europeans to understand. Jahn wrote that *Le Regard du roi* illustrates an African cosmology and shows an incompatibility between African and European mentalities. This novel is "the high point of neo-African literature in French prose" and shows how a European is "initiated into African thought." Professor Ulli Beier, who was actually initiated into a Yoruba cult and has a right to be addressed as a chief, commented that the "ravings" of Jahn and others seem more incredible now than they had years ago.[18]

Although, as Wauthier has said, "the author [of *Le Regard du roi*] seems determined in a thousand different ways to suggest that Africa is impenetrable to the European mind," such an attitude is very different from what Laye often said he was attempting in *L'Enfant noir*; he wanted to explain Africa to Europeans and to find similarities between their artistic and cultural traditions and his own.[19] In the form submitted to Plon with the manuscript of *L'Enfant noir*, for example, Laye said his purpose was "to show the Malinké culture of Upper Guinea in contact with French culture." He spoke of how Europeans and Africans were more similar than different: "they are both sons of man." In an interview in 1971, Laye said, "Man is the same everywhere"[20] Wauthier concluded that Jahn read his own mythology into the text and that "The difference in tone, style and, doubtless, intention between these two books [*L'Enfant noir* and *Le Regard du roi*] is such that one is led to wonder whether they are really by the same hand" (71).

Other scholars of African literature, both African and European or American, have expressed doubts about *Le Regard du roi*. Palmer felt that *Le Regard du roi* emphasizes the most unpleasant aspects of traditional and modern African society, making Clarence appear better than the Africans with whom he associates. Blair wrote, "My doubts as to Camara Laye's authorship of the three novels published under his name—doubts shared by many Africanists be it said—were based on the fundamental stylistic differences, variation in quality of the writing, as well as thematic variations." Albert Gérard had doubts in 1971 when he wrote the introduction for the English-language translation, *The Radiance of the King*: "I had doubts about the authenticity of the book, whose theme and style seemed to me strangely different from those of *L'Enfant noir*. But as you know it was really not politically correct to announce such reservations." Sorel, who worked for Radio France Internationale and interviewed Laye, feels that the spirit of *Le Regard du roi* is not African.[21]

Roger Chemain commented on the difference in style. In *L'Enfant noir*, he noted, the style is transparent. In *Le Regard du roi* there is a "polysémie foisonnante" [teeming polysemy] and a dreamlike quality, not a realistic portrayal of colonial life, and no conformity to any external reference. Chemain found, however, a political message in the reverse humiliation, the inversion of the experience of Africans in European society. Clarence misunderstands the language of the Africans and finds the justice system of a different culture absurd; as a stud he represents a reversal of the racial stereotype of black sexual prowess. This message could reflect Laye's experience, but it is also a portrayal of racism that a European might have written. Similarly, Chemain found an initiation scenario that is a mixture of African and Christian symbolism. Divinity symbolized by the king is Christian, but it is Africanized by the sun symbolism and the role of sacrifice.[22] Sacrifice, of course, is not specifically African and is essential to Christian theology; Clarence's experience of feeling inadequate, of reaching a depth of self-doubt, is related to the negative way of seeking God. Interestingly, Chemain did not mention any Islamic symbolism. Chemain mentioned Kesteloot's note about a European author but neither accepted nor rejected her claim.

In his analysis of the symbols, references, and correlations in *Le Regard du roi*, a Polish scholar, Janusz Krzywicki, found many images more closely related to Western than to African culture. The need for suppression of sexual instincts is characteristic of a European, Christian tradition. This is the problem that Senghor saw in his early review of the novel, and it continues to trouble those who look for an African vision of sexuality. Krzywicki also commented on how sexual activity is ambiguously portrayed, either as leading to God or as a depravation of the senses. He found passages in the text that might be read as critical of the vision of sex and procreation in the Christian tradition: the attitude of Samba Baloum and the boys and the conjunction of the sexual act and the vision of the coming of the king in the episode with Dioki. These passages have suggested to other critics an underlying homoerotic vision. It is possible to find the allusions to homoeroticism more favorable than those to heterosexual activities and particularly to procreation.

READING *LE REGARD DU ROI* THEN AND NOW

Reading *Le Regard du roi* in 1980, I felt it embodied the same essential themes as *L'Enfant noir*: "cultural conflict and the quest for salvation."[23] Clarence has to learn to find his way in a world where his previous values have been undermined. This, I thought, could be seen as a reversal of Laye's experiences as an African in Paris, as he later described them in *Dramouss*. I now wonder whether Laye was using parts of the earlier novel as models when he wrote *Dramouss*.

Cultural conflict in *Le Regard du roi* cannot, I now realize, be compared to the conflict that the young Laye experienced on leaving his family. Clarence's disturbed, drug-induced voyage to the south has little to do with differing cultural values in Europe and Africa. His life in the village of Aziana is an idyll in many ways. I also now believe that the quest for salvation in *Le Regard du roi* is quite different from that of *L'Enfant noir*, where orthodox Muslim belief in following the path God has set out does not entail the feelings of guilt and the soul searching that Clarence undergoes.

In 1980 I read the novel as a gentle parody of Negritude, since the Africa portrayed is an essential African culture, not one that exists in the real world. "There is surely mockery of Negritude in the description of the one tangible product of Clarence's stay in Aziana: the numerous half-caste children in the harem. The result of the combination of Africa and Europe is mulatto babies, not the idealized 'cultural mulatto' of Senghorian polemics" (43). When I mentioned this interpretation to Laye, he laughed; I now think it obvious that it had never occurred to him to see any relationship to Negritude, either positive or critical. As Kesteloot said in a letter to me, Laye "never tried to pass for a champion of black mysticism. It was the European critics, especially Jahn, who took this line. Laye never encouraged them, as he was not very mystical himself."

I read the theme of the quest for God in terms of a blending of animist and Muslim world views and of the Christian culture to which Laye was exposed through French education. Some images were biblical:

> Il y a temps pour tout . . . Temps pour méditer et temps pour se laver. (153)
>
> [*There's a time for everything . . . A time to meditate and a time to wash oneself.*] *(169)*

The king is to arrive at the appointed hour, one that he knows but his vassals do not, an allusion to Matthew 25:13, "for ye know neither the day nor the hour wherein the Son of man cometh" (13, 10). I assumed such images could have come from Laye's attendance at a school modeled on the French system. I did not consider that French government schools are strictly secular and that as a Muslim, Laye would have had no reason to be familiar with the Bible. More striking than a few images, of course, is the implied parallel of the king to Christ, obvious to many European readers.

It was apparent from a first reading that the Africa of *Le Regard du roi* was a universal Africa, impossible to set in any specific time or place. I cited a critic who had found that the names of characters came from various ethnic groups. I thought, however, that the reader might see a similarity to Guinea in the more Islamized north and the dense rain forests in the south. I suggested that Clarence's trip might have started near Kouroussa or Kankan. Trying to make the story fit Laye's own experiences, I did not consider that there is no seacoast near Kouroussa or Kankan.

Like most critics approaching *Le Regard du roi*, I was anxious to find parallels to African tales as well as to Kafka. The parallels to Kafka had already been studied, particularly by Deduck, and Laye's reliance on Kafka had been criticized by several African critics. Finding a pattern of an African tale seemed essential. I commented on the way the novel, like a folktale, satirizes various social types, uses a common folktale device of metamorphosis, is set in an unspecified time and place, and uses the village and the bush to represent communal values and the darker passions. I found an animist metaphysics underlying *Le Regard du roi* and cited Laye's reworking of Clarence's dream of the fish-women in a paper he gave at the Conference on Manding Studies in London in 1972 as showing that his method in the novel "was based on traditional oral sources and traditional metaphysics."[24] It now seems likely that what I thought I found was simply Laye reusing material from the 1954 novel in his conference paper.

I was conscious, however, that I was trying hard to see the African elements. "I do not want to suggest that Laye was consciously following a form of Mandinka folk tale; consciously he was using the work of Franz Kafka as a model. Perhaps he chose Kafka, however, because he felt a similarity between Kafka's work and how an African vision is recorded in folk tales" (58). I quoted Laye's comment that Kafka's technique was used to recount an African dream. Now, of course, my explanation seems weak. It is not a technique of presenting a dream, as Laye had said in interviews, but many details that are taken from Kafka.

I was also aware of the way in which the images often come from European culture. Some mechanical ones could be explained because of Laye's training in automotive mechanics. While I wrote that the dance scene was obviously inappropriate for West Africa, I thought this was an example of Clarence humorously using European diction. I did not consider that the naked dancer, dressed only in a few leaves, was out of place in an area where Clarence wears a boubou.

In 1980 I tended to see the homoerotic elements as minimal. About a sentence that reads "Que fais-tu, Baloum? dit Clarence. Je peux savonner mes cuisses moi-même" (140), I wrote, "A passage concerning Samba Baloum's bathing Clarence might seem to have a possible homosexual overtone—'What *are* you doing, Baloum? I can soap my thighs myself' [154]—but it is presumably intended to be simply a mockery of the fact that Baloum is a eunuch."[25] I suggested in a note that the emphasis in the translation on *are* was uncalled for and found other instances in which Kirkup's translation exaggerated the homosexual possibilities, relying partly on homosexual themes in Kirkup's own work as a reason for this. Undoubtedly there was exaggeration in the English translation, but my explanation ignored the strength of the homoerotic.

Rereading *Le Regard du roi* now I find that it is still a powerful novel, a spiritual quest. Soulié understood that the comedy in Kafka is about the approach to God or the divine. The spiritual quest is combined with the exotic and with the sexual. Africa is really only an imaginary setting. The novel is one of many

European tales about finding salvation in an exotic culture. *Le Regard du roi* may be read as Soulié's desired escape from European culture. Clarence's dismissal by his fellow Europeans may be an expression of the bitterness Soulié felt for the harshness of the Belgian court's judgment against him. Clarence's acceptance by the king is Soulié's hope for redemption. Perhaps the children Clarence sired express a desire for descendants, which Soulié could attain only indirectly, through adopting an African.

RUMORS ABOUT WHO WROTE *LE REGARD DU ROI*

The first suggestions in print that Laye might not have been the author of *Le Regard du roi* were made by Wauthier in *Afrique des Africains* in 1964.[26] He commented on the differences in tone, style, and probable intentions of the two books, which suggested some doubt as to whether they were written by the same hand. More substantial rumors about the authorship did not appear in print until after Laye's death. The allegation that the author was European was published by Beti in 1980 in his review *Peuples noirs, peuples d'Afrique*.[27] It had not been evident from Beti's initial comments in 1955 that he considered *Le Regard du roi* anything but a confirmation of Laye's lack of talent. One might, however, see a suspicion in one sentence: "We no longer even recognize the author of *L'Enfant noir*."[28]

The first extended published discussion of the allegations appeared in 1982 in *Notes africaines*, the journal of the IFAN in Dakar, in an issue in commemoration of Laye. Autra, who had directed Laye's research in Guinea, wrote an obituary. After commenting on the young woman who wrote down Laye's memoirs, Autra continued: "A bit later the author of *L'Enfant noir* published a novel, *Le Regard du roi*, of a completely different technique and in a quite different style."[29] In this issue of *Notes africaines* Kesteloot wrote an appreciation of Laye and especially of *L'Enfant noir*, only briefly mentioning *Le Regard du Roi*: "Then a very fine novel, *Le Regard du roi* appeared under his name, with a style and a subject matter quite different. The clear reference to Kafka, the mystical quest, were very little in the thoughts of the Laye we had known; the sophisticated expression, as well as the reference to Mossi culture, coming from a region that Laye hardly knew, were other elements that divided critics on the authenticity of this book. For us a conversation with him on the subject convinced us that he had loaned his name to support the work of a French friend."[30]

Kesteloot's allegations, however, are known to a larger audience primarily through a footnote in her *Anthologie de la littérature négro-africaine*: "Camara Laye died in 1980. He had told me (and I must say so here, finally) that *Le Regard du roi* had been written by a white man. This does not take anything away from his personal stature but should stop the clever speculations of European critics on the black soul and mystique with respect to this novel. It is not by chance that African critics remained strangely silent about this beautiful work. Someone should have asked them why."[31]

In 1984, in a review of Lawson's *The Western Scar*, David Dorsey wrote that Lawson should have "avoided psychological conjectures about Laye as author of a book which we now know was written by a European."[32] Lawson replied the next year: "Perhaps he [Dorsey] employs the royal 'we,' for I know no other scholar who shares this special knowledge. This now discredited idea arose from the notion that ROK was too literary to have been written by an African or from the fact that its style is so unlike that of his other works. But Laye published so infrequently that he was a different kind of writer for each of his books. Throughout his life he changed in many ways, but he was never a European. . . . I, for one, remain convinced that the Camara Laye I knew wrote the novel."[33] Dorsey replied that his statement was based on the "shocking" footnote in Kesteloot's *Anthologie* and stated that he was "profoundly wrong to treat this assertion as though it established incontrovertible fact. At most it merely induces some reserve about the book's authorship."[34] I quote from this exchange to show that the issue has been important to scholars of African literature. It is interesting to note that Lawson felt that Laye's style could have changed radically between 1953 and 1954.

In 1984 Roger and Arlette Chemain wrote about the rumors and the confusion: "Unique in its era among African novels, *Le Regard du roi* also occupies a singular place in the author's work, to such a degree that some critics do not hesitate to question that the author is Camara Laye. The absence of any written proof published so far in favor of this thesis makes a strange contrast with the assurance in conversations that we have heard in the corridors at various conferences and seminars."[35]

By 1997 the *Dictionnaire Universel Francophone* was published by Hachette for the Agence Francophone pour l'Enseignement Supérieur et la Recherche (AUPELF-UREF), an agency with French government funding that supported research and teaching in Francophone literatures. The entry on Laye says that *L'Enfant noir* seemed stereotypical to African critics, mentions Laye's exile in Dakar and the publication of *Dramouss* and *Le Maître de la parole*, and does not mention *Le Regard du roi* as his work.[36]

For political reasons, some Francophone African writers have been shocked by the allegations that Laye did not write *Le Regard du roi*. Such was the reaction of Blaise N'Djehoya, who told me in an interview in 1994 that Laye had defended himself at the Second International Congress of Black Writers in Rome, held in March 1959, and that there was a mention of this defense in James Baldwin's *Nobody Knows My Name*. He was wrong; I could not find evidence that Laye attended the congress or any such references in Baldwin's work.

A number of non-African scholars have also been reluctant to consider claims that a European was involved in the writing of *Le Regard du roi*. In suspecting that an African work of art is really the work of a white person, one can be seen as trying to discredit Africans' ability to create worthwhile works of art. Ingse Skattum submitted a doctoral dissertation to the University of Oslo in 1992 titled "Repetition as an Aspect of Orality in Traditional and Modern Mandingue Literature." Although the dispute about the authorship of *Le Regard du roi* is only a part of Skattum's work, she tried to show that the stylistic unity of Laye's work is much more important than the variations among his novels.

The first letter I received from Kesteloot about the subject is dated February 22, 1992. She mentioned that Autra knew Laye well in Guinea and that one could have confidence in what he had written in *Notes africaines*. I spoke to Kesteloot on July 10, 1992. In addition to restating what was published, she told me that Laye had suggested that the real author was a reader at Plon, "mon lecteur chez Plon." This would seem to be Poulet, who wrote the first reader's reports on both *L'Enfant noir* and *Le Regard du roi*. Kesteloot added that Laye told her, "Je n'ai jamais écrit que ma vie" [I have never written anything but my own life], which she felt meant that he did not write *Le Regard du roi*. Kesteloot also claimed that the beginning of *Le Regard du roi* is a description of Ouagadougou and that Laye had not visited Ouagadougou. One might reply, however, that there is no reason to assume that any editor at Plon had visited

Ouagadougou.[37] She also questioned Laye's knowledge of Kafka. Finally, Kesteloot told me that she had not denounced (her term—"dénoncé") Laye, "because he is not an intellectual." At that time, I wanted to believe that Kesteloot was mistaken.

In a letter dated December 13, 1995, from IFAN, Kesteloot wrote me:

The explanation that Laye gave me concerning his friend at Plon: he had an unpublished manuscript. Knowing the difficulties that an unknown European novelist faced to be published, he would have proposed to Laye to publish *Le Regard du roi* under his name (with of course the royalties as compensation). It was a favor that Laye gave him. The *same year* Laye had published his *L'Enfant noir* that this man had read (and revised?). There was a good relationship between them.

No one said that the author had already submitted the manuscript to Plon. If he had done so, the ruse would have been obvious immediately. Laye, not knowing about literary procedures, accepted without seeing anything wrong with it.

So it was not a white "ghost writer"; the novel already existed. Besides, Laye would not have had the time to write it between the publication of *L'Enfant noir* and that of *Le Regard du roi*. That would also explain that the flagrant difference in style cannot be accounted for by the author's style having matured.

Laye never tried to pass for a champion of black mysticism. It was the European critics, especially Jahn, who took this line. Laye never encouraged them, as he was very little mystical himself.

This is why I spoke of his "naive frankness, his constant sobriety and his discretion about this novel" [quotation from a letter to me by Mohamed Salif Keita, citing what Kesteloot had told him]. This was a wise course, certainly, for Laye was quite ill at ease talking about the novel, as his interview with Jacqueline Leiner shows.

Why did I not speak about this while Laye was alive? This is easy to understand. Laye would have been attacked with questions and criticisms. He would have been very embarrassed. This could have damaged his reputation and his financial situation. . . . There are academic reasons, but there is also the life of a man with limited education and who was soon to fall sick, who had confidence in me. After he died, Ray Autra, his compatriot, took the responsibility to write the truth in the issue of "Notes africaines," and I added a comment, but in a sentimental context which excluded any polemics about this subject.

I continue to think that for Laye this "fake" was not a fault. He had signed it in all innocence. It was not right that he would suffer for this.

Today we can tell the truth without his suffering, and he will not have to justify himself before intellectuals who would like to organize an inquisition.

In another letter from Kesteloot, dated February 15, 1996, she adds:

What you have told me about this Robert Poulet has made me think. First of all why did Laye tell you that he [Poulet] was dead? Wouldn't it be to keep you from trying to meet him? And what he told me—"an unknown novelist"—was perhaps a mask. Then if this Poulet was already a writer that explains the high quality of *Le Regard du Roi* and the enormous gap existing between this book and Camara Laye's other writing. Particularly *Dramouss*, which we know was not revised—*L'Enfant noir* having already been the fruit of a close collaboration between Laye and his girlfriend (Swiss or French, I no longer remember exactly). But why would Poulet, who was already publishing at this time, have made this curious deal? Perhaps a taste for a challenge: "Can my novel be taken as written by a Black?" There have been other examples, like that of Christine Garnier who, using the name Doéllé, published *Va-t-en avec les tiens*. I almost put it in my thesis on Black Writers at the time! . . . With a real person such as Camara Laye, his white man would have no risk of being found out, at least at the beginning. And also he would be helping a pleasant young black man, who needed the money and was a bit naive. . . . I think that today the truth can hurt no one, as long as you keep a measured and objective tone. It is only an academic problem in literary history.

This is the first time I learned that Laye had said "an unknown novelist" rather than just a reader at Plon. Kesteloot's recollection here is another confirmation of the role of Soulié, an unknown writer and a person of whom she had never heard before I wrote to her.

WHY WRITE UNDER SOMEONE ELSE'S NAME?

Krzywicki's close reading of *Le Regard du roi* and the various interpretations that the text has engendered suggest that many critics have looked hard for a myth based on African views of the world or, alternately, on a rejection of European feelings of superiority but that such a straightforward interpretation is not possible. It is the atmosphere of contradictions, the distortion of reality, the multiplicity of possible interpretations, and the undefined subjectivity that led Krzywicki to state that *Le Regard du roi* "does not fit in an obvious way into a single cultural tradition."[38] Thus, from purely textual analysis, Krzywicki is skeptical of attributing the authorship solely to Laye. After learning from my book that Poulet was Laye's editor at Plon, Krzywicki read some of Poulet's work, trying to find some similarities. Deciding that the style of *Le Regard du roi* is radically different from that of Poulet, he concluded that "no matter what the contribution of different persons to the creation of this novel was, it remains an example of an extraordinary product of an intercultural encounter."[39]

The question remains why this intercultural encounter took place, why the author of *Le Regard du roi* (Soulié, not Poulet, who, as Krzywicki says, was quite a different type of writer) did not publish under his own name. Similar cases can be found in various literatures. There are several reasons why the true author may not be the person whose name appears on the cover. An author may use someone else's name or invent one simply to get published or to receive more publicity and perhaps more sales. Several such cases of impersonation have occurred in Australia. Leon Carmen, an Australian from Sydney, published *My Own Sweet Time* under the name Wanda Koolmatrie, supposedly a part-Aborginal woman, and won a prize for his work. Carmen said he did it because he did not believe it would be published if he submitted it under his own name. In 1996 Paul Radley, who had won a prize in Australia in 1980 for *Jack Rivers and Me*, an unpublished manuscript by a young writer, admitted that the real author was his uncle Jack, who felt that young authors had a better chance to get published than older ones.

For less commercial reasons, the author may attempt to portray himself or herself as belonging to a different ethnic group in order to claim what would be a bogus "authenticity." In Australia Helen Darville wrote *The Hand That Signed the Paper* (1994) under the assumed name Helen Demidenko, appearing therefore to be of Ukrainian descent and from a family supposedly brutalized by Jewish Bolsheviks. This novel, too, won a major literary prize. When the identity of the author was discovered, Australian critics debated the question of the importance of the name on the cover. In this case the identity of the person who wrote a defense of Croatian Nazis seemed important.

Western writers might take the identity of a member of a disadvantaged ethnic group in an attempt to allay feelings of guilt for having privileges or perhaps to assume a cultural claim to victimization. Binjamin Wilkomirski's memoirs of a Jewish childhood in the concentration camps of Poland, *Fragments*, which won several prizes, was criticized when birth records showed that he was born in Switzerland to a Protestant woman. While Wilkomirski has denied the authenticity of the birth records, it is now accepted that his work is imaginative, drawing on books he read, films he saw, and stories actual survivors told him. One critic considers that Wilkomirski's assumed identity "gave him a new sense of meaningful destiny." His book was successful because of a hunger among readers for testimony and "a sense of vicarious excitement imagining oneself with those who were thrust by fate into the heart of ultimate evil."[40] This "sense of meaningful destiny" might be one reason why Soulié wrote as an African. In finding a new identity, he could reject the Soulié who collaborated with the Nazi occupiers of his country.

Kesteloot mentioned Garnier, who published under an assumed African name, Doéllé. Presumably the work showed sufficient knowledge about Africa to have been written by an African. Closer to the case of Soulié and Laye are those books that are often assumed to be the work of Europeans although published under the name of real Africans. When Bakary Diallo's *Force Bonté* was published in 1926, suspicions were aroused about a possible ghostwriter because Diallo had had little formal education. It is often believed that he had much help from the wife of a French colonial administrator, Madame Lucie Cousturier, who served as a nurse and treated Diallo in France for wounds he received fighting in the First World War. Often considered the first novel written by a black man in French, it was not political; rather, "Diallo reassured with his comforting message of gratitude to his White benefactors, and of peace, goodwill and understanding among men."[41]

Born in 1876, Cousturier spent her childhood in Africa. She was the daughter of a high colonial official in French West Africa, Paul Jean François Cousturier, governor of Guinea from 1900 to 1904. He worked to break the unity of Fulani forces in Fouta-Djallon, which he considered a danger to the public peace. Lucie wrote two books about the relations between Africans and Europeans, *Des Inconnus chez moi* and *Mes Inconnus chez eux*. She was a pupil of Paul Signac and also wrote a number of books on art history. Since Poulet mentions her in his review of *L'Enfant noir* in *Rivarol*, it is possible Laye knew something of this woman and used her life as one of the models for Tante Aline in *Dramouss*, who is said to have spent some time in Siguiri before 1925. Lucie Cousturier died in 1925.

Pierre Halen cites a number of Belgians, particularly missionaries during the colonial period, who wrote under African names, primarily to create a collection of books published in Africa for Africans and when possible by Africans; they may even have considered themselves to have become African. During the opening of an exhibition of watercolors by Lubaki in Paris around 1930, a false rumor was spread that the works were really by a white man. The European supposed to have painted the watercolors, a Belgian named Georges Thiry, did gather watercolors by Lubaki and others and sent them to Brussels for sale. Thiry also asked his "clerk," Badibanga, to collect and translate African tales. They were published in 1931 in Brussels, with a preface by Thiry and Gaston-Denys Périer, who had also promoted the African art that Thiry sent. Thiry wanted to be considered the author of the book, but Périer insisted it should appear under Badibanga's name. Jahn later said that Badibanga's book, *L'Eléphant qui marche sur les oeufs*, was false, suggesting that authenticity can come only from an author belonging to the group being described.[42] Beier, however, who wrote plays and published them under the pseudonym Ijimere to give the impression that the author was a Yoruba, considered his impersonation a "joke you share with those to whom you offer the plays." He felt only a narrow-minded person would believe that "only a Yoruba can comprehend the Yoruba world view."[43]

In the United States, when it was discovered that *The Education of Little Tree*, supposedly the autobiography of a Cherokee Indian, was written by Asa Earl Carter, who wrote segregationist speeches for Alabama governor George Wallace, there was an outcry. In " 'Authenticity' of the Lesson of Little Tree," Henry Louis Gates Jr. commented on the problems of demanding autobiographical or any kind of group authenticity (racial, ethnic, gender) in literature. While a book is a cultural event, and the identity of the author is part of that event, "fact and fiction have always exerted a reciprocal effect on each other." Thus, Gates said, all writers are "cultural impersonators."[44]

A case close in some ways to Laye's is that of Rigoberta Menchú, the Nobel Peace Prize winner whose memoirs, *I, Rigoberta Menchú*, were transcribed from interviews with a Venezuelan anthropologist and left-wing political activist, Elisabeth Burgos. David Stoll, an American anthropologist, has shown that Menchú said she witnessed incidents when she did not and that the political perspective is skewed to suggest that only the military tormented civilians. Burgos, rather like those who helped with *L'Enfant noir*, added biblical quotations and metaphors that would not have occurred to Menchú, who was an illiterate Guatemalan peasant. In an interesting left-wing reversal of the activity of conservatives helping Laye, Burgos wrote the autobiography to support the revolutionary front in Guatemala; *L'Enfant noir* was written to support the French Union. Both fictionalized autobiographies, however, are valuable. Stoll argued that Menchú is a "legitimate Mayan voice." *L'Enfant noir's* picture of Upper Guinea in the 1930s and 1940s presents a legitimate Malinké voice. A review of Stoll's book suggests that in spite of his revelations, he has succeeded in making Menchú "more human," showing that behind her public persona, "a lonely person strives to remain in touch with her roots."[45]

While suggesting that Kesteloot's claim that a European wrote *Le Regard du roi* may be false, János Riesz considered possible scenarios in which a European might be the author and yet never claim this recognized work of literary merit. Perhaps, he speculated, the manuscript by the European had been turned down, or perhaps he did not want his reputation changed by publishing a radically different work. Riesz continued: "Let us finally mention a wholly idealistic (though very unlikely) motivation. The true author 'gives' the book to the African author in order that the latter can continue a literary career successfully started without a long interruption. Out of gratitude? Out of affection? Pure altruism? An analogy with adoption suggests itself: the natural parent gives up the child to someone else for adoption perhaps because s/he believes the adoptive parent(s) will improve the child's prospects for development."[46] Riesz is, interestingly, close to the truth. Soulié gave the novel out of affection for Laye, a young man whom he had wanted to adopt. Whether Soulié had feared the novel would not be published under his name (as he seems to have suggested to Laye, according to Kesteloot's comments) or whether he was living very discreetly because of his past cannot be determined with certainty.

Poulet undoubtedly would have enjoyed helping him to pass as an African author as a game for its own sake.

Riesz found several works of French colonial literature similar to *Le Regard du roi* in treating what he termed "reverse acculturation"—among them *La Maîtresse noire* (1928) by Louis-Charles Royer and *Le Blanc qui s'était fait nègre* (1946) by René Guillot.[47] Guillot's novel is the story of Barail, a Frenchman who has returned to the scene of a violent battle in which he and other soldiers destroyed a village thirty years earlier and where he now helps the villagers. He is described as a primitive, hardly human, no longer white. The perspective is always that of the white colonial narrator who meets Barail. The Africans are simply types. *Le Regard du roi*, in contrast, does create African characters, who are never described as being of a different species from Clarence. Perhaps because he had never been to Africa, Soulié in *Le Regard du roi* moves beyond the realm of colonial literature.

READING *DRAMOUSS* THEN AND NOW

Dramouss is several intertwined stories: that of Laye's life in Paris and after his return to Guinea upon completion of his studies; a folk tale about marital infidelity; and a dream of the coming of a tyranny and the eventual salvation of the country. Reading *Dramouss* in 1980, I saw it as a story of how the African child learns to blend his two cultures, Malinké and French. Françoise and Mimie were symbols of France and Guinea. Fatoman, the hero, must choose Africa while assimilating some elements of French culture. His rejection of Françoise, I wrote, "might be explained by her being less a character than the embodiment of a theme."[48] With new information about Laye's life, I now see that she was a character based on a real person, about whom he wanted to give limited information. Similarly, Tante Aline is more than a figure to "capture some of the warmth he wishes to attribute to the French people" (65). The very vagueness with which these two women are described shows that Laye was, as he often said, writing about his life but that he did not want to admit the depth of his relationship with these women and how they helped him.

An attentive reader of *Dramouss* would be aware of certain unresolved discrepancies in the chronology of the novel. In 1980 I commented on some of these discrepancies, presumably the result of Laye combining material written at several different times. Fatoman describes his life in Paris without giving dates. On returning to Kouroussa, he says he left Guinea in 1947 and returned after six years but then describes a political meeting that took place after 1956.

I also found some echoes of *Le Regard du roi* in the description of the prince in the folk tale that is inserted rather arbitrarily into the novel. This reliance on reusing passages from *Le Regard du roi* is much more evident in Laye's work after *Dramouss*. There are also echoes of "Les Yeux de la statue" in the dream sequence. It now seems obvious that when possible Laye wanted to rely on what had already been published.

Finally, I saw *Dramouss* as an expression of the tensions of Laye's generation, during an era when one culture was breaking down and a nightmare tyranny was established. The novel has value that, I said and would still say, "outweighs its formal weaknesses" (83). Especially important, it is Laye's own voice, attacking the dictatorship of Sékou Touré, at some risk to himself.

READING LAYE'S LATER WORK THEN AND NOW

In retrospect, Laye's reworking of material from *Le Regard du roi* seems to show that he was unhappy with his own work and relied heavily on copying what had already been published under his name. A writer would not normally repeat an episode from an earlier novel in several texts written twenty years later. Laye, however, reworked the dream of the fish-women in "Le Rêve dans la société traditionnelle malinké" (1972) and in a short story, "Prélude et fin d'un cauchemar" (1976). In each case the dreamer is confronted with a being whose exact nature he cannot identity: woman or fish (*Le Regard du roi*), man or lion ("Le Rêve"), cow or buffalo ("Prélude"). The dreams in the three texts are almost identical:

> Au milieu du fleuve, à proximité d'une île qui était au milieu du fleuve, une vague forme de femme émergeait. Une forme vague; car si les seins étaient visiblement des seins de femme, la tête était bien plus une tête de poisson qu'une tête de femme. Le jour était malheureusement devenu trop faible pour qu'on pût clairement en décider. (*Le Regard du roi*, 194)
>
> [*In the middle of the river, close to an islet that was in the middle of the river, a vague female form was slowly emerging. It was only vaguely fe-*

male, for if the breasts were obviously women's breasts, the head was very much more like the head of a fish than the head of a woman. Unfortunately the light had grown too dusky to be able to make out the shape clearly.]
(Radiance of the King, *219)*

Au milieu du fleuve, à proximité d'une île qui était au milieu du fleuve, une vague forme d'homme émergeait. Une forme vague, car si la poitrine était visiblement la poitrine d'homme, la tête était bien plus une tête de lion qu'une tête d'homme. Le jour était malheureusement devenu trop faible pour qu'on pût clairement en décider. ("Le Rêve," 2)

[*In the middle of the river, close to an islet that was in the middle of the river, a vague male form was slowly emerging. It was only vaguely male, for if the chest was obviously a man's chest, the head was very much more like the head of a lion than the head of a man. Unfortunately the light had grown too dusky to be able to make out the shape clearly.*]

Au milieu du fleuve, à proximité d'une île qui était au milieu de ce fleuve, "Djoliba," une vague forme de boeuf émergeait. Une vague forme; si les cornes étaient visiblement des cornes de boeuf, la tête était bien plus une tête de buffle qu'une tête de boeuf. Le jour était malheureusement devenu trop faible pour qu'on pût clairement en décider. D'autant qu'un boeuf, ce n'est qu'un buffle rabougri. ("Prélude")

[*In the middle of the river, close to an islet that was in the middle of the river, a vague form of an ox was slowly emerging. It was only vaguely an ox, for if the horns were obviously an ox's horns, the head was very much more like the head of a buffalo than the horns of an ox. Unfortunately the light had grown too dusky to be able to make out the shape clearly. All the more so as an ox is only a stunted buffalo.*]

Looking at the dream sequence in 1980, I considered that it "suggests a frightening uncertainty about reality. . . . it is perhaps not unreasonable to consider this dream as Laye's expression of the instability of the modern world and of his belief that some force beyond the individual is needed for salvation."[49] While this reading remains a valid interpretation of the dream, I would now argue that it expresses Soulié's sensibility, which can be attributed both to his affinities to surrealism and, especially, to his own experiences of escape and exile.

What I did not consider in 1980 was how the close copying of passages showed not only Laye's need to publish texts in order to retain his reputation and to earn much needed money but also his lack of imaginative power to go beyond an earlier text. Now, realizing the extent to which he relied on others for his writing, I see more clearly how much he must have felt abandoned by those who had supported him in the 1950s and depressed by the situation in which he found himself after having made the courageous move from Guinea to Senegal.

When Laye wrote *Le Maître de la parole* the borrowings from his earlier works were evident. In 1980 I found sentences taken directly from both *L'Enfant noir* and *Le Regard du roi*. I also commented on how Laye used techniques from the European novel form in a story filled with miraculous events, which produced a disconcerting amalgam. Laye combined, for example, the voice of a limited narrator who does not know what his characters are thinking with an epic tale in which there is no ambiguity. I concluded: "As a transcription of a traditional tale, it is perhaps too modern and literary. As a novel within the European tradition, the narrative contains too many long genealogies, secondary characters and interventions in the plot" (96). I realize now that *Le Maître de la parole* shows an insecurity regarding structure and narrative voice similar to that of *Dramouss* and differs significantly from the first two novels.

Krzywicki has found a number of almost identical passages in *Le Regard du roi* and *Le Maître de la parole*.[50] One example:

> On eût dit que ses dents limés déchiraient, au passage, les éclats de rire qui sortaient de sa gorge. (*Le Regard du roi*, 176)
>
> > [*You would think his sharpened teeth were tearing the laughter to pieces as it left his throat.*] (The Radiance of the King, *197*)
>
> On eût dit que ses dents rares déchiraient, au passage, les éclats de rire qui sortaient de sa bouche. (*Le Maître de la parole*, 47)
>
> > [*It was as if her three or four teeth were tearing the bursts of laughter as they issued from her throat.*] (The Guardian of the Word, *43*)

Kesteloot wondered why Laye wanted to recreate the Soundiata legend in literary terms in *Le Maître de la parole*; perhaps he did so in order to use parts of *Le Regard du roi* and avoid too much writing.[51]

4

Stylistic Evidence in *Le Regard du roi*

Although it is not possible to prove or disprove authorship by examining the style of a work of art, many readers, soon after the publication of *Le Regard du roi*, felt that it could hardly have been written by the person who wrote *L'Enfant noir*. Some critics, however, have suggested that stylistic devices found in *L'Enfant noir* recur in *Le Regard du roi*, especially the use of repetition and the overt search to find the right word. Of course, such similarities in style might be explained by the involvement of Soulié in both *L'Enfant noir* and *Le Regard du roi*. (There are fewer such stylistic traits in *Dramouss*. As for *Le Maître de la parole*, when Laye wrote this last book he very often was influenced by earlier work published under his name.) Similarities, however, are less important than the many differences, particularly in the choice of diction.

Laye said in interviews that he wrote for the ordinary African reader, that he wanted to be understood. The vocabulary in *Le Regard du roi*, however, is far from simple and includes a number of expressions or terms unknown to many educated French readers. A few examples considered unusual: "lutiner" (124), meaning bothering or harassing; "piriformes" (144), meaning in the shape of a pear (a fruit not found in West Africa); "couri[r] le guilledou" (148), a rather old-fashioned familiar expression meaning "to chase women" (nicely translated by Kirkup as "spending the night on the tiles" [164]); "calembredaines" (211), meaning "pleasantries"; "claquemuré" (233), meaning "enclosed."[1] In the hut he shares with Akissi, Clarence "se laissa glisser le long du bourrelet qui sert de chambranle" (180); literally the "bourrelet" is a circle of cloth used to carry something on one's head, an appropriate image for Africa, and the "chambranle" is cloth put around a door to cut the draught. The use of the two somewhat obscure words might make the passage difficult for the French or the African reader. (The English translation is simply "he slithered down the jamb of the door" [201].) There is also the use of "carême-prenant" (152), presumably in the sense of someone wearing a disguise, a rather unusual meaning deriving from the literal expression meaning the three days before the beginning of Lent, a term that would normally only be understood or used by religious persons. Several French persons I asked did not know the meaning of "carême-prenant." (The English translation is simply "idiot," [169].) "Le caquet rabattu" (41) is a poetic reworking of "rabattre le caquet" ("to make someone be quiet") and is not common usage.[2] Similarly, "un tintamarre jeté à la chaleur" (20), meaning "loud noise thrown into the heat," as a description of the music Clarence hears, was considered vague and poetic by several speakers, both French and Belgian. The English translation captures this unusual tone: "a loud din that had to be flung against the barrier of heat" (20). Another unusual metaphor is "comme la gueule trop rose d'un chien bâtard" (60); in the English translation it also seems odd, "like the rosy jaws of a mongrel dog" (65).

At least two words do not exist in many standard French dictionaries. "Enquinauder" (57), meaning to deceive, is listed only in a multivolume French dictionary, as an old usage. In addition, "coquecigrues" (154), presumably meaning "illogical statements," is rare and perhaps Rabelesian. It is worth looking at the passage in which it is used, two sentences with several slang expressions and a rather recherché word order.

Clarence revoyait la salle d'audience d'Adramé, et le vieux filou accroupi sur la table, égrenant son chapelet. En avait-il débité des coquecigrues, le coquin! (154)

> [*Clarence seemed to see again the courtroom at Adramé and the old rogue of a judge crouching over his table and telling his beads. What a lot of balderdash he had talked!*] *(172)*

Besides these rather obscure words, there are familiar, or occasionally literary, expressions that would not normally be used by Africans who learned French in school; because they feel unsure about the tone, they are often less willing to use slang than most native speakers. There are a number of idiomatic or familiar expressions in the novel, many more than were used in *L'Enfant noir*. Among the slang expressions, "tintouin" (174) is a familiar term for "noise"; Samba Baloum is called a "poussah" (122), a familiar but rather old-fashioned term for a fat man; and "De la frime" (173; "make-believe," 194) is an idiomatic term for "counterfeit" or "simulation."

While praising the pure style of *Le Regard du roi*, Senghor noted that Laye's language in *Le Regard du roi* is too metropolitan, not reflecting African usage of French. Among metaphors borrowed from Europe, he gave as an example "ne quitter pas d'une semelle," which occurs twice (36, 70) and is translated as "We haven't stirred an inch from your side" (38) or "I did not stir one step from his side" (77). "Semelle," however, refers to the sole of a shoe and is thus not an African image.[3] One might also mention "Je ne vais pas mettre des gants" (237, literally "I'm not going to put on gloves," translated as "I'm not here to spare your feelings," 266).

There are also a number of images in *Le Regard du roi* that are European:

Une frénésie qui transformait les carrefours et leurs brasiers en autant de clairières de sabbat. (61)

> [*a pitch of frenzy which transformed the brazier-lighted crossroad into scenes from a witches' sabbath.*] *(66)*

pour peu qu'on observe ses traits, c'est à un enfant qu'on pense; à un enfant que ses parents traînent par des rues de banlieue, un dimanche soir, au retour d'une promenade. (91)

[*But if one were to look at his face, one would think it belonged to a child being dragged through suburban streets by his parents on a Sunday evening.*] *(101)*

une vapeur chaude, fade comme l'haleine du métro. (157; this image—"hot fumes, stale as breath in the underground"—is omitted in the English translation [175], perhaps because it seems so obviously out of place.)

une cour profonde, une sorte de fosse aux ours comme on en voit dans les jardins zoologiques. (162)

[*a deep yard, a sort of bear-pit such as one might see in zoological gardens*] *(180–81; the bear is not an African animal.)*

Such comparisons can perhaps be explained because they are often used by Clarence or indirectly from his point of view, though it would be unusual for them to occur to Laye. We must, of course, beware of attributing European authorship on the basis of imagery. When I inquired of Lamine Kamara about Laye's references to non-African fauna and flora, such as the swans in "Les Yeux de la statue," he pointed out that all Laye's first education, like that of Kamara himself in Guinea a generation later, would have been with French literature and culture. It would be difficult to prove that swans are not often used by African authors, but I doubt that they are.

An African author would have seen a cultural error when the untutored African characters use some clearly Western expressions.

Des alouettes? dit le mendiant. Des alouettes à ces polissons? (41)

[*"Larks?," said the beggar. "Larks for rogues like these?"*] *(43)*

Quoi! votre veste pour cette misérable Saint-Charlemagne qu'il nous a servie? dit celui [Nagoa ou Noaga] qui avait sa main sur l'estomac. (59)

[*"What!" exclaimed the one who had been holding his stomach. "You gave your coat for that wretched cat's-piss he served us?"*] *(65)*

Larks are European birds. Saint-Charlemagne is presumably used to compare the drink served with a French wine. The translation "cat's-piss" seems less out of place for Africa.

Even while admitting that the author wants to establish Clarence's feelings of difference from the Africans, and initially of superiority over them, one may question the need to have descriptions that so clearly suggest a sort of animal-ity among Africans. I now find it difficult to imagine Laye himself describing the odors of Africans as "l'odeur du troupeau" [the odor of the flock] (63, 68) or writing about hair, "Mais il avait le nez à hauteur de leurs cheveux crépus; une lourde odeur de suint s'en dégageait" [But his nose was on a level with the tops of their heads, from which gave off a strong smell of rancid grease] (19, 16; the translator omitted "cheveux crépus" [frizzy hair], perhaps because it sounded too derogatory). In *L'Enfant noir* Laye is often concerned to stress how he and his family are like any family in the world. In *Le Regard du roi*, however, there is a strong feeling of an essential difference of cultures. In particular, there is a suggestion that Africa is the south, a land of sensual temptations, irrationality, and odors.

Critics have often found the description of the king, with his heavy gold bracelets, to recall the Benin statues.[4] Although Laye could well have been familiar with these statues, so could any educated European. Less often discussed are the frescoes. Alain Fresco, however, has suggested that they were not inspired by Africa at all:

> Prof. Roy Sieber, a specialist in African art in the Fine Arts Department at Indiana University, feels that the images described by Laye Camara could not have been patterned after Benin or West African art. African art is figurative and sculptural. Further, in Benin art, those who support the king are not pages but functionaries of the court and usually there are only two individuals, not four. Secondly, the idea of a two-dimensional mural or fresco with a narrative content is alien to Benin art, which was commemorative rather than descriptive. (Some of the frescoes described by Laye Camara retell the lives of the kings.) Prof. Sieber further maintains that, to his knowledge, human sacrifices were not depicted on murals. He feels that Laye Camara might have drawn his inspiration from Aztec murals.[5]

At the least, this judgment by a specialist in African art suggests that anyone might well have written the descriptions. Many African readers have said that the use of flowers in the hut at night as a sort of drug to confuse Clarence seems out of place in Africa. This image may well have been taken from Paul Gauguin's *Noa noa*.

More difficult yet to explain are incidents in the narration that cannot be reconciled with the customs of traditional Africa. Particularly wrong are the phrases used to describe dancing, which is made to sound like the activity in a

European dance hall: "un couple ouvrit le bal" [a pair of dancers opened the ball] (112, 125). A woman invites Clarence to dance: "Elle le serra dans ses bras" [And she pressed him to her] (118, 132). Dancing in couples is quite out of place in Africa. In *L'Enfant noir*, Laye states:

> Nous dansions avec infiniment de retenue, mais il va de soi: ce n'est pas la coutume chez nous de s'enlacer; on danse face à face, sans se toucher. (186)
>
> [*Of course we danced very circumspectly. In Guinea it is not customary for couples to dance in each other's arms. We danced facing each other, but without touching.*] *(161)*

Laye is describing dancing with Marie to a record; how much less probable is dancing in one's partner's arms to traditional music in a village.

The reader is also supposed to imagine that some women in the village are naked: the woman who invites Clarence to dance "arracha une demi-douzaine de feuilles au dais et s'en fit un espèce de pagne" [She pulled a handful of leaves from the canopy and made herself a sort of diminutive apron with them] (118, 132). References to total female nudity often seem exaggerated if we assume that the novel is set in the savanna area of West Africa. There was much less clothing, if any beyond a covering for the genital area, for both men and women in Central Africa than in West Africa; in the Congo there wasn't any suitable material with which to make cloth. Clarence, however, wears a boubou frequently, so the setting seems rather to be the savanna region. I wonder if Soulié, looking at photographs such as those Marc Allégret took for André Gide's *Voyage au Congo*, didn't assume a degree of nudity that does not fit the area he is presumably describing. Clarence several times refers to the filed teeth of the citizens of Aziana. While the practice was sometimes used in other parts of Africa, it was particularly prevalent in the Congo. Again, Soulié may be mixing two regions of the continent.[6]

There are, of course, details that are definitely African and perhaps furnished to Soulié by Laye. There is an echo of *L'Enfant noir* in the list of "menu services" [every kind of small service] Clarence thinks he could perform: "éloigner des champs de mil les oiseaux" [scare away the birds from the millet-fields] (120, 135). More obvious are the Malinké numbers: tan, mouan, and tan saba (166–68, 185–86). As these are the only Malinké words in the novel, we might wonder if they were added only to make the novel seem to be the authentic work of a Malinké speaker.

There are also geographical inconsistencies. This is an archetypal Africa; it is not Guinea, the only region Camara knew, but the Africa of many European anthropologists. The period in which the story takes place is also vague. The reader assumes, because Clarence initially feels superior to the black people on the esplanade and has lived in a European hotel, that the story takes place during a period of colonial rule. By the time he goes to the south, however, there is no suggestion of the presence of any colonial government.

An obvious difference between Laye's other works and *Le Regard du roi* concerns the treatment of sexuality. Laye's first feelings toward Marie in *L'Enfant noir* are very discreetly portrayed. Descriptions of Laye's visit to the sea are used to suggest nascent passion, but he also tells us that he and Marie were too shy, too reserved to eat in each other's presence. In *Dramouss* the wedding night is described with much discretion:

> j'étais à présent au lit, avec elle près de moi. Je ne crois pas que nous causâmes longtemps. Et je m'endormis à poings fermés. (38)
> [*I was now in bed, with her beside me, very close beside me. I don't think we talked very long. I soon dropped off and slept like a log.*] *(25)*

A few pages later it is not clear whether he has even had sexual relations with Mimie, who is presented as almost unbelievably shy. Since he never admits what his relationship is to Françoise in Paris, this scene is the only sexual activity described in the novel, except for the passage in which Fatoman is outraged at the advances of a homosexual in a Paris bar and the folktale, where there are several episodes of sexual intercourse in which the beauty of the naked female form is evoked but little detail as to what takes place is offered.

> Elle était belle au sens africain du mot, avec les douze signes de la beauté: les dents blanches, le cou mince, long et enrobé de plis, les chevilles minces, les main effilées, les épaules tombantes, le bassin large, les avant-bras minces et longs... (135–36).
> [*She was beautiful in the African sense of the word, bearing upon her body*

the twelve signs of beauty: white teeth, slender neck (a long neck garlanded
with little folds of flesh), narrow heels, fine hands, sloping shoulders, broad
pelvis, long, thin fore-arms . . .] *(86)*

He does not complete the list, which does not contain twelve signs. Because naked breasts are common in many African villages, they are not considered sex-
ually stimulating to the extent they are in Western society. In *Dramouss*, however, Laye is too shy to mention any sexual parts of the female body.

In *Le Regard du roi*, Clarence describes women's faces in general terms.
Akissi's face is a "minois" [pretty little mug] (150, 168). He is, however, often
aware of women's breasts, an awareness that seems more Western than African.
In Adramé before he goes to the south, Clarence observes a dancer: "Comment s'y prend-elle pour avoir tant de poitrine?" [How on earth does she man-
age to have such prominent and pointed breasts?] (77, 85). Later, the manatees
"tendaient ignoblement la poitrine" [kept pushing their dead-white, ungov-
ernable tits] (198, 224); in his dream Clarence is frightened of touching these
breasts, with "cette gluante mollesse" [their glutinous softness] (199, 225).
Lack of interest in describing the female body, except in negative terms, might
suggest a homoerotic orientation.

Jokes about the eunuch are frequent, and with them an atmosphere that can
readily be seen as at least partly homosexual. There are many allusions to
Samba Baloum as a eunuch and many allusions to his love of touching Clarence's body:

—Alors cessez de me palper, dit Clarence.
—Oh! de ma part, cela n'a pas grande importance, dit Samba Baloum. (126)
[*"Then stop feeling me all over," replied Clarence.*
"Oh, that's nothing at all," said Samba Baloum.] *(141)*

—Que fais-tu, Baloum? dit Clarence. Je peux savonner mes cuisses moi-
même. (140)
[*"But what are you doing, Samba Baloum?" demanded Clarence. "I can*
quite well soap my thighs myself."] *(154)*

Clarence comes to appreciate Samba Baloum's help with his shower:

S'il était ici, il me laverait le dos; ce n'est pas que j'aime beaucoup ses mains:

elles sont molles, trop douces et trop molles; mais il faut voir l'intention. (153)

> [*If he were here, he'd wash my back for me. Not that I care much for his hands: they are too soft, too tender and too caressing, but you have to give him his due.*] *(170)*

The hands seem to be like female hands, which Clarence doesn't much care for.

Often references to Baloum's sexual gestures are combined with allusions to Clarence's sexual activities during the night:

Allons, dormez bien. Reposez-vous, acheva-t-il en donnant une légère claque sur le derrière de Clarence. La nuit qui vient, vous aurez du travail! (127)

> [*"Have a good rest,"* he concluded, *giving Clarence's behind a light smack. "There will be work for you tonight!"*] *(142-43)*

—Mais non, reprit-il, pas comme une volaille. Ma parole, vous me tâtez comme on tâte un étalon!

—Un étalon? s'écria Samba Baloum. Ah! voilà qui est drôle! Il faut que je rie. (149)

> [*"No, not like a bird,"* he went on. *"You keep going over my points, feeling me as if I were a prize stallion!"*
>
> *"A stallion?"* cried Samba Baloum. *"Oh, that's a good one! I've got to laugh."*] *(165)*

There is a suggestion of homosexual attraction when Clarence speaks of "la même adorable fragilité" of the king [the same adorable fragility] (250, 281). The description of the beating of the master of ceremonies may also seem like sadomasochism. Clarence's choice of color for his boubou—olive green with white flowers—might have homosexual connotations. At the least, it is not a common textile design for men's clothing in West Africa.

The book is often misogynist or at least shows little awareness of women, even to the point of considering that a sexual advance toward a woman would be a way of mistreating her. As Clarence says to Dioki: "il ne me viendrait pas à l'idée de te maltraiter. Tu n'as plus l'âge où un homme voudrait te maltraiter" ["it would never enter my head to treat you otherwise," he said. "You're past the age when men would want to ill-treat you"] (217, 242).

Bernard Mouralis saw a puritanical attitude in Clarence's feelings of revulsion about human flesh and speculated on Clarence's sexual orientation. Discussing the final scene, in which Clarence is taken into the king's bosom, Mouralis wrote:

> On constatera ainsi que ce qui s'exprime ici dans ce passage sur lequel se clôt le roman, ce n'est pas seulement l'évasion hors du monde réel, à travers un motif qui relève du fantastique, mais, plus fondamentalement, le rejet de la femme et une homosexualité qui probablement est une des clefs de la marginalité de Clarence.
>
> [*The reader notices that what comes through in this passage at the end of the novel is not only an escape from the real world, through a motif based on the fantastic, but, more basically, rejection of woman and a homosexuality that is probably one of the keys to Clarence's feeling of marginality.*][7]

Mouralis felt that Clarence's relationship to Africa shows both attraction and repulsion and considered him to have a schizoid personality.[8] In a letter to me Mouralis added that he wondered if the question of the paternity of the novel might be linked to the homosexual dimension of Clarence's experience, which Laye might have invented or might have based on a real experience.

There are also suggestions of sexual activity expressed in a more complex fashion than we would find in *L'Enfant noir.* Do the odors of the flowers and the odors of sexual activity have a relationship to the animal odors Clarence notices in Adramé? Why does Clarence's vision of the arrival of the king depend upon some kind of sexual activity of Dioki with her snakes (and perhaps with Clarence)? There are a number of symbols in the novel functioning at a more complex level than anything in other work signed Camara Laye, with the exception of the short stories. These include the reef, the ocean, the odor of flowers and of sexuality, and the snakes. What is the relationship between the ocean, which Clarence thinks of initially as an enemy keeping him from crossing the reef into Africa, and the drums announcing the arrival of the king? These symbolic resonances cannot be explicated simply and lend an atmosphere of mystery quite different from that in *Dramouss.*

The structure of *Le Regard du roi* is also considerably different from that of *L'Enfant noir* or *Dramouss.* The order is still chronological, but the story is not presented as a series of isolated incidents. There is a continuity between chapters. Laye told me that there were two levels in the novel—social comedy and the quest for God—and that both are important to create interest for the reader. There is nothing like such social comedy in his other work. In *Dramouss*, he said, the political message is important and the rest, the personal story, was merely "des agréments" [embellishments].

Rereading some scenes I was reminded as much of *Alice in Wonderland* as of Kafka:

> leurs mains, devenues énormes, s'allongeaient, largement ouvertes, comme prêtes à se refermer! Clarence courut de plus belle. Deux ailes, cette fois, lui étaient inopinément mais tres réellement poussées dans le dos. (78)

> [*their hands, grown suddenly enormous, were reaching out, their great, broad palms wide open, ready to seize them! Clarence ran even faster. This time, a pair of wings had unexpectedly but quite positively sprouted between his shoulder-blades.*] *(86)*

> Clarence aperçut le naba en conversation avec le mendiant. Mais le décor n'était plus le même: les fauteuils et leur contenu avaient disparu comme par enchantement. Le naba, à présent, était assis sous une galérie, au fond de la cour . . . parfois, il laissait tomber sa barbiche. (111)

> [*Clarence noticed that the naba was in conversation with the beggar. But the setting was different: the arm-chairs and their occupants had disappeared as if by enchantment. The naba was now seated under an arcade at the rear of the courtyard . . . occasionally he wagged his beard as if in agreement.*] *(123)*

Indeed, the atmosphere throughout much of the novel is not Kafkaesque, is not frightening, but rather amusing. The naba with his beard might almost be a character from the pack of cards in Lewis Carroll.

A more frightening Cheshire Cat image, however, occurs in Clarence's dream:

> ce qu'il découvrit, ou ce qu'il imagina découvrir, ce fut le sourire du maître des cérémonies; ce sourire uniquement, bizarrement, incompréhensiblement détaché du reste. (179)

> [*what he saw, or imagined he saw, was the smile of the master of ceremonies—a smile that was curiously, incomprehensibly detached from the rest of his face.*] *(200)*

Poulet compared *Le Regard du roi* to *Alice in Wonderland* in his reader's report, but most critics have not mentioned any similarities. One can only speculate now that Poulet had good reason to notice the allusions to Carroll because he had written them or, more probably, suggested them to Soulié.

Anise Postel-Vinay mentioned to me that Laye said Poulet, who believed in using very formal French grammar, taught him how to use the imperfect subjunctive. While Laye did not say when Poulet taught him grammar, it is probable that Poulet corrected the manuscript of *L'Enfant noir* before it was submitted to Plon. Others also referred to this tense in defending Laye's ability to write French. Blancard, discussing the stories Laye wrote in the early 1960s for Radio Guinée, made a point of telling me that Laye knew how to write French, including how to use the subjunctive. It almost seems as if those wanting to defend Laye, such as Blancard, picked on the subjunctive as a way of proving that Laye could write. Many students of French can use the subjunctive correctly, however, without being able to write a story of any value in French.

Imperfect and pluperfect subjunctives, except for the third-person singular, sound ludicrous to the modern French ear and are avoided by most native French authors. Work signed by Camara Laye uses more imperfect and pluperfect subjunctives, particularly in conversations, than would most twentieth-century French novelists. *Le Regard du Roi* was published only two years before Camus's *La Chute* (1956), where the listener's reaction to Clamence's use of the imperfect subjunctive is a proof both of his grammatical knowledge and of his recognition that using such forms in modern French is awkward. Using very correct grammar may reflect a conservative temperament, such as Poulet's, or a desire on the part of any non-French writer, African or Belgian, to be precise and accurate, seeking not to sound foreign. Belgians are often aware of needing to avoid Belgianisms.[9]

Some of the conversations in *Le Regard du roi* that use the subjunctive seem particularly stilted (emphasis mine):

Croyez-vous qu'après cela *j'eusse* encore *voulu* servir le roi? (38)
[*"Do you really think that after all that I would want to enter the king's service?"*] *(40)*

Mais peut-être *eussions-nous bu* plus utilement à la santé de celui-ci. (124)
[*But perhaps it would have been better if we had drunk to the health of this young man.*] *(140)*

Et vous en avez eu la preuve: comment *eussé-je présenté* votre requête, s'il n'y avait pas eu de porte? (87)

> [*And the proof of that is: how could I have presented your request, if there had been no door to go through?*] *(96)*

Alors, oui, *c'eût été* un métier contre lequel *j'eusse peut-être troqué* le mien. (97–98)

> [*Then, I admit, it would be the sort of job for which I would have willingly exchanged my own.*] *(109)*[10]

Similar examples occur in *Dramouss*, where Laye used the formal grammar that Poulet had taught him and that was used in *Le Regard du roi*:

Alors je demandais au bon Dieu de faire retomber le voile sur mon esprit . . . afin que *je fusse* dans l'incapacité de me souvenir. (25)

> [*So then I asked the good Lord to let the veil fall over my mind again . . . so that I might be incapable of remembering the past.*] *(17)*

ton beau-père, avant de nous quitter pour rejoindre son nouveau poste d'affectation, tenait à ce que les cérémonies religieuses de votre mariage *eussent* lieu. (33)

> [*your father-in-law, before leaving us to take up his new post, insisted that the religious ceremonies for your marriage should take place.*] *(22)*

There are, however, so many improbable conversations in *Dramouss*, obviously inserted to give the reader information and almost impossible to imagine anyone saying, that these do not stand out.

There are weaknesses in *Le Regard du roi* that may result from the author's lack of familiarity with the two cultures being compared. Another weakness is the sentimental treatment of the relationship between Clarence and Akissi in the final chapter:

—Toi, Akissi, va, dit-il. Va, oui . . . Laisse-moi.
—Je demeurerai près de toi, dit-elle.
—Non, va . . . Je serai mieux seul.
—Sais-je combien de temps je te verrai encore? (241)

> [*"You go, Akissi," he said. "Yes, you go . . . Leave me alone."*
> *"I shall stay beside you," she said.*
> *"No, go away . . . I'll be better alone."*
> *"How do I know how much longer I shall see you?"*] *(270)*

This seems particularly inappropriate because in previous chapters there has been almost no description of any intimate relationship between the two. In fact, Clarence usually treats Akissi more as a servant, asking her to bring water, pour a shower, cook the food he likes, or find palm wine. Clarence is, however, taking on a role as a servant of the king, a role that might be compared to that of Christ. This conversation continues with an echo of the biblical phrase "and, lo, I am with you always, *even* unto the end of the world" (Matthew 28:20).

> —Tu me verras chaque jour et chaque heure. Désormais, tu me verras toujours. Il ne dépend plus de moi que je te voie ou que je ne te voie pas. (241)
>
> [*"You shall see me every day and every hour. From now on, you shall always see me. It no longer depends on me whether I see you or whether I don't see you."*] *(270)*

The mysticism at the conclusion of this novel seems Christian, not Manding or Sufi. The love of God devours the sinner and embraces him forever.

A major theme in *Le Regard du roi* might well have come from the mind of an author who had been condemned to death by a system of legalistic justice:

> Ou serait-ce que la sordide justice des hommes ne peut se rendre que parmi les immondices? (161)
>
> [*Or could it be that the sordid justice of mankind can only be meted out in foulness and filth?*] *(179)*

More significantly, the whole story is a search for grace, in which actions count for little and faith counts for everything. This is a position consistent with Laye's own belief and with Poulet's religious outlook. Soulié never discussed religion when writing before the war. During his life in Paris, however, as an outcast from his former society and living at least initially in some secrecy, the search for love and redemption would have been of importance to him.

Le Regard du roi is overtly a story about the universality of faith. Finally, Clarence is no longer a white man looking for employment with a black king. He loses any feeling of racial superiority. This theme is implicit in the religious faith of the child in *L'Enfant noir*. It was also expressed by Poulet in his 1976 memoir: "Geographical, ethnographical and ideological affiliations play a small role in this life. They have no place in eternity."[11]

5

Aude Joncourt and Marie-Hélène Lefaucheux

Two women played prominent roles in the creation of *L'Enfant noir*. About one of them, Aude Joncourt, I have only a little information, provided by Simon Njami, whose father met Joncourt when she came with Laye to visit him in Lausanne. She was a student of anthropology, very anticolonial, and had lived in West Africa at some time, where her father was a civil servant. She was about the same age as Laye and a good friend of his. Rich and cultivated, she helped with the manuscript of *L'Enfant noir*, presumably writing it according to Laye's memories. It is Joncourt to whom Autra refers as the Frenchwoman to whom Laye told the story of his life. When Laye told a Nigerian student in 1974 that a white woman wrote *L'Enfant noir*, he was speaking of Joncourt. She is the source of the rumors Wauthier heard and rejected, about a Jewish woman who helped Laye write and introduced him to the work of Kafka.

About the second woman, whose help was for the most part in establishing contacts for Laye with the Ministry of France Overseas and helping him to get published, I learned a great deal. She was an exceptional woman whose life testifies to her devotion to Africa and to women of the Third World. Marie-Hélène Lefaucheux was the major link between Laye and the French government, particularly the Ministry of France Overseas, which gave support to both the publication of *L'Enfant noir* and the possible film. This support came through the French agency for financial support to the colonies, the Caisse Centrale de la France d'Outre-Mer, of which Lefaucheux's brother, André Postel-Vinay, was the director.

Marie-Hélène Postel-Vinay Lefaucheux was born February 26, 1904, into an upper-middle-class family. Her grandfather, Paul Delombre, was an eminent economist and statesman who played an important role during the Third Republic. Her father was a business executive. She was one of the first two women admitted to the Ecole des Sciences Politiques. In 1925, however, she married Pierre Lefaucheux and did not continue her studies. Pierre, who was born in 1898, held an engineering degree and a doctorate in law. During the First World War he had been a volunteer and received the Croix de Guerre with two citations. In 1924 and 1925, presumably prior to his marriage, he worked in sub-Saharan Africa for a commercial company.

One of Lefaucheux's brothers, Roger, was killed in May 1940, at the beginning of the war. Another, André, fought in the Resistance movement, was captured by the Gestapo, and eventually escaped to England, where he worked for de Gaulle.[1] Both Pierre and Marie-Hélène were also active in the Resistance. Among other activities, they organized a network to help Allied pilots. Pierre was arrested and deported in August 1944. After his deportation, Marie-Hélène tried unsuccessfully to follow the German bus transporting the prisoners to the east, then returned to Paris and to her position as a member of the Comité de Libération at the Hôtel de Ville. After the liberation of Paris she managed to go east, between the advancing American army and the retreating German army. She was very resourceful and bribed a German Gestapo official in Metz in order to get her husband freed. Later, by going to the camps in Buchenwald and Bergen-Belsen, she helped to get a number of French deportees freed. Pierre was awarded the Légion d'Honneur, the Croix de Guerre, and the Croix de la Libération. Marie-Hélène was also awarded the Légion d'Honneur and the Croix de Guerre, as well as the Médaille de la Résistance. After the war, Pierre became the director of Renault, a position he held until his death in 1955. Renault was nationalized by de Gaulle in January 1945 and was in the forefront of modernization in France, being the first car plant to give a third week of paid vacation to its workers.

Unable to have children because of an accident in her youth, Lefaucheux devoted herself to various political, cultural, and philanthropic activities. As a result of her Resistance activities, she entered political life. She was a member of the two Constituent Assemblies in 1945 and 1946, which developed the constitution for the Fourth Republic. There were only thirty-three women in the First Constituent Assembly. She was affiliated with the MRP, largely left-leaning Catholics and Christian trade unionists, which won 25.6 percent of the seats in the assembly in the October 1945 elections. It was one of the three parties aligned in the "Tripartisme," with the Communist Party and the Socialist Party. Along with her male colleagues in the MRP, but to a much greater extent than most, she believed strongly in the importance of the family.

In the debates of the Constituent Assembly on March 26, 1946, on colonial policy, as listed in the *Journal officiel*, Lefaucheux spoke of the importance of the overseas colonies and of the interest that her constituents (mostly "workers or peasants" in the Département de l'Aisne) showed in the colonies. She also said that during the Occupation the news from Africa helped sustain those whose loved ones were in danger because of the Resistance. This speech was greeted with much applause. Lefaucheux mentioned that she provided information on overseas territories to her comrades in other regions, an early indication of the knowledge of the colonies that she was developing, particularly about Africa. When a vote on the first proposed constitution was taken April 19, 1946, however, she and the other MRP delegates opposed it, in spite of its favorable proposals for the territories, because its monocameral legislature gave too little power to the executive.

Lefaucheux held an important role in several spheres concerned with human rights and especially with the rights of women, although she was not a modern feminist.[2] In a speech in 1962 she said that the role of the International Council of Women was "in no way revolutionary."[3] Working with Sister Marie-André du Sacré-Coeur, a missionary to Africa, she helped establish better conditions for marriage and for dowry in the colonies. Later, for a brief period (February 1959 to August 1960) she worked on women's rights in Islamic countries, in the office of Miss Nafissa Sid Cara, a secrétaire d'etat aux affaires musulmanes (secretary of state for Muslim affairs), in Michel Debré's government. Like Lefaucheux, Sid Cara, an Algerian, was a strong personality, and the two clashed eventually.

After the Fourth Republic was established, Lefaucheux had three main areas of activity—the Assembly of the French Union, the United Nations, and the Conseil National des Femmes Françaises (National Council of French Women, founded in 1901). She was a member of the Assembly of the French Union from 1947 to 1958 and for a time its vice president, a delegate to the United Nations from 1946 to 1959, a French representative to the UN Commission on the Rights of Women, president of the National Council of French Women from 1954 to 1964, and president of the International Council of Women from 1957 to 1963. She was also a member of the French Conseil Économique et Social from 1959 to 1962.

In the Assembly of the French Union many of Lefaucheux's motions and speeches were related to Africa. In 1949, for example, she presented a motion to suppress the age limit on social security benefits for scholarship holders from overseas and another motion to make newsreels and documentaries about the French Union. She was a member of the committee for the Dahomey-Niger railway. While supporting international endeavors, she also said that the assembly must remember that France does not take orders from the United Nations.

During the session of 1950, Lefaucheux was elected vice-president of the assembly. She presented many motions during this year, among them a motion to help Muslims get to Mecca. She spoke of seeing French schools functioning well in Morocco. By this time she was traveling frequently to Africa.

Lefaucheux worked with Marcel Griaule, who was president of the Commission on Cultural Affairs at the Assembly of the French Union from 1948 until his death in 1956. Griaule was a noted ethnologist whose studies of the religion and philosophy of the Dogon culture of Mali were, along with the work of Placide Tempels on Bantu philosophy in the Congo, the most influential European work on African culture. Griaule would have been aware of Laye's work through Lefaucheux.[4]

During the session of 1951, Lefaucheux was again vice president of the assembly. Both she and Griaule were members of the MRP delegation, which put forward a motion advocating "publication of writings which will develop mutual knowledge and understanding among peoples and races." During a debate on this motion there was more discussion of literature than was common in the assembly. Monique Lafon, a representative of the Communist group, spoke of Aimé Césaire and several African poets, including Bernard Dadié, and said that the French government did not want to guarantee liberty of expression to colonial peoples. This was followed by applause from the extreme left. Paul Hazoumé, representing Dahomey, spoke of the difficulty Africans encountered in getting published. Hazoumé had published a novel in 1938. He was, in 1951, a moderate spokesman for Africa, and he undoubtedly knew Lefaucheux. Although her only contribution to this debate was an ironic comment mocking the idea that the Soviet Union was doing a good job erasing illiteracy in Uzbekistan, the discussion would have made her aware of the need to help African writers. Encouragement of Laye's *L'Enfant noir* would obviously have been a way of publishing works that, in the words of the MRP motion, "will develop mutual knowledge and understanding among peoples and races."[5]

In 1953 some MRP members, including Lefaucheux, presented a motion asking the government to preserve the French Union from certain tendencies apparent in the European Council. In her presentation, Lefaucheux spoke of the problems of reconciling the French Union and the European Council as two federal systems but insisted that "every task is secondary in relation to the important job of supporting the French Union." This speech was following by applause from the center and the left. During 1953 Lefaucheux also presented a motion stating that France should recognize medical degrees from the overseas territories.[6]

In 1978 Postel-Vinay gave me a copy of a two-page, typed, unpublished document, "Jeunesse, avenir de L'Union Française," signed by Laye. It is remarkable for its expression of an uncritical belief that a union between France and the colonies on a basis of equality could exist. Laye begins by stating that the idea of a French Union is generous and even "revolutionary." Unfortunately this idea is better accepted in France than in the overseas territories. Yet its establishment is essential; through the union people of different ethnic groups will be united and understand their similarities and differences. As this understanding can best be inculcated in young people, Laye suggests that an exchange of children be established, which would lead to harmony and the destruction of prejudice. Children from France and children from the overseas territories should be sent to visit different regions. At present, he feels, in the territories whites live separately from blacks. This is not because of "discrimination" but simply a result of class differences, as everywhere in the world. Coming to metropolitan France, children from the territories will learn that not all whites are bosses, but some are also employees, and that the life of these whites is not so different from their own. Children from France going to the colonies will learn that their co-citizens in the French Union have the same solid family support as they do. Children from France and from the colonies will learn the richness of the different regions in a way that they could not learn from books. From these exchanges "brotherhood" will be born. This brotherhood comes most easily to children, who are confident and without prejudices. The document concludes that the future of the French Union is in the hands of young people. Laye continued his praise for the French throughout his life.

Lefaucheux was the main link between the National Council of French Women and the Association des Femmes de l'Union Française (Association of Women of the French Union), which began in May 1946 and in which she was very active. She probably met Laye through the association's foyer for women students from overseas territories, the Fondation Jane Vialle. The group's activities for December 1953 may give a clue about how, in an earlier year, Lefaucheux met Laye: "Saturday December 26, we had a party at our Foyer Jane Vialle. It has become a tradition to get together around a Christmas tree and a well-stocked buffet with the students residing in the Foyer, our young scholars on holiday, and our friends, students of both sexes from Overseas."[7]

Lefaucheux contributed regularly to the association's bulletin, *Les Femmes de l'Union Française*. In the second issue (January–February 1947) she wrote an article on private schools in Morocco as a good example of what could be done for education overseas. In the fifth issue (March–April 1948) she wrote of the need to respect Muslim traditions while moving toward monogamy. In issue nine (February–March 1949) she contributed the literary column on the poetry of Flavien Ranairo.

As vice president of the Assembly of the French Union and president of the Commission on Women of the UN, she presented a paper on "L'Evolution féminine aux Nations Unies" in the September–October 1951 issue of *Les Femmes de l'Union Française*. She had reported to the UN commission on the laws recently adopted by the French Parliament for the benefit of African women. She quoted at length from a document submitted to the UN by the International Federation of Catholic Women's Leagues, which attacked polygamy and bride price and stated that monogamous marriage is important for the development of African societies. The document suggested a number of measures that governments should undertake. Without agreeing or disagreeing with the position of the Catholic women, Lefaucheux invited her readers to submit their ideas on the subject. In both the document and her concluding sentence, women in French Africa are presented as part of the French Union, referred to as "Françaises de toutes origines." Similarly, in 1952 she wrote of the need to invite the youth of the French Union to come to France, as "our culture remains their best hope."[8]

Of greater interest, however, is a review of *L'Enfant noir* by Christiane Léopold published in *Les Femmes de l'Union Française* in 1954. It is one of very few book reviews in the bulletin, and it shows the influence of Lefaucheux. The review begins with biographical details, indicating that Laye had earned his living at the Simca plant (actually for only a few months) and was taking courses in aeronautics. Léopold then speaks of the "astonishing mastery of French prose" by a young Guinean of only twenty-six and recommends that readers study his "subtle command of tenses, especially his delicate use of imperfect subjunctives and the second form of the past conditional." These are the tenses that, as Laye told Lefaucheux's sister-in-law, Anise Postel-Vinay, among others, he learned from Poulet. They are also the tenses to which others referred in defending his ability to write French. It is, I believe, doubtful whether Léopold, writing a short review for a general audience, would have signaled this "subtle command of tenses" had she not been aware of how several persons had helped Laye. She also knew that Plon had asked for the rights to Laye's next five books, a detail she could hardly have learned from anyone except the author or, of course, from Lefaucheux. (I learned of Plon's request for the first time when I read this review in 1999.)

After her husband died in a car accident in 1955, Lefaucheux traveled throughout the world in her work for women's rights. In 1962 she organized a study circle at Yaoundé, Cameroon, for representatives of thirteen African states. In the 1960s, after the African colonies gained independence, she organized many national councils of women in Africa. In the foreword she wrote for *Women in a Changing World: The dynamic story of the International Council of Women since 1886*, on which she was still working at the time of her death, she spoke of how the International Council of Women strives for the abolition of discrimination on grounds of sex, race, class, and creed and of the fundamental need to consider marriage as a union of partners equal in duties and rights. Lefaucheux died in a plane accident in the United States on February 25, 1964, while traveling for the International Council of Women.

After Lefaucheux's death a requiem mass was held at the Invalides. Maurice Schumann, president of the Committee on Foreign Affairs in the National Assembly, presided at a memorial March 29, 1964, and homages were presented by the organizations in which Lefaucheux had been active—the National Council of French Women, the secretariat of the Commission on Women of the United Nation, and the French delegation to the United Nations. Also presenting homages were a friend who had worked with Lefaucheux during the Resistance and the ambassador from Senegal. A letter was read from Sister Marie-André du Sacré-Coeur as well as a message from a social worker in Yaoundé, who praised Lefaucheux's work for the women of Africa.

The Fondation Marie-Hélène Lefaucheux was later established to help African women. In 1998 the president of the National Council of French women, Françoise Bouteiller, who had traveled for the council in Africa in 1975, said she met many African women who still spoke of the important work Lefaucheux had accomplished.

Postel-Vinay did not mention his sister to me either in 1978 or in my first conversation with him in the 1990s. He spoke of her only after I had learned enough about her to question him. I assume her role in helping Laye was so important that he would have preferred not to discuss it. He said that his sister could not have been Tante Aline because she had no children. He did not mention when his sister met Laye but said that he met Laye because he admired *L'Enfant noir*. His close connection later with Laye, however, is undoubtedly a result of his sister's interest in Africa. Several times he told me that I was mistaken in my search for a ghostwriter, and he cited as proof the false rumors that Alexandre Dumas had worked with a ghostwriter.

The Postel-Vinays became friends of both Laye and Marie and gave them much support over the years. André knew that Poulet was the reader at Plon who helped Laye (though in 1978 he thought the name was Gaston), and Anise remembered that Laye had told her that Poulet helped him with the use of the subjunctive. Neither of the Postel-Vinays had ever heard of Soulié. This seems strange, as Marie, whom the Postel-Vinays helped on her arrival in Paris, told me that she and Laye lived in Soulié's studio at 15 rue Molière when she first came to Paris. Laye might have said very little about his friendship with a Belgian who had collaborated during the war to friends who had actively fought the Germans. (Pierre Lefaucheux had been deported. Anise Postel-Vinay, whose sister was shot by the Germans in 1944, had also been deported, in 1943.) Perhaps Laye did not know about Soulié's past, as Soulié was very discreet after he arrived in France. Lansiné Kaba, who met Soulié a few years later, was not told the truth about Soulié's collaboration during the war. Lefaucheux, however, may have had some contacts with Soulié and almost certainly did with Poulet, contacts it is now impossible to verify.

Le Regard du roi was dedicated to "Monsieur Bernard Cornut-Gentille, Haut-Commissaire de la République en A. O. F. . . . as a token of respectful friendship." Cornut-Gentille arranged a reception for Laye in Dakar in 1954. Lefaucheux and André Postel-Vinay would have known Cornut-Gentille. The son and grandson of naval officers, he was a prisoner of war in 1939 and later fought in the Resistance. He was high commissioner in French Equatorial Africa in 1949–51. In 1952 he was high commissioner in French West Africa, where he was instrumental in founding *Traits d'union*, a magazine that linked cultural centers in French West Africa and published folktales and fables. Later he was ambassador from France to the UN Security Council and minister for France overseas in de Gaulle's government in 1958. He broke with de Gaulle when the general advocated Algerian independence.

There were other women interested in African students during the 1950s who possibly could have helped Laye and served as a model for Tante Aline in *Dramouss*. Of these, by far the most interesting was Madeleine Rousseau, a lively but eccentric art critic and editor of *Le Musée vivant* who wrote many books, had a large collection of African art, and represented France at UNESCO. She befriended many African students and often met them in a left bank café, as did Tante Aline. She was drummed out of the Communist Party for taking a black rather than a Marxist approach to colonial politics. When I first read *Dramouss* I was certain that the character of Tante Aline was inspired by Rousseau, whom I had met in 1954. She lived on the rue du Val de Grâce, very near the rue Saint Jacques, where Tante Aline is said to live. She believed strongly in the value of traditional African culture. Rousseau was well known to French intellectuals interested in Africa and to many African students. The first African my husband met in Paris in 1952 took him to see Rousseau. Other possible models for Tante Aline are more obscure. One woman who helped Africans in France was Catherine Bailly, who had lived in Togo for two or three years. Madame Morel, who knew Lefaucheux well, also spoke to me about her activity helping Africans, inspired by disgust for the racist comments she and her late husband had heard from French people. In thirty-nine years, she had invited over nine thousand foreign students to her house.

Laye needed financial support during his years in France in the 1950s, and he also needed emotional support. Many people who knew Laye have spoken of his dependence upon women who would pamper him and help him conquer the insecurities he claimed he felt upon leaving the warm world of the African child. Aude Joncourt gave Laye affection and helped write his memoirs. Marie-Hélène Lefaucheux gave him much more—the possibility of earning his living in France and a sense of dignity as a writer and as a voice for the French Union. She worked unselfishly for the causes in which she believed, and she believed in Laye. He was indeed fortunate to have met this remarkable woman.

6

Introducing Francis Soulié

According to Kesteloot, the manuscript of *Le Regard du roi* was completed before Laye saw it. Liliane Elsen has speculated that perhaps Laye helped Soulié with it. While the exact nature of Laye's contribution will never be known, Soulié is the principal author of the second novel credited to Laye. An obscure figure in Belgian literary history, Soulié wrote what is often considered one of the early masterpieces of African literature.

Francis Henri Charles Marie Soulié was born in Antwerp, July 21, 1897. Although Antwerp is in the Flemish part of Belgium, he was raised in a French-language environment. By the time he was in his twenties, he was living in Liege, which during the 1930s was an impoverished region.[1] Soulié's mother, however, was wealthy.

During the 1920s, from the age of about twenty-five, Soulié was writing regularly for various little magazines, using the pseudonym of Gille Anthelme (Gille is a name from Italian comedy). Belgium had an astonishingly large number of literary magazines for a country of its size. There were, between 1916 and 1940, 140 Francophone literary magazines in Belgium, though many lasted for only a few issues. Such publications were important because less money was needed to start them than to start publishing houses, for which there was not a large enough national market. Many of the magazines were financed by art galleries, and this strong link between literature and the visual arts was particularly attractive to Soulié, who wrote art criticism as well as literary criticism. The magazines were not always strictly allied to any political position.

The earliest magazine publications I have found by Soulié are articles from the first issue of *Créer*, a "bi-monthly review of art and literature" founded in 1922 in Liege, for which Arthur Petronio was the director and Soulié the editorial secretary. In the early issues, Soulié contributed an article on Constant Permeke, a Belgian artist, and short book reviews on works by such authors as Max Jacob, Roger Martin du Gard, and Jean Cocteau. Although Soulié accepted the anti-Semitic positions of *La Légia* and *Terre wallonne* during the war, there is no mention of Jacob's identity as a Jew and only praise for his work. *Créer* lasted for four issues in 1922 and four in 1923. Among other contributors was Georges Thialet, a pseudonym of Georges Poulet, who was the brother of Robert Poulet and was later famous as a literary critic. In 1929, in a letter to Robert Guiette, Soulié wrote that *Créer* "belonged to me and a few friends at the time." In 1923 he published one poem in *Créer*, "Infidélité," a monologue by an Asian chieftain among "Tatars" on the steppes. This is an early instance of Soulié's interest in exotic cultures and also of his somewhat unconventional sexual themes. The warriors awake with:

> filles dans les jambes.
> J'en poignardai une;
> .   .   .
>
> J'offris la ville à mes Tatars:
> Toutes les vierges furent pourvues
> Et nos chiens lappaient le sang.

[*girls in our legs.*
I stabbed one;

. . .

I offered the town to my Tatars:
All the virgins were provided
And our dogs lapped up the blood.]

After *Créer* folded Soulié wrote for more enduring and better supported literary magazines, contributing primarily criticism of literary and artistic works but also occasional poems and fiction. The first of these magazines was *Sélection: Atelier d'art contemporain*, which began publication in 1920, had a permanent exhibition space in Brussels, and was distributed in Paris and Amsterdam. Soulié joined the editorial board in 1923.[2]

The contents of *Sélection* indicate the interest in Africa, particularly of course in the Belgian Congo, among literary and artistic circles in the 1920s and 1930s. The colony, many times the size of Belgium, played a greater role in the country's imagination and in periodicals of the 1930s than Africa did in French publications. In 1935 the Exposition de Bruxelles attracted many visitors to the colonial exhibits. In the first two years of its existence *Sélection* published articles on Congolese art and a review by Franz Hellens of Blaise Cendrars's *Anthologie nègre*. Hellens was one of the best-known Belgian writers of the period; his reputation was in part based on the magazines he edited and in which he published the work of his French friends.[3] Hellens wrote two children's books on Africa, *Bass—Bassina—Boulou*, published in 1922 and translated into Russian, German, and Czech, and *Bamboula: Le Petit Homme noir*, published in 1942. *Sélection* also published a review of the work of a young painter, Auguste Mambour. Soulié, who was a friend of Mambour, had written a study of Mambour's art for the catalogue of his exhibition in Liege. In a letter dated June 10, 1922, to Melot du Dy, a poet, Soulié sent a photograph of himself standing in front of a poster by his friend Mambour, as well as photos of other works by Mambour. After receiving the Prix de Rome, Mambour went to the Congo in 1923, when he was only twenty-four. Mambour's works, often used for illustrations in *Sélection*, were one source of Soulié's interest in Africa.

Soulié's first contribution to *Sélection*, which appeared in November 1923, was a story, "Cécile ou l'aventure en chemin de fer." This is one of only two pieces of Soulié's creative prose that I have been able to find. It is a first-person narrative by a man who meets a woman on the train. He is sure she is his former fiancée. At first, in spite of his rather direct approach ("Don't you remember when I bit your neck," he asks), she denies knowing him. Later she tells him rather indirectly and discreetly about the sexual habits of the man for whom she left him. After the marriage her husband was upset that she did not submit as prostitutes would. Soon there were many women, adulterous scenes, gambling debts. Finally she left him for a man who loved her but, "easily charming on the surface, he had no spark at night."[4] There is a latent homosexual theme in the description of this man. The story ends with a passionate kiss between the narrator and the woman, Cécile. There is little of interest in the style; the similes are rather banal (she cried "like a child who wants sweets between meals"); and the psychology seems rather simple.

Soulié also wrote a few poems for *Sélection*, with some rhyme but no regular meter and relying largely on a series of images. "Anvers" is about sailors and prostitutes in the port. Several poems, such as "Raspoutine," include exotic imagery. He also wrote many reviews. These were often short, and initially he was not given the best books to review. Between 1924 and 1927, however, he published a substantial article on Drieu La Rochelle, a long study of Charlie Chaplin, an analysis of surrealism entitled "Contre André Breton," and a study of "Le Roman."

The essay on Chaplin, "Ebauche d'un Charlot," compares Chaplin's work to that of many writers and artists of varying political persuasions, mostly French. Soulié cites Cocteau, Gide, and Louis Aragon, as well as Hellens and Igor Stravinsky. His analysis of Chaplin shows a considerable knowledge of the cinema, comparing Chaplin's lack of expressionist techniques of filming to their use by the prominent French director Louis Delluc, who had recently died and to whom the article is dedicated. Soulié wanted the cinema to move toward a completely expressionist art. The style in this essay is, however, somewhat rambling, and the structure is not always clear. There are over two pages of notes for a fifteen-page essay, which seems excessive for a literary magazine.

"Contre André Breton," written while Soulié was "far from a library, far from all civilization, I should say," with the army in occupied Germany, attacks Breton as a priest who propagates his faith and is too dogmatic.[5] Soulié liked the imagination, the marvelous, the dream, to which surrealism has given importance: "the fabulous is the sole compensation for all the unbearable barriers by which society is given order" (374). He believed that surrealists, however, have neglected to recognize that reason is also essential and have denigrated the importance of the novel. From this essay it is clear that Soulié was skeptical of automatic writing, of literature that seems unintelligible, and of novels without clear characters and plot. Writing, he believed, requires both imagination and reason. Why did Soulié write? "Literature seems to me the ideal way to understand" (381); the characters he could create would be a way of understanding his own subconscious.

By March 1925, Soulié's name appeared on the cover of *Sélection*. In 1925 and 1926 he reviewed such authors as Luc Durtain, Raymond Radiguet, Gide, and Drieu. He also reviewed Hermann Hesse's *Siddhartha*, a work that may well have influenced the conception of *Le Regard du roi*. Soulié's writing at this time shows no pronounced political bent. Worth noting, considering his later career during the war, is a favorable review of the Communist critic Léon Moussinac's *Naissance du cinéma*. There is also, however, a rather unfavorable review of the work of Scholem Aleihem, which is tinged with anti-Semitism.

Soulié's ideas about the novel can be seen from his reviews and from his essay "Le Roman," part of a series by four young critics from Liege. While he stated that there is no set form for the novel and each writer must invent it, he was unhappy with Drieu's *Le Jeune Européen*, which he thought was too much a confession, introducing extraneous elements to literature. He was full of praise, however, for Drieu's *La Valise vide*. Two rules he suggested for the author of a novel were to give the work "a feeling of real life which touches the reader's emotions" and to be intelligible.[6] He believed in the importance of giving an impression of felt life and cited the work of Stendhal and Flaubert as preferable to that of most of his contemporaries.

When *Nord* appeared in April 1929, Hellens mentioned in his editorial preface that he had engaged as collaborators a group from *Disque vert*, which he edited for a few years with Henri Michaux, and a group of four young critics who had written a special issue of *Sélection* on the novel. That issue was reviewed by the French critic Edmond Jaloux in *Nouvelles Littéraires* in Paris. (A Belgian sense of inferiority in relation to the hub of French-language culture is evident here.) The four young critics, all from Liege, were Gille Anthelme

(Soulié), Léon Duesberg, Robert Mathy, and Georges Thialet (Georges Poulet). Robert Poulet also wrote for *Nord*. The second issue, devoted to the novel, began with Poulet's essay on the "Roman poétique," which evokes *Le Grand Meaulnes*, followed by Anthelme's (Soulié's) "Sous le signe de la jeunesse."

"Sous le signe de la jeunesse" begins as an autobiographical story of a boy going into the woods, first with other young children, later as an adolescent, and still later as a young soldier on duty with the army of occupation on the Rhine. He compares his adventures to those in Alain-Fournier's *Le Grand Meaulnes* and seems fascinated by the innocence of childhood friendships and the life of bucolic youth. He also compares Alain-Fournier's novel to the films of a rather obscure American silent filmmaker, Charles Ray, whose *The Old Swimmin' Hole* (1921), about a group of boys going swimming, was famous at the time for using no intertitles with which to tell its story. Soulié had considerable knowledge of films, particularly silent films, as is evident in much of his journalism in the 1920s.

In letters written in late 1929 Soulié described to his correspondent in Antwerp, Guiette, how he and others went in a group to see Hellens, who was unable to continue the direction of *Nord* "because of bad reviews in the NRF" (*La Nouvelle Revue française*, the preeminent French literary magazine; October 21, 1929). The judgments that counted seemed to come from France. The interview finished badly. Duesberg was to take over, and the third issue would appear soon. In the third issue of *Nord* (1930) the first item was "Caligula" by Anthelme (Soulié), described as a novel although it was only thirty-two pages. Although "Caligula" was written in 1926, Soulié told Guiette, "I still like it." The story is more interesting than "Cécile" and shows a spirit of play and a mixture of the realms of fantasy and reality.

"Caligula" is written in a deliberately flat style, with short sentences, present-tense verbs, few adjectives, and no introspection. The hero, Caligula, easily loses his identity. He gets a new hat, for example, and no longer recognizes himself in the mirror, or he has his photograph taken and must destroy the plates so as not to be duplicated: "Dédoublé, tu n'es plus Caligula" [Split in two, you are no longer Caligula].[7] Many of the incidents are surreal. Caligula thinks about the home of a woman he has met, an episode that ends with all the furniture in his own room disappearing out the window. He decides that a stuffed bear in a hotel lobby is going to attack the guests at night. He has

CAMARA LAYE, 1967

© *Archives La Documentation française, M. R. Cornevin.*

MARIE-HÉLÈNE LEFAUCHEUX
Photo courtesy of André Postel-Vinay.

FRANCIS SOULIÉ

Photo courtesy of the Archives & Musée de la Litterature,
Bibliotheque Royale Albert I, Brussels.

ROBERT POULET

*Photo courtesy of the Centre de Recherches et d'Études
historiques de la Seconde Guerre Mondiale, Brussels.*

ANDRÉ POSTEL-VINAY (*RIGHT*)

Photo courtesy of André Postel-Vinay.

SIMON NJAMI

Photo courtesy of Simon Njami.

strange dreams and believes in the reality of imagined beings: "Il n'y a de réel encore que ces êtres qu'on imagine" [There is nothing real except the creatures that you imagine] (245).

Soulié wrote book reviews occasionally for *La Meuse*, the Liege daily paper. In 1929 he was also working with *Liège*, a weekly "Artistique, Mondain, Sportif" paper, for which he wrote on boxing. In letters he wrote to Guiette in 1929 and 1930, he stated that he was working on a novel, "a rather mad novel in which Antwerp plays a part" (March 7, 1929). In June 1930 he was working on "Tigrana", which he describes as "nothing precisely Asiatic; Tigrana is an Eskimo"; it would soon be one-third written, and he planned to send it to Grasset. In the midst of this journalistic and literary activity, however, Soulié told Guiette that he would like to find more to do, as boxing was not doing well, and asked Guiette if there was a journal in Antwerp for which he could write reviews (June 5, 1930). He appeared to need money.

The letter to Guiette about the problems with *Nord* is written on letterhead of the Commission des Sports. A rubber stamp affixed below the printed letterhead lists "Anthelme" as director of the secrétariat. On later letters written on the same printed letterhead, the stamp gives the name "Francis Soulié" but the signature is Gille Anthelme (November 8, 1929; June 5, 1930). In 1934 Soulié had printed letterhead with "Francis Soulié" on it. This seems to be a man with some problems of identity, judging from his shifting pseudonym.

In 1933 *La Revue réactionnaire* began in Brussels with Poulet as director. The journal lasted only two years, until April 1935. Anthelme (Soulié) had a column titled "Les Romans nouveaux" in the first issues. Among the novels he reviewed was Céline's *Voyage au bout de la nuit*, which may have inspired some incidents in *Le Regard du roi*.

Soulié was for a short period a collaborator on *Cassandre*, a political weekly that began publication in December 1934 and that had among its aims to fight against foreign intellectual domination. It was directed by, among others, Paul Colin and Gaston Derycke, who were both to work with right-wing publications during the German Occupation. It was a respected journal in its early years; at least until 1937 most Belgian writers were proud to be published in it. Many of the collaborators on *Cassandre* had worked with *Sélection*, including Poulet, Hellens, and Thialet, who was already a professor of literature at the University of Edinburgh. The quality of writing in *Cassandre* was quite high, and the literature reviewed was mainly French. Gaston René Joseph Heenen, a "Vice-gouverneur général honoraire du Congo Belge," contributed regular articles on the Congo in 1935.

At the beginning, *Cassandre*'s political orientation was middle of the road. An editorial compared Hitler to Stalin and Mussolini as dictators threatening half of Europe. Another told of how Jews were being hunted down in Germany. A sports column on the Joe Lewis–Max Baer fight spoke of the primitive tribalism apparent in Goebbel's telegram of support to Baer. Later the political tendency became conservative. A number of collaborators left because of the change in political orientation. Then, during the war, Derycke, who later escaped to France and took the name Claude Elsen, became editor-in-chief, and the magazine came under the thumb of the German *Propaganda Abteilung*.

Soulié's articles in *Cassandre* included one on a triple murderer and an article praising Liege, followed by an occasional column called "Feuillet de Liège." He compared Liege to Aix-en-Provence, which he had visited. He was not a major contributor. After mid-1936 he wrote no more articles for *Cassandre*.

THE POLITICAL CLIMATE DURING THE WAR

Before discussing Soulié's collaborationist journalism during the war, it is useful to consider the situation of Belgium, which was rather different from that of France. At the beginning of the German invasion of Belgium, May 10, 1940, two million Belgians (20 percent of the population) had fled to France temporarily. For most Belgians at that time the priority was to preserve Belgian unity, and they wanted to find some form of accommodation with Germany.[8] Memories of heavy losses in the First World War contributed to their initial assessment of the situation. Later the majority of the population supported the Allies. The situation in Belgium, as in most of Europe, was complicated and cannot be reduced to an account of resistants and collaborators; neither collaborators nor resistance fighters were more than a small portion of the population. Resistance in Belgium was never so mythologized as in France, at least partly because in Belgium there were many resisting groups, from Communists to Catholics, with no real cooperation among them. Many Belgian writers and critics also cannot easily be categorized. Hellens, a major literary figure in

prewar Belgium who was not a German sympathizer, published in the single issue of *Disque vert* that appeared during the war (July 1940) an anti-Semitic article about rich Jews who collect art.[9]

King Leopold III did not follow his government in exile to London but remained in Brussels. He surrendered quickly and was widely assumed to have
been a covert German sympathizer. Taken to Germany in 1944, after the invasion of the continent, he could never return permanently to Belgium. He abdi-
cated the throne in 1951.

The most outspoken advocates of the German Reich were the Rexists, led
by Léon Degrelle, who had come to prominence in the 1930s as an opponent of
the established political parties. Once the Germans invaded Belgium, Degrelle
saw them as a force against a corrupt democratic order. He advocated the position of the SS: the creation of a Burgundian state, to include the Netherlands,
Belgium, and part of Eastern France, which would be allied to a larger German
Empire. Degrelle spoke of reinstituting the fifteenth-century empire of the
Dukes of Burgundy and used the cross of the old Burgundian empire for his
flag. In his interpretation of history the Walloons were "a Germanic frontier
people struggling over the centuries against the alien influences of French culture."[10] The Catholic Church kept a *modus vivendi* with the German occupiers
but refused to allow Rexists in uniform to receive mass.

Belgians were less cooperative than the French about the deportation of
Jews. At the beginning of the German occupation, the Belgian administrators
in Brussels refused to distribute the yellow star to foreign Jews, and it was
never distributed to Belgian citizens. Police forces in Brussels, in contrast to
those in Antwerp, did not participate in the rounding up of the Jewish population in the summer of 1942. During the night of September 3–4, 1943, however,
the immunity granted to Belgian Jews was canceled and many were caught in
a raid. In two years 44 percent of the Jewish population of Belgium was deported, in contrast to 25 percent in France.[11]

During the war it was not possible to depend upon French publishers and
French books, which led to some increase in French-language publishing in
Belgium. There were, however, half as many magazines as there had been before the war, at least partly because of the shortage of paper. The German authorities favored the creation of new publishing houses, promoted Belgian authors, and attempted to publish works by German or Nordic rather than French

and Anglo-Saxon authors. One prominent publishing house during the war, Toison d'Or, was founded by Edouard and Lucienne Didier in March 1941; 135 of the 150 shares were held by the Mundus group, which was connected to the Ministry of Foreign Affairs of Joachim von Ribbentrop. Others who held stock included Raymond de Becker and Pierre Daye, both on the far right politically. Toison d'Or published a fairly wide range of authors, considering its German-controlled stock. Although a number of the authors were on the extreme right, such as Céline, Robert Brasillach, and Poulet, it also had a list of classic authors, including Diderot, Stendhal, Baudelaire, Cervantes, and Voltaire. Lucienne Didier had a literary salon, attended by writers of a wide range of political positions: many Rexists but also Henri de Man, Poulet, Henri de Montherlant, and Emmanuel d'Astier de la Vigerie, a prominent French Catholic critic.[12]

SOULIÉ'S JOURNALISM DURING THE WAR

Soulié spent the war years in Liege, a major site of extreme-right groups and assassinations. The prewar offices of *La Meuse* were taken over by *La Légia*, a daily paper established under German pressure that reached a circulation of seventy-five thousand.[13] The editor-in-chief, René Letesson, was associated with Poulet, Colin, and others who worked with collaborationist papers in Brussels. The staff was in general pro-Nazi and ultra-collaborationist. The newspaper's position was that the Walloons, people of south and southeast Belgium, were a Germanic race and there was no such thing as Belgium. Wallonia was to be incorporated into the greater German Reich. An editorial of October 6, 1941, by André Comhaire concerning Belgian soldiers fighting with the Germans against the Russians shows the political orientation: "The Führer said a word, only one it is true, which gleams in our eyes as a message of hope." According to an undated report in Soulié's file at the Auditorat Général près la Cour Militaire in Brussels (Military Court), in May 1940 Soulié called *La Légia* a "sale torchon" [dirty rag] because it was poorly written and edited. He was more enthusiastic about Poulet's *Nouveau Journal*, for which he wrote a few articles. He wanted to start a Liege edition of this paper, but when that proved impossible, he decided to write for *La Légia*.

Soulié contributed to the daily *La Légia* and the weekly *Terre wallonne* as well as to the French-language radio station, which was under the control of the Germans and actively supported the concept of a New Order in which Germany and Belgium would be linked. It was for these activities that Soulié would be prosecuted and condemned to death after the war. In his condemnation in 1945, preserved in the files of the Military Court, he was described as "one of the most zealous collaborators with the enemy."

Soulié's articles for *La Légia*, preserved in his file at the Military Court, include praise of Hitler and of Pierre Laval and advocacy of a united Europe in which France would be an ally of the Germans and Belgium part of a Burgundian state. In 1942 Soulié predicted frequent bombings of the United States by Japan. He denigrated any enemies of the Reich. Britain, South Africa, and America were seen as menaces to the Belgian Congo. "Al Capone aviator" (June 8, 1943) claims that the Americans are deliberating bombing Belgian houses, because they are not as civilized as Europeans.[14]

At Radio National Belge the technical installations were sabotaged and the personnel evacuated after May 10, 1940. "Belgium was therefore the only occupied country where radio propaganda had to be provided during the whole war by mobile transmitters belonging to the German army."[15] Radio Bruxelles, directed from 1940 to 1942 by Louis Carette (who quit in May 1942 and went to Italy; after the war he became a prominent writer in France under the name Félicien Marceau), was under the direct control of the German occupiers. Among the main themes of its programs were attacks on supposed enemies—England, the Jews, the Communists, the Freemasons—and praise for Belgians working in Germany. Soulié wrote scripts for the programs "Arts et lettres dans les provinces" (for 300 Belgian francs per manuscript) and "Présence de l'Europe." He was told to concentrate on Wallonia and the Germanic world.[16] He wrote a series of 135 articles for Radio Bruxelles, from 1942 through 1944, for which he earned 27,500 francs. His papers were normally ten minutes in length and broadcast at 5 P.M. Among his subjects were the need for a directed economy, praise of fascism for raising the spiritual level of the masses and replacing the individual in his natural familial setting, and criticism of Marxism for reducing all individuals to the lowest level. He expressed opposition to the ideas of the French revolution, to class warfare, to Marxism, and to Judaism. As in his articles for *La Légia*, he advocated a united fascist Europe, in which the particular qualities of each country would not be sacrificed but would be reinforced through national architectural styles.[17] Another theme was the need for more births, which in turn entails more space, gained initially through colonies in eastern Europe opened up by the "victorious march of the German army." In an article broadcast January 5, 1942, Soulié regretted that Belgians were allowed to emigrate to the Congo only with the permission of the financiers who control it. He advocated a system without bankers.[18]

Notre Terre wallonne, retitled simply *Terre wallonne* in 1942, was a weekly published by the *Légia* society from August 2, 1941, to August 26, 1944, with a circulation of about one thousand. While it showed some independence initially, after 1943 it wrote largely propaganda for the German occupiers. It covered many of the same themes as *La Légia*. There were regular cartoons advocating going to work in Germany. One cartoon shows a woman paying her bills readily because her husband works in Germany; in another a young woman is told to choose the most courageous of her two suitors, the one who is working in Germany.

Soulié was among eleven principal editorial staff members of *Terre wallonne*. He had a column, "Vie sportive" (later titled "Chronique sportive"), from August 9, 1941. Topics included sport in ancient Greece, the need for professionalism, and even the need to reduce the length of some sporting events because of dietary restrictions during the war. Several times in the sports column he praised the volunteers working in Germany. One sports column advocated more power for referees (January 24, 1942). Another proclaimed that bodies, character, and intelligence could be formed only with the aid of the state (June 6, 1942).

From August 1941 Soulié was also responsible for long book reviews, in a column usually titled "Livres," of about eight column inches, and a column called "Carnet des editeurs," mostly short notices of new publications. Sometimes his articles were signed Gille Anthelme, sometimes simply G. A. Most of the articles show a decided opinion, but almost everything he read was given some praise. He is not as interesting a critic as Poulet, whose work he often cited with admiration. Soulié praised novels by such varied authors with differing political persuasions as Elsa Triolet, de Montherlant, John Steinbeck, and Colette. His literary criticism was considerably less doctrinaire than his other work for *Terre wallonne*. Considering the amount of work he was doing, it is understandable that in the longer columns he quoted a good deal. He obviously had to read, or at least skim, many books. By August 1, 1942, another journalist took over "Chronique sportive." Also in August 1942 the format changed and Soulié usually only wrote "La Vie littéraire."

Foreshadowing *Le Regard du roi* or at least showing similar interests is Soulié's review of poems by Hubert Dubois, in which he said that "celebrating the redemption of the flesh by the spirit, of the body by the soul is a way of touching God" (September 20, 1941). He also commented that the "fantastic" makes for the originality of Walloon writing in French. He reviewed a novel by Hellens that he compared to Poulet's *Handji* (March 14, 1942). In a review of Poulet's *L'Ange et les dieux*, Soulié saw a religious message (July 18, 1942).

Many of Soulié's reviews show his interest in African culture, especially in the Congo. He praised Belgian policy in the Congo, where "Belgians have encouraged maintaining the original style of life of the Negros" (November 22, 1941). Reviewing a book on Belgian colonial literature, Soulié praised this literature as humanistic, not exotic (May 9, 1942). There are also references to Africa in various other reviews: of a book by a governor general of the colonies (July 3, 1943); of a collection of articles by Daye on the Congo, in which Soulié said that colonization has added to the Belgian personality (September 11, 1943); and of a collection of tales by a magistrate in Katanga (November 20, 1943), which sheds light on "the hearts of the blacks." A review of *Les Regards sur notre Congo*, by Julien Vanhove, lead Soulié to say that Belgium must affirm its right to the Congo by the work it has accomplished there (December 11, 1943). In 1944 he mentioned Léon Damas's *Veillées noires* (January 1, 1944). He reviewed *Tempête sur la brousse*, a novel by Sylva de Jonghe translated from the Flemish and published in 1943 in French, which he praised for seeking to understand the Congolese (January 22, 1944).

Tempête sur la brousse is the story of a Congolese chief who is tempted to convert to Christianity after the arrival of white missionaries who speak of "the evil life of the blacks and the terrible punishment they will suffer for all their misdeeds: murders, superstitions, adultery and debauchery."[19] The white missionaries believe that sensuality is for all Africans the only reason for living. There are scenes of the torture of an adulterous woman and of a tribal conflict leading to many deaths and the mutilation of the corpses, which, a footnote assures the reader, are based on real events. The chief, however, is said to possess intelligence, to be, like his fellow tribesmen, practical and clever. He is given a certain nobility and dignity when he dies, a conclusion that appealed to Soulié.

It is clear that de Jonghe knew the Congo, because of the many details in the novel, which are much more specific than anything in *Le Regard du roi*. The names, descriptions of the seasons, and many metaphors are clearly based on the Congo: "separating the people of a single tribe was as difficult as making cassava grow on bamboo" (79); contact with civilization marks a man "as indelibly as the tattoos after the initiation ceremonies" (215). Especially obvious, in comparison with the vagueness of *Le Regard du roi*, are the detailed descriptions of weather and of animals.

Political commentary is less prominent than literary explication in Soulié's work. René Tonus, the editor-in-chief of *Terre wallonne*, wrote that the war was "desired by the Jewish plutocracy."[20] Soulié accepted the anti-Semitism of the paper, stating in one article that the "cosmopolitanism of Jewish inspiration tried to ruin our own cultural sensitivity" (October 25, 1941). He mocked Joe Louis's political comments during the war but more strongly criticized the managers of black boxers, who, he claimed, exploit them and are "invariably Jews" (May 30, 1942). He quoted with approval a comment about Walloon artists who went to Germany and found "a neglected source of their own sensibility." He also mentioned that Pierre Hubermont, the director of the Communauté Culturelle Wallonne, was struck by the "the monumental art of the new Germany" (November 29, 1941). Considering Soulié's previous art criticism, it is hard to believe he could really have approved of Nazi art, but he quoted Hubermont without apparent irony. Comparing Soulié's work during the war with his writing before the war, I have the impression that he was writing for *Terre wallonne* without any conviction.

From October 1941 to August 1944 Soulié also wrote a book column for *Wallonnie*, a magazine edited by the Communauté Culturelle Wallonne, a primarily cultural organization founded by the *Propaganda Abteilung* and directed by Hubermont (the pseudonym of Joseph Jumeau). Hubermont, director of the Communauté Culturelle Wallonne and publisher of *Cahiers de la Communauté Culturelle Wallonne* in Liege from October 1941 to August 1944, was a proletarian writer who opposed any French influence. In his articles in *Terre wallonne*, Soulié supported the Communauté Culturelle Wallonne in general terms but without denying French cultural influence. It is difficult to decide to what extent Soulié wrote what he believed and to what extent he followed what we might say was the line of least resistance. His earlier writing, before the war, seems definitely pro-French. In 1924, for example, he wrote that Paris "est le pôle des arts et chaque nation y contribue" [is the center of the arts and each nation contributes to it].[21] As a member of the Liege branch of the Communauté Culturelle Wallonne, Soulié was involved in efforts to get rid of Hubermont in August 1941.[22] This coup failed, and Soulié seems to have made some kind of peace with Hubermont.

In an article titled "Esprit et leçons des journées culturelles wallonnes 1942" Soulié spoke of a Walloon renaissance, which was to be part of a New Order, with Germanic energy and the white race as the "summits" of achievement (April 4, 1942). He reviewed a book by Daye, *L'Europe aux Européens*, praising its argument that Europe must be united against the dangers presented by the United States and Asia. Europe, however, increasingly did not seem to include France. In "Au seuil des journées culturelles wallonnes" Soulié complained that before the occupation of Belgium by the German forces "propaganda organized by the Quai d'Orsay tended to denationalize Belgium. . . . they were preparing a Marxist and Free Mason celebration. . . . we must look toward Germany" (March 28, 1942). This is from a writer whose greatest praise for Liege in 1935 was to compare it to Aix-en-Provence. More significantly, he had often praised the work of Hellens and Poulet, both part of the "Groupe du Lundi," which in 1937 edited a manifesto stating that the French-language literature of Belgium must, to avoid provincialism, remain part of "la France littéraire."[23] By 1942 Soulié claimed that the history of Liege shows that its people are happy only in an imperial climate (April 18, 1942).

At times Soulié wrote front-page articles in *Terre wallonne* in support of the New Order. On August 2, 1941, in "Le Travail pour restaurer la patrie," he said that class warfare must give way to a new society with three bases: family, profession, and nation. On January 2, 1942, Anthelme (Soulié) signed a front-page article titled "Liberté, liberté chérie . . . ," which was the most right-wing article he had written so far. Liberty, he wrote, is a problem of order and reason. Previously artists were free to die of hunger but not free to say what they wanted; for example, if they worked for a newspaper they could not offend advertisers. He also cited the condemnation of Céline during the Popular Front. It is easy to refute the arguments, of course. Most artists are not journalists. Céline's work was published and well reviewed even in the left-wing press. There was a favorable review of *Voyage au bout de la nuit* by Paul Nizan in *L'Humanité* (December 9, 1932). Nizan called it a major work, although he wondered where Céline's "pure revolt" would lead. In very vague terms, Soulié spoke of a tolerance whose limits are those that preserve liberty from license. He quoted Maurice de Vlaminck about how well artists were treated in Germany. He wrote in favor of national socialism, the corporations of Italy, and a "communitarian" spirit.

By 1944 Soulié mostly reviewed books published in Belgium, often by Toison d'Or, for *Terre wallonne*. In the last review Soulié wrote, on August 12, 1944, he commented that *Grapes of Wrath* is "the only novel that has crossed the Atlantic since the thunder of May 10." Soulié said of Steinbeck, "his good will is evident and his anger legitimate"; he judged that this is not a Communist book.

In December 1943, Soulié seemed to suggest that he was just doing a job: "A journalist writing at present continues to do his job. This does not imply any particular ideology, as it could also imply one, however." What was his own ideology? It is hard to make any clear evaluation of some of his cultural statements; his rejection of French influence and implied praise of Nazi art, for instance, seem to be parroting of a party line. On the other hand, his hatred of democracy and his anti-Semitism seem to be expressions of his own beliefs.

HOW SOULIÉ'S WRITING SUGGESTS
LE REGARD DU ROI

Soulié's own style in writing fiction and some comments from his criticism suggest parallels to *Le Regard du roi*. Soulié's study of Chaplin shows his interest in a type of comedy similar to certain scenes in *Le Regard du roi*, a comedy that is not found in other work signed by Laye or, for that matter, in work by Poulet. Soulié praised, for example, the effect that Chaplin obtained by putting someone in an embarrassing situation, someone who refuses to admit what has happened and insists on keeping his dignity.[24] This analysis could be seen as an explication of why Clarence is a comic figure to Samba and the boys.

One dream in Soulié's short novel "Caligula" may remind the reader of Clarence's dream of the manatees in *Le Regard du roi*:

Caligula repose.

Il est sur un quai, sous le toit vitré d'une gare, un cintre immense, ex-
cessif, ou peut-être dans un tunnel, mais démesuré . . . Un trottoir roulant
l'emporte en toboggan vers une bouche lointaine, inconnue, invisible encore mais formelle. C'est un trottoir gluant, pâteux, où l'on tombe assis et qui
entraîne à une allure folle. L'angoisse monte à la gorge de Caligula, comme
une bille. C'est effroyable! . . . Le cauchemar atteint sa cime. Caligula
étouffait, quand il s'éveille en nage. ("Caligula," 244)

[*Caligula is resting.*

*He is on a platform, under the glass roof of a station, an immense, ex-
cessively large vault, or perhaps in a tunnel, but one that cannot be measured. . . . A rolling sidewalk carries him like a toboggan toward a faraway
mouth, unknown, still invisible, but definite. It is a sticky, pasty sidewalk,
where you fall onto your seat and which carries you at a mad speed. Anguish
rises to Caligula's throat like a marble. It is frightening. . . . The nightmare reaches a climax. Caligula is suffocating, when he wakes up in a cold
sweat.*]

Clarence vit le moment où il n'allait pas seulement les frôler, mais les heurter;
heurter en plein leurs seins blanchâtres . . . et sentir sur ses mains et sur son
front et sur ses joues, cette gluante mollesse et cette envahissante tiédeur. Il
poussa un grand cri, il fit un suprême effort, il dégagea si rudement ses pieds
de la boue et du courant qu'il ressentit un choc. (*Le Regard du roi*, 199)

[*Clarence could see that the moment would come when he would not just
brush against them, but actually bump into them, bump right into those
pallid mounds of urgent flesh . . . and feel on his hands and on his head
and on his cheeks their glutinous softness and their overpowering warmth.
He uttered a loud cry, he made a supreme effort, and disengaged his feet so
forcibly from the mud and the current that he felt a great shock.*] (The Radiance of the King, *225*)

Reviewing *Sainte Beauté* by Jean Libert, a book he compared to *Le Grand
Meaulnes*, Soulié cited a passage showing pantheism that seems very similar to
the conclusion of *Le Regard du roi*:

Alors je me suis mis en route pour joindre, à l'extrême pointe de la visibilité,
l'océan de feu qui rugit dans le coeur de Dieu, cette océan de flammes vives
qui arrachait à l'apôtre son cri presque intraduisible: Dieu est amour! (*Terre
wallonne*, January 8, 1944)

[*So I set out to join, at the furthest point I could see, the ocean of fire that was roaring in the heart of God, that ocean of hot flames that tore from the apostle his almost untranslatable cry: God is love!*]

Quand il fut parvenu devant le roi, quand il fut dans le grand rayonnement du roi, et tout meurtri encore par le trait de feu . . . Clarence tomba à genoux. . . . C'était ce feu qui brûlait et cette lumière qui rayonnait. C'était cet amour qui dévorait. (*Le Regard du roi,* 252)

[*When he had come before the king, when he stood in the great radiance of the king, still ravaged by the tongue of fire . . . Clarence fell upon his knees. . . . It was this fire that sent its tongue of flame into his limbs, and this radiance that blazed upon him. It was this love that enveloped him.*]
(The Radiance of the King, *283–84*)

More than his own writing before the war and his interest in Africa, however, it was Soulié's experience after his condemnation that is most clearly reflected in the themes of *Le Regard du roi.*

7

Francis Soulié after the War

When the Germans began their retreat from Belgium in August 1944, thousands of Rexists and other collaborators joined the exodus, often after looting what property they could. Some managed to escape to France, Spain, or South America. With the liberation, the process of judging the collaborators was carried out in an orderly and legal fashion.[1]

Soulié went into hiding several weeks before the liberation of Belgium. An arrest warrant was issued for him on October 11, 1944. A long, undated report on Soulié submitted to the Military Court summarizes how he was viewed by his investigators. The report describes him as a "pretentious dilettante" who frequented avant-garde artistic circles in Liege, admired Futurists and Dadaists, and played at being an esthete. Before the war he had his portrait painted by Mambour, who also became a supporter of the New Order. He first wrote sports columns for *La Meuse*. His interest in physical education was said to be consistent with his study of totalitarian regimes, which stressed the culture of the body along with that of the mind. The investigators found his political articles to be written with more subtlety than those of Letesson, the editor-in-chief of *La Légia*. They considered his praise for young writers an attempt to create sympathy between them and the New Order. Finally, they noted, Soulié could not say that he had to work to earn a living, as he was going to inherit from a very rich woman.[2]

Documents in Soulié's file at the Military Court report various attempts to find him. A resistance agent went to see his mother several times. In November 1944 she showed the agent a letter from her son stating, "the Belgium of tomorrow will be a National-Socialist dictatorship. I am a royalist and I admire everything the king does." Although the king was widely believed to be supporter of the Germans, Soulié's mother felt that this letter proved her son innocent, because he called himself a royalist. The agent commented, "Madame Soulié must really be insane to show me such documents."

There were several later reports that Soulié had been seen in Charleroi and Wéris. Among those questioned about his whereabouts was Mariette Falla, who told the investigators on August 22, 1945, that Soulié was a friend of her father's. Both Soulié and her father had been delegates to the national Olympic committee, but they never spoke about politics. She said she had seen him three or four weeks before the liberation but not more recently. She was lying, as she kept Soulié hidden in seclusion in an apartment in Belgium for some time. He could not be found at the time of the trial of the *La Légia* staff.

The *Jugement du Conseil de Guerre de Liège*, dated September 29, 1945, case number 1171, against twenty-nine defendants describes the twenty-sixth as follows:

> SOULIE François [*sic*] Henri Charles Marie, journalist, using the pen name Gilles [*sic*] ANTHELME, son of François Soulié and Marie COURTOIS, born in Antwerp, July 21, 1987, living in Liege at Quai Saint Léonard, No. 53
> *FUGITIVE, UNDER THE CONSTRAINT OF A WARRANT OF ARREST*

All twenty-nine defendants were accused of having "disturbed in wartime the fidelity of the citizens toward the king and the state and evilly served the politics or the plans of the enemy" after May 10, 1940, and in 1941 and 1942. The same charge was laid against twenty-four of the defendants, including Soulié, for 1943 and 1944, with the additional precision that these defendants engaged in propaganda directed against the Belgian resistance movement.

Soulié was condemned along with many others to pay a fine of one million Belgian francs. He was said to have been a political collaborator with *La Légia* and *Terre wallonne* and to have given articles to these pro-German papers as well as having taken an active part in shaping the political orientation of the papers. Soulié was also accused, along with one other, of particularly serious offenses, because of the odious nature of what he wrote and his collaboration with the French-language German radio in Brussels.

As a result, the war council condemned Soulié along with three other defendants to death. He was deprived of all titles and public offices. He was also ordered to pay 205,170 francs in expenses and civil charges of 500,000 and 2 million francs. (According to Conway, Soulié's official salary as a journalist would have been a modest 3,000 francs a month.) Finally, his immediate arrest was ordered, as there "was reason to believe that he would try to escape punishment." Soulié is described as one of the most zealous collaborators with the enemy and one who had escaped from Belgian justice.

Those from *La Légia* condemned to death followed various paths. Tonus, the head of drama for the Communauté Culturelle Wallonne, escaped to Germany. Several others who were caught submitted psychiatrists' reports in defense of their wartime activity. Letesson was arrested after escaping to Germany. He defended himself by saying he wrote in a spirit of political realism and out of the necessity of fighting against bolshevism. His psychiatrist's report mentioned his alcoholic grandfather, that Letesson did not walk until the age of two, and that he had had a nervous depression in 1943. Hubermont's file includes a doctor's report stating that Hubermont's mother had dementia praecox and that he tried to hang himself when she was sent to an asylum. Another letter in his file, from an acquaintance, suggests that Hubermont was going to claim he was "dingo" but that was just an excuse and he has always been "nasty, lying and cowardly."

At some point Soulié made his way to France. According to Liliane Elsen, who knew him in Paris, he hid for seven years, partly in Belgium and partly in France. He finally had to come out of hiding, according to Elsen, because he was having severe trouble with his teeth.

SOULIÉ IN PARIS

After the war a number of right-wing Belgians had literary careers abroad. Perhaps the best known is Carette, who took the name Félicien Marceau and was later elected to the Académie Française. De Man, who translated books for Toison d'Or and was a literary critic for *Le Soir*, where he published some anti-Semitic articles, became a famous professor at Yale. Derycke became, as Claude Elsen, a prominent translator of a number of major English-language works, including books by Norman Mailer, Kingsley Amis, R. D. Laing, Colin Turnbull, and Evelyn Waugh. A number of Belgians had careers in French publishing. Those on the right, such as Poulet and Elsen, were often connected to Plon or to the extreme-right journal *Rivarol*. Poulet needed all the jobs he could get. Elsen did many translations, which paid poorly, but he worked fast. Another Belgian in France, Jean Libert, became well known as a writer of spy novels under the name Paul Kenny. Soulié, who did not need money, appears not to have had any job with a literary review or publisher in France.

There are two documents in the archives of the Prefecture of Police in Paris concerning Francis Soulié. The first, dated October 18, 1952, is a report responding to a note of June 10, 1952, asking for an investigation of Soulié, born July 21, 1897, in Antwerp. He had been residing at 36 rue des Ecoles in Paris (thus in the Latin Quarter, where he met Laye). According to this document, Soulié was a bachelor but was engaged to Falla, who was thirty-eight to Soulié's fifty-five and a resident of a suburb of Liege. Liliane Elsen said that although he was a homosexual Soulié married Falla in gratitude for her help in keeping him hidden.

The report continues by stating that Soulié had entered France "irrégulièrement" in January 1952, with a Belgian identity card that had expired in October 1944. On April 26, 1952, Soulié went to the Service des Etrangers de la Préfecture de Police, where he stated that he had been condemned to death in Belgium on November 6, 1945, for working for the enemy and that he had also been fined 500,000 Belgian francs. The police contacted the Belgian Department of Justice to see if Soulié should be extradited. Soulié would have known that by 1952 the Belgians no longer demanded extradition. In addition, in Belgium there was no appeal. The French were therefore reluctant to expel those who had been sentenced to death and were willing to give them political refugee status.

Between 1944 and 1949 the Belgians had prosecuted over 57,000 persons, of whom 53,000 were found guilty. Of 1,247 death sentences, 241 were carried out. Most sentences were eventually commuted. Would Soulié have been executed had he remained in Belgium? It is difficult to guess, but those who had contributed to the German-controlled press were generally given harsher sentences than others.[3] The situation had changed considerably, however, after a Catholic government was elected in 1950 and followed a more moderate policy toward collaborators. A law passed in February 1953 made it easier to release and pardon collaborators.

While waiting to hear about extradition, the French imprisoned Soulié for violation of the laws concerning foreigners. When they learned that the Belgians no longer wanted Soulié, the French freed him provisionally on May 4, 1952. They gave him a card authorizing him to remain in France for fifteen days, which he could renew until October 27, 1952. In the meantime, however, he was condemned to a month in prison and a fine of ten thousand francs for illegal entry. He appealed this judgment. On May 6, 1952, he moved to 15 rue Molière, described as a small apartment ("petite résidence"), which his fiancée had purchased for him. He stated that he had been a journalist in Belgium but had had no job in France.

The police report of October 1952 also noted that Soulié had inherited property and other objects upon the death of his mother, consisting of buildings valued at 4,993,550 Belgian francs and furniture and other objects valued at 408,645 francs. He could dispose of the property because he had paid the fines for which he was liable in Belgium. (The sum Soulié mentioned to the French, 500,000 Belgian francs, was, however, much less than what had been demanded in the judgment of 1945.) Soulié stated that he had an income of 370,000 Belgian francs per year. He did not have any police record in France. He made the following declarations to the police: While he had studied at an advanced level in Belgium, he had no university diplomas. He began as a journalist with the daily *La Meuse* in Liege, for which he wrote the sports column. Later he wrote the literary column. He also wrote art reviews for various Belgian publications. During the occupation he wrote the literary column for *La Légia*, founded in Liege in 1941.

The final paragraphs of the police report are of particular interest: "At the Liberation, he hid in a room near Liege and wrote novels as well as a historical narrative about Louis XI and Charles the Bold." This is Soulié's own declaration to the police. It is hard to judge its veracity, but it is interesting to speculate about the novels he mentions. There is nothing published under the name of Francis Soulié or Gille Anthelme in the Belgian or French national libraries. The subject of the historical narrative, Charles the Bold, the last duke of Burgundy, who was defeated by the French king in 1477, shows Soulié's continued interest in the possible restoration of a Burgundian state, as advocated by some of the collaborators with the Germans during the war. At least, having defended this policy in *Terre wallonne*, he would have had the opportunity to study the history of the Burgundian rulers.

The police report of October 1952 ends: "Since his arrival in Paris, Soulié has not attracted attention, from a political or national point of view. He lives quietly, goes out seldom, and only receives a few visits." Obviously, under the circumstances, Soulié would have been very careful in his private life.

The second police document, dated January 10, 1962, is a report on Soulié's activities in France that corrects some of the information in the first report. Soulié married Falla (whose birth date is given as 1912 instead of 1914) on June 8, 1954. He entered France illegally in January 1952 (though at one point on the report the entry date is listed as June 1952). He had a residence permit valid until January 20, 1963, but no work permit. Since September 12, 1957, he had lived at 50 rue des Francs-Bourgeois, in the Marais district, in a four-room apartment that he bought in June 1950 for 3.5 million old francs. Formerly, the report says (without noting the contradiction of the earlier statement that Soulié had entered the country in 1952), he lived in the Oise region, near Paris, from 1946 until May 1952 and then at 15 rue Molière (where Laye was living at the time he submitted his manuscript of *L'Enfant noir* to Plon).

Soulié had considerable revenue from renting property in Belgium—358,350 Belgian francs in 1955. His wife was the administrator of his property and lived most of the year near Liege. According to the information available in 1962, his death sentence was revoked May 31, 1946. He lost his Belgian nationality. In the January 1963 report he again told the police that he had been required to pay 500,000 Belgian francs in fines plus interest.

The French police required Soulié to reside in the Oise department until June 11, 1955, after which he was allowed come to Paris to do historical research in the Bibliothèque Nationale. He would not be allowed to publish any writings in Belgium. The blatant contradictions in the reports (how had he been required to live in the Oise when his address was 15 rue Molière or 50 rue des Francs-Bourgeois?) make one wonder about the rationality of the French police. Soulié himself, obviously, did not mind inventing whatever stories might help him.

SOULIÉ, LAYE, AND KELEFA KEITA

Marie Lorifo, Laye's first wife, thinks Laye met Soulié by chance in the Latin Quarter (at the Bar Pergola, where Fatoman meets the homosexual in *Dramouss*?). Marie and Laye lived for about two years in Soulié's studio at 15 rue Molière in Paris and visited him in Chantilly on Sundays. The family, Marie said, was very rich. Soulié's wife lived in Belgium, where she sold the paintings he owned. Marie claimed that rumors of Soulié's homosexuality were just "histoires." Liliane Elsen and others, however, confirmed that he was homosexual. Marie also claimed that Soulié wanted to adopt Laye. While Marie knew Poulet, who had "corrected Laye's writing," she never saw him at Soulié's. Neither Marie nor Elsen thought that Poulet and Soulié had much contact in Paris, at least before the publication of *L'Enfant noir*. The two men had, however, known each other in the 1930s in Belgium, as they had contributed to the same journals, and Soulié wrote for *La Revue réactionnaire*, of which Poulet was the editor.

Elsen did not often see Soulié, whom her husband found "emmerdant" [irritating] but she knew that Laye lived with him. When it became known that Soulié had adopted a son, most people thought the adopted son must be Laye. Elsen knew that Soulié was passionately interested in Africa and had spent his time in hiding reading about Africa. She described Soulié as "an inhibited or frustrated writer." She also mentioned that Soulié had a strong Walloon accent.

The Guinean whom Soulié adopted was Kelefa Keita, now a businessman in Guinea, who, along with Falla, Soulié's wife, inherited Soulié's property and papers upon his death in 1976. Keita's sister, Malon Keita Kouyaté, lives in Paris in a house where Soulié's papers are stored in the basement. The basement was damaged by fire, and the papers have never been sorted. I have not been allowed to see them, nor has Kelefa Keita replied to any of my letters.

The Keita family lived in Kankan. The father had given money to Laye to help with his trip to Paris in 1947. To reciprocate, Laye later introduced Kelefa Keita to Soulié. When this introduction took place is unclear, but Soulié brought Kelefa to France to study in 1955, according to Malon. At this time Laye was still living in Soulié's studio. Soulié later also took care of Malon and another sister. Malon had a room in his apartment on the rue des Francs-Bourgeois. She does not remember ever having seen Poulet.

Later Soulié and Kelefa wrote some tales together, which Malon thought had been sent to the Paris publisher L'Harmattan. Denis Pryen, the director of L'Harmattan, who has been with the publishing company since its founding in 1975, remembers hearing about Soulié, knew he was Belgian, and knew he attended functions with Africans and had friends among the African writers in Paris at that time. Pryen, however, had no knowledge of any manuscript that might have been submitted by Soulié and Kelefa to L'Harmattan. If it had been submitted, there would be no retrievable files. Kelefa had been planning to take Soulié to Africa, but Soulié died in 1976, before he could ever visit the Africa he saw in his imagination.

Dr. Lansiné Kaba, now dean of the Honors College at the University of Illinois at Chicago, came to France in 1956. He was initially a student at the Lycée Henri IV in Paris, where he studied literature and humanities. He met Soulié in 1957 and often talked to him about literature and about Africa. According to Kaba, Soulié was "un homme de lettres" with a wide acquaintance in literary circles in France. He had at least once talked to Kaba about Poulet. Soulié was also very knowledgeable about Africa. Kaba, who is from Kankan, said that Soulié, although he had never been to Guinea, could talk in detail about Kankan. Soulié was also a great collector of African art. He was a "rentier" [person of independent means] but did not live as a wealthy man. He had properties in Liege and Antwerp. Kaba knew that Soulié had played a role in politics in Belgium. Soulié told him he was condemned as part of a group of journalists who worked for the abdication of the king. Kaba thought Soulié had no connection with the collaborationists. It seems obvious that Soulié did not talk about his past during the war. Kaba said there was "not an ounce of racism" in Soulié.

Kaba remained in contact with Soulié until his death and has kept at least one letter from him. Soulié's style in the letter is simple, direct, and "correct"; Kaba compared it to the style of *Le Regard du roi*. Kaba knew that Soulié had written novels but thought that nothing had been published under his name. He knows Keita, who did a degree in commerce at Le Havre. He did not consider Keita a writer and knew nothing about the manuscript that Keita's sister, Malon, had mentioned.

With regard to *L'Enfant noir*, Kaba is convinced that although Soulié knew Africa very well, this book is Laye's story. There are too many details that only a Malinké would know. Soulié, however, told him that there was a manuscript of the book at least partly in Soulié's handwriting. Nevertheless, according to Kaba, Laye is the authentic author of *L'Enfant noir*.

Le Regard du roi is a different matter. Kaba said he was aware that there were not many descriptions in the book. It was not African, it was "surrealist." He found that the style shows the influence of Soulié very strongly. Malon Keita Kouyaté, who knows Kaba, confirmed to me that this suggestion was "possible" and added that Soulié was always "very discreet."

THE CULTURAL MILIEU REFLECTED IN *LE REGARD DU ROI*

If *Le Regard du roi* appealed to a French reading public interested in preserving ties with the former African empire, it also reflects the cultural milieu in which Soulié worked for years, which was only partly inspired by his interest in Africa. He was influenced by the modern Francophone Belgian tradition of literature based on dreams, fantasies, and the surreal, exemplified in the work of many artists and writers of the interwar period, including Henri Michaux, René Magritte, and Poulet. Numerous surrealist magazines were published in Belgium during the interwar years, and Soulié worked for several of them.

Hellens, an editor of *Nord* and *Le Disque vert*, was a major figure in twentieth-century Belgian literature. In his *Réalités fantastiques* (1923), the ordinary is mixed with the chimerical. In several stories in *Réalités fantas-*

tiques there is a moment of luminosity at the end: "a ray of light in the sky"; "Pierre went up to heaven on a chariot of fire."[4] "La Vie trouve toujours son chemin" is a strange story of a man walking through the mountains. He follows a pair of lovers who disappear into an abyss. The imagery of a misty, indeterminate natural world is similar to that used later by the writer of *Le Regard du roi*: "At each turning of the road, as I went upward, I saw other black pine trees appear, whose trunks seemed to take root in the obscure tops of those below. . . . Here and there a few blades of light cut through the shadow and broke on the hard ground of the road. . . . At every instant I saw a wall grow dimmer, a wall that I thought I could not cross; but suddenly a narrow passage opened between the rocks and the road continued, playing with all the obstacles, a road endowed with a clear and unpredictable will" (189).

An interest in escaping from the confines of European culture had been a temptation in European culture at least since the time of Flaubert and Baudelaire. One of the most popular authors in French during the late nineteenth and early twentieth centuries was Pierre Loti, whose descriptions of exotic cultures—Tahiti, North Africa, West Africa—appeared in many of the forty volumes of prose he published between 1879 and 1923. Other French writers of the period with an interest in exotic cultures and their encounter with colonialism include Ernest Psichari and Pierre Mille. These works were concerned with the French traveler or colonist in reaction to the colonial government as well as to the exotic culture. There is no colonial government in *Le Regard du roi*.

After Paul Gauguin went to Tahiti, he described in *Noa Noa* his disgust with French civilization, including the colonial regime in Papeete, and his need to live simply, in the wilderness. He lived almost nude, saying that "civilization is falling from me."[5] He fought off a homosexual temptation: "I was reborn; or rather another man, purer and stronger, came to life within me" (22). *Noa Noa* might well be a source for a few details in *Le Regard du roi*, perhaps indirectly, through Poulet's South Pacific novel, *La Hutte de cochenille*. In particular, Gauguin's frequent descriptions (and paintings) of flowers in the hair of young women might have been copied in *Le Regard du roi*, as they seem quite out of place in West Africa. *Noa Noa* was first published in 1900; by 1903 it was in a third edition.

Some passages in *Noa Noa* may strike the contemporary reader as indirectly racist, since Gauguin saw the natives of Tahiti as essentially different, even not quite human: "My guide seemed to follow the trail by smell rather than by sight, for the ground was covered by a splendid confusion of plants, leaves, and flowers which wholly took possession of space. . . . With the suppleness of an animal and the graceful litheness of an androgyne he walked a few paces in advance of me. And it seemed to me that I saw incarnated in him, palpitating and living, all the magnificent plant-life which surrounded us. From it in him, through him there became disengaged and emanated a powerful perfume of beauty" (19). Similarly, some passages in *Le Regard du roi* clearly show Clarence's feeling of an essential, though not so pointed, difference between himself and the black bodies with which he comes in contact, particularly in the first part of the novel.

By the 1920s the work of Hesse, invoking the superior moral climate of the East, was becoming popular. In 1925 Soulié reviewed the French edition of *Siddhartha* (originally published in German in 1923). The novel, set in India, is the story of the conflict within a young Brahmin about various ways of life. He travels through a forest during part of his journey, giving his clothes away, and progresses from strict Brahmin obedience to the law through saintly asceticism to a life of sensual pleasure with Kamala, a well-known courtesan. He then lives with "ordinary people" whose simple ways he admires and finally retreats into contemplation. Siddhartha looks for Atman, the Only One, and asks himself, "where did His eternal heart beat."[6] He describes the Buddha as "childlike and mysterious" (35). At times he feels that the ordinary world melts away. He has a vision by a river bank, in which he becomes aware of his own "wretchedness" (89). He then realizes, "I had to experience despair, I had to sink to the greatest mental depths, to thoughts of suicide, in order to experience grace" (97). The admiration of Govinda, Siddhartha's friend, may remind the reader of Clarence's attraction for the king: "He loved everything that Siddhartha did. . . . And if he ever became a god, if he ever entered the All-Radiant, then Govinda wanted to follow him" (4–5). As Siddhartha is dying, Govinda kisses him and is overwhelmed with love.

In *Steppenwolf* (1927) Hesse also examined the need to go beyond the ordinary self:

> the power to die, to strip one's self naked, and the eternal surrender of the self bring immortality with them. (62)

The return into the All, the dissolution of painful individuation, the reunion with God, means the expansion of the soul. (64)

While I am not suggesting exact parallels between *Le Regard du roi* and Hesse's Eastern mysticism expressed through a modern European sensibility, his work could be more influential than Sufi or Manding beliefs on writing signed Camara Laye.

Another influence on Soulié would have been the Belgian interest in the Congo. In 1946 Hergé (Georges Rémi) published a completely revised edition of *Tintin, reporter au Congo* (1931) as *Tintin au Congo*. The Congo was in the imagination of all Belgium; to some extent it was considered a rejection of materialist civilization.

French interest in Africa was also considerable during this period. In the 1920s and 1930s Soulié often wrote with admiration of the work of Gide. Given his interest in Africa and his homosexuality, Soulié certainly knew Gide's *Voyage au Congo* (1929), illustrated with sixty-four photographs by Gide's lover, Allégret. Soulié may have had in mind Gide's description of women "vêtues d'une sorte de tutu fait de fibres de palmes tressées" [dressed in a kind of ballet skirt made of plaited palm-fibre] (35, 37) when he described the woman who asked Clarence to dance; she "faisait bouffer son tutu de feuilles" ['fluffing up' her leafy tutu] (124, 139).

Céline, whose work Soulié knew and reviewed and who became a friend of Poulet, sets part of *Voyage au bout de la nuit* in Africa, primarily in Togo. *Le Regard du roi* may well have been inspired in part by Céline's novel. Céline's hero, Bardamu, goes to Africa because he needs money. He gambles, playing cards on the ship, where he has the feeling that everyone hates him. Later, in the deep bush in Bilomimbo, he has a group of young boy servants and there are vague homosexual references. Bardamu is conscious, as is Clarence, of the "odeur âcre d'Afrique" [the acrid odor of Africa].[7] Later Bardamu is sold by a priest to the captain of a ship, where he becomes a galley slave.

There was increasing fascination in the 1930s and 1940s with the work of Kafka, whose influence on *Le Regard du roi* has often been studied. *The Trial* and *The Castle* were translated into French and published by Gallimard, in 1933 and 1947 respectively. Soulié, who read widely, knew Kafka's work and would have seen how Kafka's spiritual quest, combined with comedy, including sexual comedy, could be a model for a story reflecting his own emotional concerns. There may also have been other literary sources. Kirkup, in the introduction to *The Guardian of the Word*, his translation of *Le Maître de la parole*, mentioned another work similar to *Le Regard du roi*—Dino Buzzati's *Il deserto dei tartari*. It is possible that Soulié knew this work, published in French translation in 1949, as he was interested in Asian culture. Kirkup also found some details in *Le Regard du roi* that are similar to Jules Verne's *La Mission Barsac*.[8]

All these influences on the literary sensibility of the period can be seen in *Le Regard du roi*. There might also have been more direct influence on *Le Regard du roi* in the work of Leiris, particularly *L'Afrique fantôme—De Dakar à Djibouti, 1931–33*. *L'Afrique fantôme* was published in 1934. The first edition was destroyed under Vichy in 1941, and a new edition was published in 1951. Parallels between *Le Regard du roi* and *L'Afrique fantôme* were noticed in 1991 by Cornélie Kunze, who speculated on a possible literary plot between Laye and Leiris, who was a member of a committee supporting Présence Africaine. Kunze found *Le Regard du roi* to be closer to modern European surrealism than to Negritude and more specifically found that Clarence's experience—his inability to understand Africa, the strangeness of the forest in which he cannot find his way, his disgust with his sexuality—is close to what Leiris described in the journal that became *L'Afrique fantôme*. She also mentioned the way in which sexuality is related to death and to the sacred. For Leiris, sexual desire, death, and possession were closely linked.[9]

Kunze found direct parallels to Leiris's work in the descriptions of African huts, clearly seen from a European perspective, the palace decorated with frescoes, the fat eunuchs, the protocol of the court, and even a figure corresponding to Dioki with her serpents in *Le Regard du roi*. She concluded that there can be no probable explanation for the parallels and the similar emotional state of Leiris and Clarence except Leiris's collaboration with Laye on the novel. Equally probable, of course, is that the author of *Le Regard du roi* took episodes from *L'Afrique fantôme* and that he was, like Leiris, a surrealist with similar problems concerning his sexuality.

Other details that Kunze did not mention include the descriptions of the armored horses Leiris sees in a procession in Cameroon, which are similar to those Clarence notices in the opening scene. One of the photographs that accompany Leiris's text shows dancers masked as antelopes and another is a castle in Gondar, with crenelated towers. Nagoa and Noaga are masked as antelopes in their dance for the king at the conclusion of *Le Regard du roi*. Both photos could well have spurred the imagination of Soulié.

The themes of *Le Regard du roi* are based on more than Soulié's interest in Africa and in surrealism. They often relate to his own situation after his escape from Belgium, a white homosexual banished from his native land. Clarence has been banished from his hotel. He can no longer return, as "chacun lui tournerait le dos" [they would all turn their backs on him] (14, 11). Clarence looks at the young black king and thinks he could "aimer d'amour ce frêle adolescent" [love this frail adolescent] (23, 22). Later, when the Aziana police have arrested him, some of the white men see him and are certain that he is guilty. Soulié, by the 1950s, appears to have been sure that he was misjudged and was not guilty of any crime. The novel often includes discussions of the errors of human justice:

> —Est-ce qu'un premier président n'est pas un homme honorable? demanda Clarence.
> —C'est un homme qui a des fréquentations suspectes, dit-elle. (80)
>> [*"Isn't a lord president an honourable man?" asked Clarence.*
>> *"Those sort of men have all kinds of dangerous contacts," she replied.*] *(88)*

> Eh bien, dit Diallo, les hommes justes seraient beaucoup moins justes, je suppose, si leur justice flattait moins leur cruauté. (187)
>> [*"Well," said Diallo, "I suppose just men would be much less just if their justice pandered less to their love of cruelty."*] *(209)*

The love of the king overrules humans' sense of justice.

> —Le maître des cérémonies? Tu écoutes le maître des cérémonies, à présent? Je croyais que tu savais à quoi t'en tenir sur les hommes justes. . . . Tu es aussi digne de te présenter que n'importe quel autre. Si tous ceux qui se présentent devant le roi devaient être dignes de lui, le roi vivrait dans un désert. (246)
>> [*"The master of ceremonies! Do you take any notice of what* he *says? I thought you knew what to expect from these so-called 'just' men.". . . You*

are as worthy of being presented to the king as anyone else. If all those who present themselves to the king had to be worthy of him, the king would live alone in the desert.] (276–77)

In Belgium Soulié was a willing collaborator with the Nazi regime and was thought a "pretentious dilettante." After he escaped to France and met Camara Laye and other young Africans, he developed a deeper interest in African culture. He wanted to justify his actions during the war by criticizing the system of justice that had condemned him and by imagining a world in which he could find salvation. These psychological needs, when combined with his interest in surrealism and in social comedy and with his desire to help Laye led to *Le Regard du roi*, a work of far greater value than anything else Soulié produced.

8

The Life of Robert Poulet

Robert Poulet, born in Liege in 1893, was a student in the Faculté des Mines in Liege in 1913. He fought with honor in the First World War, where he served as a night patrol, preferring the independence of this work and scorning his own personal safety. After the war he did various odd jobs on farms and in factories, sometimes in France. He spent some time in the early 1920s working for Metro-Goldwyn as a technical assistant in Africa, at least partly in Côte d'Ivoire. If his own experience of Africa was rather limited, he at least had some general knowledge of the very unspecified area in which *Le Regard du roi* is located. According to those who knew him in Belgium before the war, he did not, however, show any particular interest in Africa prior to his departure for France in 1951.[1]

By the 1930s Poulet was well established as a journalist and a critic. His first novel, *Handji*, published in 1931 in Paris, brought him great recognition and is often considered a major example of Belgian surrealism. In 1936 Hellens, as a member of the jury for the Prix Albert, said that there were only two names possible for the prize: Henri Michaux and Robert Poulet.[2]

Poulet wrote for *Sélection* at least occasionally from 1924. When *Sélection* became devoted solely to visual arts, he worked on *La Revue européenne* and *Variétés* and with Hellens on *Nord*, where part of *Handji* was published in the first issue in 1929.[3] His essay on "Les Conditions du roman et la question du 'roman poétique'" appeared in the second issue. In 1933 he became director of *La Revue réactionnaire*, the policy of which he defined in the preface to the first issue in April 1933 as "against the power of the state, against materialism, against the reign of money, against barbarism and decadent taste."[4] His opening essay was "Le Mythe démocratique." Georges, Robert's brother, contributed to early issues of *La Revue réactionnaire* under his real name rather than his pseudonym, Georges Thialet, and at least one scholar considered the review to belong to "the Poulet brothers."[5] The journal disappeared in 1935.

Poulet was also a collaborator from the beginning on *Cassandre*, although he had a secondary role compared to Hellens or Derycke. He was in charge of the cinema page and reviews of French literature. In the first issue (December 1, 1934) he reviewed Aragon's *Les Cloches de Bâle*, which he found "extraordinary," calling it a "religious novel" and noting that it was not Aragon's fault if his religion (Communism) was rather poor. In an interesting review in *Cassandre* in 1936, Poulet's opinion on François Mauriac is strikingly similar to Sartre's famous judgment that "God is not a novelist, nor is Monsieur Mauriac." Poulet, like Sartre, found there to be too much comment by the narrator, too much philosophical demonstration. Poulet's reading is intelligent and perceptive, and his wit is clever: in one hundred years, he wrote, Mauriac, who lived in Bordeaux and set his works there, might be "un Bordeaux de la bonne année" [a Bordeaux from a good year] (February 8, 1936). Poulet admired Bernanos. In his film criticism he often preferred silent films by Chaplin, Buster Keaton, and Harold Lloyd, but he also liked Disney and considered Jean Renoir's *La Grande Illusion* a masterpiece. He praised Cecil B. de Mille's technique in *Bozambo*, a film shot in Central Africa.

Poulet was part of a prominent movement of the period between the wars that was critical of the regional novel. From 1936 to 1939 he was a member of the "Groupe du Lundi," united around Hellens, which published a manifesto in 1937, probably written by Poulet, stating that French-language literature in Belgium was part of "la France littéraire." "The *Manifeste du lundi* became the ideological Bible of literary discourse after the war."[6] The manifesto advocated a universal humanism and an attachment to a mythic, ahistorical France; it criticized folklore and superficial, picturesque writing. Poulet also was a defender of what he termed "magic realism," of which *Handji* is an early Belgian example. The two tendencies—toward universalism and toward the fantastic—both contrast with a regionalist literature, a literature specifically set in Belgium.

Poulet's attachment to France from the point of view of literature was allied to his strong support of political independence for Belgium and his desire to avoid conflict. In September 1939 Poulet wrote a neutralist-pacifist manifesto that called for "Belgian neutrality, against the prolongation of the European war and for the defense of the values of the mind."[7] This manifesto was signed by journalists from the left as well as the extreme right. It was rejected, however, by Communist journalists, since it implicitly accepted that the German Reich had a free hand in Eastern Europe.

POULET DURING THE WAR

Poulet was in France in the summer of 1940 and returned to Brussels because, according to one defender, he received a message that he was needed there.[8] He was director of political services for *Le Nouveau Journal* from its inception to January 1943. He played a role of some importance in the various schemes of those attempting to conciliate the German occupiers. Poulet was among the group that controlled the New Order press in Brussels, who "behaved with the arrogant self-confidence of men who felt that they were the opinion leaders of their country."[9] Another in this group was Paul Colin, an art critic and historian who was the director of *Le Nouveau Journal* and *Cassandre*.

Poulet's primary concern was preserving the independence of Belgium. He was a patriot, a Catholic, and a royalist, influenced by Charles Maurras's Action Française. He commented later that he came to politics through Maurras, whose work offered him a way of combining charity with a sense of order.[10]

(Interestingly, the works of right-wing Catholic authors such as Maurras were banned by the German authorities during the occupation of Belgium, presumably to conciliate the Catholic Church, which had put Action Française on the Index as early as 1926.)

Poulet was not in agreement, temperamentally or ideologically, with Léon Degrelle, whose populist Rexist Movement, which was excluded from the main body of Catholics, had moved to the extreme right in the late 1930s. Poulet deplored the fawning tone of Degrelle's speeches. Rémi (Hergé), a close friend of Poulet, refused to give *Tintin* to Degrelle's paper but published his strip in *Le Soir*, a New Order paper with which Poulet was in sympathy. In 1941 Poulet supported the plan of de Becker, the director of *Le Soir*, to create a broadly based single party, the Parti des Provinces Romanes, which would be committed to the New Order and to the "construction of a federal Belgian state based on authoritarian and corporativist principles."[11] Those who supported the idea felt that this party could be an important force in Belgian political life, but by August 1941 they had to retreat, as the Germans disapproved of their plan. In September 1942 José Streel, the most original thinker of the Rexist group and, like Poulet, a believer in Catholic tradition and a strong state as necessary to regenerate society, created a political council to try to unite the various collaborationist groups. While Poulet did not join the council, he wrote a series of articles in which he called for the creation of a single party of all pro-German forces and accepted that the Rexists would have a leading role.[12]

After Degrelle gave a speech in which he called for the integration of Wallonia as part of a Germanic empire, Poulet, prevented by the German censors from publishing any criticism of Degrelle, resigned as editor of *Le Nouveau Journal*. Later, after the assassination of Colin by the Resistance, Degrelle prevented Poulet from returning to *Le Nouveau Journal*.

Poulet had regular conversations with King Leopold's secretary, Comte Robert Capelle, a basis for his claim after the war that he was carrying out the king's intentions in his journalism.[13] It is not possible to verify any of Poulet's assertions with regard to what he may have been told was the king's position, as all the archives belonging to Leopold were destroyed on his death.

In the Central Police Archives in Paris a report on Poulet dated December 2, 1943, concerns his wish to reside in France temporarily. It mentions that he is of the Aryan race (this was German-occupied France) and of the Catholic faith. He had been in Paris in September and October. The officials could not exactly situate his political ideas but noted that he was said to be "en relations" with the French minister of national education and with other Belgian journalists in Paris. Poulet, however, did not stay in Paris for long at that time.

In the 1940s Germans forbade the exchange of books between France and Belgium, which, of course, encouraged Belgian writing in French. A young writer, José-André Lacour, a student in 1939, wrote a first novel, *Panique en Occident*, about the beginning of the war. He sent it first to Jean Paulhan at Gallimard, who liked it, but the German censors in France would not approve publication for moral reasons, as they found the language too audacious. Then he sent a copy to Poulet, who replied within forty-eight hours, asking Lacour to come to Brussels to meet him. Lacour had intended to send the book to Toison d'Or. Poulet told him the publisher was affiliated with the German publisher Mundos and thus part of the propaganda network. Poulet told Lacour to send his manuscript to a friend, Jean Vanlook, whose money was Belgian. Lacour dedicated the novel to Poulet, which caused him problems after the war, when he was forbidden to publish for six months. After an investigation, the ban was lifted.[14] In spite of his advice to Lacour, Poulet himself published a novel (*L'Ange et les dieux*, 1942) and a book of literary essays (*La Fleur de l'imagination: Nouveaux Romanciers belges de langue française*, 1944) with Toison d'Or during the war.

Lacour told me that he saw Poulet at an editor's soirée during the war, in January 1944. Someone said to Poulet he would get his throat cut. Poulet replied, "We will be able to move from the collaborationist press to a new press at the liberation." While the spring of 1942 was the last moment when it was possible to believe in an outright German victory, Poulet continued to support what he assumed to be the position of the king. After Stalingrad and the defeat of Rommel in 1943, there was no realistic possibility of European cooperation in a German empire, but Poulet felt, until the end, that his work was justified.

Lacour, like others with whom I spoke, wanted to present Poulet in the best possible light or at least had considerable admiration for him. He saw Poulet as intelligent, a great critic of the cinema, a fine journalist, and a patriot whose record during the First World War was outstanding. Lacour felt that Poulet's collaboration could be explained by his patriotism. Poulet wanted to maintain a form of intellectual liberty; Lacour called this "un joli rêve" [a pleasant dream]. Poulet, he thought, was not very racist. Lacour also thought that Poulet had been the youngest soldier in the First World War (whereas Poulet was twenty-one in 1914).

Pierre Silvain, a French novelist, mistakenly thought that Poulet had corrected a manuscript for Bernanos. Bernard Delcord thought that Poulet won a prize for the body of his work from the Académie Française.[15] Marc Quaghebeur called Poulet one of the important "conseillers littéraires" at Plon in the 1950s, whereas Poulet was a freelance reader without great influence, according to those who were on the staff of Plon.[16] Poulet's personality seems to have caused strong reactions among those who knew him. Even recent Belgian historians who do not share Poulet's political views treat his work with more respect than that of others who collaborated during the war. David Lewis, a Canadian scholar of collaboration in France and Belgium during the war, considers Poulet a "gentleman fascist" or even just a royalist, essentially a literary figure, influenced by Maurras. Poulet, he said, felt that Belgium must remain independent and Catholic and that Leopold must remain king. Poulet's collaboration, according to Lewis, was essentially pragmatic, an attempt to save Belgium.

While it is certain that Poulet was never a supporter of Nazi ideology to the extent of the Rexists, one must remember that "distinctions between 'moderate' and 'extremist' definitions of collaboration are easily exaggerated." There was a "chasm which separated collaborators from the patriotic majority."[17] If Poulet's views were undoubtedly less extreme than those of many Belgians who collaborated with the Nazi occupiers, he was still very conservative, and the Germans tolerated what he wrote. He was against economic liberalism, which he saw as leading to a undignified domination of overseas countries, and for a corporate order, a contract between employers and workers. He wanted "strict but humane" regulations for the Jews in Belgium but saw Jews as foreigners, not Belgians. He wrote that in spite of any problems, the Wehrmacht kept Belgium from becoming a Russian colony.[18] Better fascism than communism. After the war, Poulet said, "I have committed grave errors of judgment, but I did so in good faith and I never wanted to harm my country."[19]

In October 1945 Poulet was condemned to death in Brussels, primarily for his role as editor-in-chief of *Le Nouveau Journal* during the war. He was one of eight staff members of *Le Nouveau Journal* to be condemned. Poulet could have fled to Switzerland, as did Henri de Man, or to France, with Derycke, but he stayed. He was imprisoned for six years and for some years thought he would be executed. Freed in 1951, he was taken to the French border. He later said he was allowed to stay in France but not to publish writings on politics. French officials, however, seemed to have done little surveillance. A document in the French Central Archives dated December 16, 1954, comments upon Poulet's career, stating that "according to some rumors in literary milieus, Poulet had been condemned to death for collaboration, particularly for having edited *Le Nouveau Journal*, the Belgian counterpoint of *Le Pariẓer Zeitung*."

POULET IN FRANCE

During his years in France Poulet published many justifications of his actions during the war, including thinly disguised autobiographical novels. One article justifying his activities appeared in *Rivarol* August 29, 1986, at the time of his ninety-third birthday. He insisted in *Ce n'est pas une vie* (1976) that he held his position as editor of *Le Nouveau Journal* with the advice of the secretary to the king. His four principles for Belgium, he said, were independence, monarchy, the Christian tradition, and social justice. He claimed, however, to have been released from prison because his wife threatened to produce documents proving that King Leopold was a full collaborator with the Germans.[20]

Poulet was a reader at the extreme right-wing Editions Denoël from January 1953 to January 1954. He had published his first novel, *Handji*, with Denoël, had read Céline's *Voyage au bout de la nuit* for them, and had known Robert Denoël in Liege. Denoël's father had been a teacher at the Ecole de Mines when Poulet was a student there. Editions Denoël was a collaborationist publishing house during the war. After the war, in 1945, Robert Denoël was assassinated under mysterious circumstances.

Poulet was also a reader for Plon at the same time. He was not part of the establishment but rather a freelance reader who came once or twice a week to pick up manuscripts. He did many jobs to earn enough money in France. He was a critic for *Spectacle du monde* from 1962 to 1983. For a time, especially when first in France, he wrote under the pseudonym of Walter Orlando, a name he also used later for *La Table ronde*, which was distributed by Plon. Walter Orlando is also the name of a character in *Handji*.[21]

Comte Ivan du Monceau was director of *Pan*, a Belgian weekly satiric magazine of the far right, for thirty-five years, from 1948 to 1983. Contributors included Lacour, Félicien Marceau, and, from about 1952 until 1986, Poulet. Poulet wrote a column, "Plume de Pan," under the pseudonym Pangloss. According to du Monceau, Poulet had a superior intellect. Marceau remembered seeing Poulet occasionally in Paris during the years after the war. He felt that Poulet was an exceptional literary critic but not a good novelist, with the exception of *Handji*, an opinion shared by many readers.

Poulet worked for the daily Catholic *Présent* as well as for *Rivarol*, the extreme right-wing Parisian paper, from 1958 to 1989. Other Belgians condemned to death after the war worked for *Rivarol*: Poulet, Claude Elsen (Derycke), and Paul Werrie. (Soulié, however, had no connection with *Rivarol*.) Initially Poulet wrote primarily on literature, later on philosophical questions. He also wrote for the monthly *Ecrits de Paris*, published from the same offices. Poulet attended luncheon meetings of *Rivarol*'s editorial board twice a week until 1980, when he suffered an infarctus. He was very energetic but also very proud; he didn't want anyone to see him in his weakened condition, so he worked from home for his last nine years and no longer came to the office. He wrote his last article for *Rivarol* in September 1989, not long before his death.

Camille Galic, now the editor-in-chief of *Rivarol*, knew Poulet for many years and described him as interested in metaphysics, with a "sentiment religieux" but not a practicing believer. He saw the church as a foundation of society. Liliane Elsen gave a similar opinion. She considered Poulet fascist but less so than her husband. She also thought he was not Catholic in any usual sense but rather a mystic. For Poulet, she felt, Catholicism represented the tradition that must be upheld. Galic also felt that Poulet was "profondément raciste" but not "un Klansman." According to Galic he believed in the difference and the inequality of the races, but he could respect individuals of other races. She noted that he liked the work of Albert Cohen, a French citizen who was Jewish and therefore, in Galic's eyes, not French. He also found Isaac Bachevis Singer's work interesting. In *J'accuse la bourgeoisie* (1978), Poulet included much irony about the loss of the colonies and mockery of those who believe in equality of races. Earlier, however, in *Ce n'est pas une vie* (1976), he had said that ethnographic affiliations have no place in eternity.

Galic, who saw Poulet at *Rivarol* editorial meetings from 1963 to 1980, could not remember him talking about Africa, except to say that the French presence must be maintained. She thought he had at one time worked in Indonesia as an engineer but did not know of his work in Africa. She did, however, remember the name Camara Laye. Poulet's reviews of Laye in 1953 and 1954 were published before she joined the editorial staff of *Rivarol*.

According to Michel-Claude Jallard, an editor at Plon for many years, Poulet was marked by his political experiences—bitter, withdrawn, and isolated. He had fought with his brother, Georges, who was published by Plon. They did not speak if they happened to pass each other in the corridors at Plon. Jallard thought that Georges's politics were at the "center," whereas he considered Robert Poulet a fascist. Poulet himself mentioned his loss of contact with Georges, which he attributed to a "vague echo of political passions."[22] According to Galic, Poulet was somewhat reconciled with his brother before his death.

Michael Neal, who met Poulet in the 1970s, described him as very intelligent, with a great love of books. Poulet wrote the book page for *Rivarol*, which Neal always found interesting and not always polemic. Poulet was, however, still a fanatic. He was violently anti-homosexual and was always anti-Semitic. In *Rivarol* in October 1985 Poulet wrote in defense of Henri Roques's thesis questioning the Holocaust. Like Degrelle, Poulet denied the existence of the gas chambers.

Poulet lived with his wife, Germaine Bouillard, from Avignon, in Marly-le-Roi, a suburb of Paris. According to Liliane Elsen, Bouillard lived for her husband. Lacour said that Poulet and his wife were united by their troubles. After the war, Rémi, who perhaps realized that he had been saved largely by the great popularity of *Tintin*, helped many who had been declared "inciviques" (denied the status of citizens) because of their collaboration with the Germans. Poulet and Rémi had been friends since they collaborated on *Le Soir* during the war, and Rémi loaned Poulet considerable money to buy his apartment in Marly-le-Roi, money that Poulet eventually reimbursed. Rémi also published Poulet's pseudonymous stories in the magazine *Tintin*.[23]

Poulet died in 1989. His daughter had committed suicide over a love affair at least twenty years earlier. His wife committed suicide shortly after his death.

POULET AS AUTHOR

In *Ce n'est pas une vie*, his autobiography published in 1976, Poulet told of having been asked, while he was still in prison, to write for a weekly journal in Brussels under several pseudonyms, since he would not have been allowed to publish anything under his own name. He added, "I only agreed to the preliminary negotiations to have fun." The person who thought up this aborted project later sent Poulet a book. Poulet's reaction included a comment on ghostwriters: "A quarter of a century later, I had news from this papa's boy—who in the meantime had moved to the extreme left. He had 'signed' a book, probably put together by a ghost writer, and submitted it to me hoping I would find that he had talent. Neither the ghost writer nor he had any."[24] These comments may suggest that literary merit was important to Poulet but strict honesty in attributions of authorship was not. According to Neal, Poulet enjoyed playing games. He was, Neal said, a practical joker ("farceur"). Neal described Poulet in the late 1970s as "*very* intelligent, cynical, antidemocratic. He was probably a compulsive reader, obtained great pleasure from books but realised their limits and, also, the limits of their authors. . . . Poulet was quite a psychologist, but who wouldn't be after being condemned to be executed in a public square in Brussels? Writing as an African author would have appealed to his sense of (cynical) humour, in my opinion."[25] Poulet presumably collaborated in the false attribution of authorship of Laye's second novel as a joke.

Because Poulet was a major figure in prewar literary Belgium historians continue to cite his accomplishments and acknowledge his prominence while recognizing his errors during the war.[26] Everyone to whom I spoke who knew Poulet has stressed the sharpness of his intellect and his fine literary criticism. In 1929 Poulet wrote an essay in which he discussed the question of the role of poetry in the novel. The novel, he stated, must first of all create an atmosphere in which the reader accepts the action as plausible, a requirement that surrealist novels do not meet, he felt. A great novel, however, includes poetry, in which the reader will also be surrounded by "strange perspectives, enchanted horizons; he will live in the mysterious and will admire his ability to feel at home there. The characters will 'live' as do the heroes of all adventures, but their charm will be unusual; what they do will seem deepened by meanings and signs. . . . A crowd of images will be enclosed in the novel. . . . after they obey for us the inevitable requirements of reason and the necessary requirements of life, we will realize that this was only an illusion, that the work depends upon a more secret logic."[27] This essay, in praise particularly of Alain-Fournier's *Le Grand Meaulnes*, can be seen to describe what Poulet himself was then writing in *Handji*. Poulet's admiration for a novel that seems to follow our usual perceptions but has its own inner logic explains not only his praise of *Le Regard du roi* but also his criticism of what he felt is too far from the "inevitable requirements of reason" in that novel.

While Poulet's ability as an editor and his contacts at Plon were important for the creation of Laye's work, *Le Regard du roi* is Soulié's book. Poulet's work, however, contains themes that undoubtedly influenced Soulié, particularly his descriptions of life in prison awaiting execution. A later reaction to *Le Regard du roi* influenced Poulet's own work in the 1960s.

Handji is the story of two men in the Austrian trenches during the First World War who invent a female companion and whose lives are increasingly complicated by their efforts to keep her existence, which they no longer admit is fictitious, from other soldiers. Finally they are killed during Russian advances, and the woman, "Handji," also dies. With many conversations, much use of the present tense and the *style indirect libre*, and many exclamation points, the writing bears little resemblance to that of *Le Regard du roi*. The treatment of invented, imaginary persons and events as if they were just as real as events in the quotidian world of the war may, however, suggest a willingness to consider the truth of dreams in a fashion similar to that of Laye, whose world is always partly that of unseen divinities and "magical" powers. Poulet's novel contains several dream sequences and an ending, as the Russian shells destroy the Austrian bunker, that may seem similar to that of *Le Regard du roi*, as the world imagined by the protagonists suddenly ends:

> A silhouette was coming out of the gaping shelter, a woman perched on high heels, with a confused look, her transparent dress floating.
> They have seen her . . . this phantom, this imaginary flesh! . . .

The barrage falls on the shelters, hits the enormous pile of shells and grenades. A small gleam appears, an absolutely unusual gleam. And the cement, the ground, the Russians, David, Walter, Handji, and everything which makes the world; all that is no longer more than the same star in the same storm of smoke.[28]

L'Enfer-ciel: Journal d'un condamné à mort (1948, republished by Plon in 1952, and recipient of the Sylvio Pellico prize) is Poulet's journal from April 17, 1947, to October 18, 1947, the period when he thought, until mid-July, that he would certainly be executed. Poulet's imaginative world is seen in this prison journal, which describes a situation similar to that of Clarence in *Le Regard du roi*. Here is a man thrown back entirely on himself, who feels that he has been ostracized by the world he knew, who is looking for a new way to live. Some of his companions in prison, he said, "dream of leaving without coming back, of fleeing toward exotic continents."[29]

Poulet's images of walls, labyrinths, the forest closing around him, and the heat of the sun are rather like Clarence's impressions on the trip toward the South. Occasionally Poulet described dreams or visions. In one he is in the church of Saint-Roch in Paris; he feels that he is flying and the earth is turning. A light enters and pierces him, and he hears a voice. Another, a dream of a statue, somewhat resembles "Les Yeux de la statue" and is similar to the sort of visions Clarence has toward the end of his adventure: "Suddenly I realize that a terrible wind is blowing on these expanses. Between earth and sky the air is breaking up into transparent cubes that move around, uncovering the lines of a wonderful statue, lying at an angle on the soft pillow of the rays of light. . . . What does this sleeping figure represent? . . . Perhaps she makes me see how the material world is softening. There will only be this: this ultimate drone at the heart of the only living cell, frozen for all centuries. . . . On the unmoving ocean, on the fading, disintegrating banks, all I see in the firmament is a raised hand with two joined fingers pointing toward the sky" (215).

The writing in *L'Enfer-ciel* is superior to that in Poulet's political essays and his later novels. While he often shows his arrogance and disgust for most of his fellow humans, he also speaks of a divine presence always with him in his cell, a presence making him feel that the material world has finished. It is the atmosphere of *Le Regard du roi*, with one important difference. Women (his mother, his wife, his daughter) are important to Poulet's emotions; he often

mentions his love and desire for his wife. He compares most men, in their base-
ness, to eunuchs: "stupid smiling eunuchs would not repulse me more" (180).
Poulet's heterosexual temperament contrasts with the homoeroticism of *Le
Regard du roi*.

In *Nuptial* (1949, reprinted 1956), the hero returns to sexual relations with
his wife after an absence of three years. Initially she puts him off. At the end of
the novel he comes into the room naked, like "Aurore pleine de Dieu" [a dawn
filled with God]. Their lovemaking is described in terms similar to the ending
of *Le Regard du roi*.

> The sun rose to the edge of the earth. Already the world was becoming
> bright. . . .
> She opened . . . she waited in trembling for the appearance of the sun.[30]

La Hutte de cochenille, set in Polynesia, was published by Plon in 1953, the
same year as *L'Enfant noir*. In it, a French governess is kidnapped by a native
tribe in Mandralie. The natives think she is a goddess and take her into the interior of the island. The kidnap party is followed by a French boy with a native
companion. Some details are similar to the first part of *Le Regard du roi*. The
tribal people are skilled in the art of narcotics, and they rely on the odors of
flowers to subdue the Europeans. The kidnappers and the boy following them
make a slow, disturbing trip into the interior. Later, when the governess, Emmanuèle, becomes a living idol, *Le Regard du roi* may be prefigured in the dei-
fication of a human being, the sexual imagery of the ceremonies, and even the
vision of a life beyond this world: "This path opened beyond the world, in a
point where all human races can be seen. The center of goodness and universal
perceptiveness could be found in Emmanuèle's face"[31] When the French boy
is dying, facing Emmanuèle, "His clothing fell open. His manliness failed and
swelled up in a wonderful fashion" (250). At the end, Emmanuèle finds peace
"at the heart of this red blotch" (255), the cochenille hut. This novel, with its
similar themes and even details and publication date in the second trimester of
1953, was certainly one of the sources for the themes of *Le Regard du roi*.
Where it differs is in its clear rejection of the culture of the South Pacific tribes,
seen as far from equal to European culture.

In later works Poulet returned to the theme of natural inequalities. His
work is for the "few," not for the "many," who are "the refuse, the failed at-

tempts," the weakest, who would have died if science had not interfered with nature's intentions. Poulet's views of human nature and natural inequalities lead him even to suggest that most people should not be taught to read. He often displays his disdain for other societies. Christian missions have failed, he stated, perhaps because in Africa, Asia, and Oceania the natives have only a "childish idea of truth," even though in those regions there is a certain form of happiness and beauty.[32]

Poulet returned to an exotic South Pacific setting in *Les Sources de la vie* (1967), the story of an Italian American aviator whose plane crashes in Papua during the Second World War and who must live with native people until he can escape. Poulet uses some details and themes that echo *Le Regard du roi* in a portrayal of the clash of "civilized" and "savage" cultures. Papuan girls, who treat Torquato, the aviator, as a god, decorate his hut with fresh purple flowers every night. Torquato spends his days with a griot and a young adolescent. One of the chiefs regularly brings him new women. *Les Sources de la vie* is written from a heterosexual perspective, and its treatment of female sexuality differs markedly from that in *Le Regard du roi*, but it might be regarded as a reply to *Le Regard du roi*. The plot is, however, overly complicated, often impossible to take seriously. Presumably it was one of the works Poulet wrote to try to make money in France.

L'Histoire de l'être, published in 1973, again includes dream sequences. The unnamed narrator is incarcerated in a cell that he believes is the whole world, a world that measures seventeen and a half paces. (The major source of the story is Poulet's own imprisonment.) The man, who refers to himself as "l'être" (the being), sees himself as the center of the universe. He tries to make a stone statue of himself, to which he talks and which he sometimes sees moving. The statue is the Other, the Non-Being. He goes through periods of despair and sometimes decides there is something beyond his cell. Finally, he decides to quit eating (food has appeared regularly in a way he cannot explain), to see what will happen if he disturbs the order of the world. Then, the door is opened. The story is a strange, sometimes powerful picture of a mind thrown entirely upon itself.

Céline wrote a preface to Poulet's *Le Livre de quelques-uns* (1957) in which he spoke of Poulet's mysticism, which cannot be understood in our materialist, rationalist world.[33] Poulet's is indeed an extreme vision but one whose themes

are related to those of *Le Regard du roi*, particularly in the rejection of the material world, the belief in seeking union with the divine, and the emphasis on
sacrifice.

In an interview conducted in 1982, when he was eighty-eight, Poulet said:
"Everything is ordered in my mind according to an idea that came to me with
great force when I was about twelve: the world does not exist. This means that
we are facing a vision produced by our mind, busy dreaming an adventure that
is not completely real. Behind this adventure there is another truth, incompa-
rably better, of a different nature. For me the novel consists of beginning with
apparent reality to try to arrive at the 'real reality.' In all my novels, I have
looked for ways to go from one to the other . . . In *Handji* it was emotional solitude. In *Les Sources de la vie* it is contact with primitive humanity."[34] The
"idea" that Poulet had when he was twelve is, at the least, one idea behind *Le
Regard du roi*. The world of the huts of Aziana seems not to exist when Clarence comes to meet the king. Krzywicki found in several of Poulet's works the
same mysticism as in *Le Regard du roi*, the same beliefs that the perception of
the world is not real, that earthly life is a transition toward what goes beyond
the knowable.[35]

Poulet kept coming back to the judgment and prison sentence he endured
after the war. In *La Conjecture: Mémoires apocryphes* (1981) he imagined a
different ending to the war, in which Churchill is defeated, Hitler dies, and the
United States makes peace with Japan after an attempt to put together the
atomic bomb fails because of the suicide of a Jewish scientist. While the narrator says he has no interest in the war and refuses to participate in political discussions, there are many anti-American comments, much general misan-
thropy, and criticism of the Allies, as well as a defense of German policy. One
character says he must admit "that concentration camps came from the Trans-
vaal, the imprisoning and deporting of enemy subjects was a usual practice in
the previous war, and that, as for indiscriminate bombing, it had been pushed
by the English in Germany. . . . the assassinations of Jews, of which some German leaders were accused, had mainly been perpetrated (for the cause, but
nonetheless disgusting) by small groups of killers."[36] While one could read
this novel as an antiwar manifesto in which the white race is said to have committed suicide by its policies, in its denial that the Holocaust was the policy of

the German government it shows Poulet's continued extreme right-wing views.

Poulet's last book, *L'Homme qui n'avait pas compris* (1988), is a final plea for comprehension and understanding between the two political sides in Belgium during the war. His statement on the back cover of the book seems less doctrinaire than most of his earlier writings. Speaking of the two antagonistic factions in the 1940s, he wrote that they were "almost completely driven, from both sides, by the same attachment to their native land and by the sincere wish to serve it. That was the age of passion." Now, however, the atmosphere has changed and passion should be replaced by pardon, again on both sides: "Having arrived, myself, at the extreme limit of my earthly life [Poulet was ninety-five when the book was published] I can now say, when the last page has been turned, how, from my side, the hour of remission of sins has sounded. By the grace of the *Pater*."

9

Robert Poulet at Plon

LIBRAIRIE PLON

In its long history, the publishing firm of Plon had many Belgian connections. The Librairie Plon began with a Danish printer who went to Belgium about 1580, perhaps because as a Catholic he preferred to leave a Lutheran country. He established a printing firm in Belgium, and some of his descendants remained there. Others went to France. In Paris the name Plon dates from 1798, when Philippe Plon established a printing firm. His son, Henri, installed the firm on the rue de Vaugirard, where it was a meeting place for such authors as Balzac and Victor Hugo. In 1852 it became a publishing company. Plon was printer to Napoleon III and also published liturgical books. The company later moved to rue Garancière, where it continued to operate until recently.[1] As late as 1952, the title page of Plon publications included the statement that the com-

148

pany was the property of the grandsons of Henri Plon. This family company with connections to Belgium and a conservative Catholic outlook undoubtedly looked favorably on employing writers who had been forced to leave Belgium for political reasons, such as Claude Elsen and Poulet.

The political persuasion of Plon is usually described as Catholic right. It published more history than fiction and had a special interest in the memoirs of political figures such as Raymond Poincaré, Clémenceau, Winston Churchill, Franklin D. Roosevelt, and Joseph Stalin. It was also the publisher of de Gaulle. Its strength in its literary list was with what were known as "the four B's": Georges Bernanos, Robert Brasillach, Paul Bourget, and Maurice Barrès, all conservative authors. Among its authors were also Julien Green, Henri Troyat, and, in translation, Saul Bellow, Aldous Huxley, and Joyce.

The Librairie Plon took over the review *La Table ronde* from 1949 to 1961; these were the best years of the review. Later the review was sold to a group close to Opus Dei. Names on the editorial board in 1953 included Mauriac, Gabriel Marcel, Jean Mistler, Thierry Maulnier, Jacques Duhamel, Orengo, and Roland Laudenbach. Among the contributors in 1953 were Julien Green, Jean Cayrol, Paul Léautaud, Marguerite Yourcenar, Michel Vinaver, Marceau, Karl Jaspers, and Graham Greene. Not all, of course, had connections to right-wing politics, but many had strong Catholic convictions. In 1954, however, Mauriac described the contributors as nonconformist and extremely right-wing; he then moved to *L'Express*. In 1954 *La Table ronde* published "Le Prince," a story attributed to Camara Laye.

Plon had been seriously compromised after the war, when perhaps half of its writers were banned or imprisoned. According to Liliane Elsen, who worked as the secretary to Orengo, the director of Plon, from about 1948 to 1950, Plon became less doctrinaire after the war. Orengo loved discovering new talent and was not political.[2]

According to Guy Dupré, an editor at Plon in the 1950s and 1960s, Plon may have decided to publish *L'Enfant noir* in 1953 because of the conservative, pro-French theme of the novel. He mentioned Mouloud Mammeri, whose *La Colline oubliée*, published by Plon in 1952, is a novel of youth in North Africa that is not anti-colonialist and thus in the same vein as *L'Enfant noir*. Plon may well have had contacts with the Ministry of France Overseas at the time of the publication of Mammeri's novel.

La Colline oubliée, the first novel of a trilogy (all published initially by Plon), tells of life in a Berber village. It explores the problems of love in a Muslim society, where wives can be repudiated for sterility, where killing an adulterous wife and her lover are acceptable vindications of the family honor, and where ancient customs dominate life. It is also a society, however, in which the religious leaders bemoan the advent of a commercial attitude and unscrupulous moneylenders force a father of six children to leave for work in the Sahara. After the outbreak of the Second World War in 1939, many of the young men are mobilized temporarily, and then again after the Allied invasion of North Africa. Some die fighting in Europe, and the community suffers from the penury of vital food supplies. There is, however, little overt criticism of the French, who for the Berbers are merely more suspect foreigners than the Arabs.

The major theme of the novel is the troubled marriage of the first narrator, Mokrane, who loves his wife but finds it difficult to oppose his family when they repudiate her because she has produced no children after several years of marriage. In perhaps the most psychologically astute comment in the novel, Mokrane meditates on the prayer of an old woman: "make their union fertile so that they will not be a burden to one another." He realizes that she has read in the hearts of himself and his wife "that we forced ourselves to love each other as we had before, that we clung together so as not to hurt one another, because we remembered feelings that no longer existed . . . but that we were tired of always vainly looking at each other, without anything coming into our love to introduce some diversity."[3] During a snowstorm, while on leave from the army, Mokrane has a mental breakdown, wanders off, has hallucinations of seeing his wife (who had been forced to leave him but then realized she was pregnant), and dies. His cousin Menach continues the story of the family, including his own unconsummated love for a married woman. These stories are of more importance than any reflections on society or on the French presence.

The novel provoked debate, rather similar to that surrounding *L'Enfant noir*. For French critics the book showed the Berber soul. A critic in *Le Jeune Musulman*, however, said that the French liked it for its formal qualities but that "A work signed by an Algerian can only interest us from one point of view: what cause does it serve? What is its position in the fight which opposes the nationalist movement to colonialism?"[4] The parallels to Beti's attack on *L'Enfant noir* in *Présence africaine* are evident. Mammeri's novel, like Laye's, is seen as appealing to a French public that did not want to face the political problems of the postwar period. Plon had chosen well-written works that portrayed African societies and would contribute to support of the French Union, a union based in Paris and controlled by the French government.

Another author published at this time by Plon whose work presents parallels to that of Camara Laye is Pham Duy Khiem, a Vietnamese whose *Nam et Sylvie* appeared in 1957 under the pseudonym Nam Kim. Khiem was ambassador to France from 1955 to 1957 and a supporter of Ngo Dinh Diem's conservative political regime. *Nam et Sylvie* recounts a romantic liaison between a Vietnamese man studying in France and a French woman. It is a story of cultural conflicts and difference but also a story of universal love, in which political issues are of little importance.[5]

POULET READING CAMARA LAYE

Dupré said that Poulet would not have been given much foreign literature to read for Plon. He was an outsider, very bitter, and ostracized by most critics because of his political views.[6] Presumably Poulet requested to read the manuscript of *L'Enfant noir*, because he had already seen it. At the time he submitted the manuscript, Laye was living in Soulié's small apartment. Poulet and Soulié had known each other at least since the 1930s. There were connections among the Belgian exiles in Paris, particularly those who had been condemned to death. Claude Elsen had a regular position at Plon, saw Poulet frequently, and occasionally saw Soulié. According to Liliane Elsen, the circle of Belgians who saw each other regularly included her husband, Poulet, and Marceau. Poulet and Paulhan had been the witnesses at the Elsens' marriage ceremony. When he read the manuscript, Poulet noted in his report that the Ministry of France Overseas was interested in promoting *L'Enfant noir*. Presumably Laye told Soulié about the help he was given by Lefaucheux and the ministry, and Poulet learned this from Soulié. It is unlikely, given his political opinions, that Poulet had direct contacts with a French ministry.

Either before or after Laye submitted his manuscript, Poulet gave the advice about style that Laye readily acknowledged. Poulet did many corrections for writers, including various politicians. Michel Tournier sent him *Le Roi des*

Aulnes for comments before submitting the manuscript. Liliane Elsen said that Poulet was very intelligent and generous in his assessments as a reader. He would be fair in judging writing styles and opinions that were quite different from his own.

Poulet told Liliane Elsen that he had discovered Laye. She said no, it was Plon that gave him the manuscript, but she did not know the whole story. Later, in a review of Lacour's *La Mort dans ce jardin*, Poulet commented that Lacour was part of the group of authors, including Laye, whom he was proud to have "discovered."[7] Poulet had read Lacour's manuscript and encouraged him to submit it to a particular Belgian publisher, and in the review he claimed to have done the same for Laye.

Poulet's typed report as reader of "L'Enfant de Guinée" (the first title of *L'Enfant noir*), dated July 28, 1953, includes a plot summary in which Poulet called Laye's family and neighbors "assez évolués" [rather modern], although they retained certain animist beliefs ("fétichistes"). He spoke of Laye having had a scholarship to a university in France, when in fact the scholarship was to a school of automobile mechanics. More interesting is Poulet's judgment of the value of a work "from an authentic Black," whose soul remains "primitive" and whom Poulet does not hesitate to term "sauvage." He found, nevertheless, "a naive but sincere and deep emotion," expressed in "a French that is almost too elegant, a bit schoolboyish." Laye's dialogues, translated rather "ceremoniously" from an African language, he considered both moving and comic. If Poulet found Laye's French too schoolboyish, he presumably decided that this was part of its charm and did not attempt to change it. Poulet considered the work to be only moderately important as literature but precious as a document. The use of the terms "primitive" and "savage" is, to our ears, racially biased. Poulet also saw the rare white person being portrayed as a "demi-dieu." Here he is reading his own ideas into the novel, as there are hardly any white persons portrayed, and they are not described in any detail. Poulet did, however, see that the novel is in no way an attack on French colonial rule.

After *L'Enfant noir* was published, Poulet reviewed it in several publications. Writing under the name Walter Orlando in the Belgian magazine *Le Phare* on September 20, 1953, Poulet repeated the theme of the good savage found in his reader's report and emphasized the spiritual tone of the book, which had been of particular importance to Poulet at least since the time of his imprisonment. "The tranquil and conscious acceptance of the supernatural in everyday life is what we notice most in this child of nature. Perhaps one of the worst effects of material 'progress' has been to deprive us of the way in which primitive and simple people stay in touch with the invisible." Another enthusiastic review of *L'Enfant noir* was written by Hellens for *La Dernière Heure de Bruxelles*, May 3, 1954. Hellens was also among the judges for the Prix Charles Veillon. He had edited several magazines for which both Poulet and Soulié had worked during the 1930s, as well as being a founding member of the Groupe du Lundi and a close associate at that time of Poulet. Undoubtedly, Poulet, and perhaps Soulié as well, suggested that Hellens review *L'Enfant noir* and consider it for the Prix Charles Veillon. It is surely not a coincidence that there is so often a Belgian connection with the early novels of Laye.

In his review of *L'Enfant noir* for *Rivarol*, Poulet began by stating that it owes nothing to the imagination. It is the story of Laye's childhood, he noted, without the "infantile" tone one often imagines in the "black soul" but full of reason and seriousness. He found the African society described to be full of good people and goodwill and attributed this to the combination of two cultures through colonization. He used his reading of the novel to attack Negrophilia, *Batouala* (Maran's novel of 1921 condemning the French colonial regime), and what he termed "l'écriture tam-tam et de la psychologie en culotte capitula" [tom-tom writing and cheap psychology]. Although his tone is paternalistic, Poulet praised the elegance of the style and the truth of the vision.[8]

Poulet also found an element of sentimentality in the novel, which he thought Europeans usually did not associate with Africa. He said that Lucie Cousturier, however, had seen that sentimentality could be linked to African culture. Cousturier was the Frenchwoman often thought to have at least assisted Diallo in the composition of *Force Bonté*.[9] Perhaps Poulet was subtly hinting at similar help for Laye. Poulet also mentioned in his review that even the author of *Le Coup de lune*, Georges Simenon, did not avoid facile exoticism. Simenon's story, published in 1933, is about a Frenchman who almost loses his mind reacting to injustice against natives in the Congo and is not similar to *L'Enfant noir*. Poulet's mention of works by two French writers that had limited relevance to the book he was reviewing is intriguing, suggesting that he connected Laye's novel to European literature.

Because *L'Enfant noir* was so favorably reviewed, Plon did not hesitate when the manuscript for *Le Regard du roi* was sent to them. Poulet's report on "Le Ciel d'Afrique" (the first title of *Le Regard du roi*) is not dated. He recounted the plot with fidelity and commented on the lack of connection with *L'Enfant noir*, saying that "la sensibilité de l'auteur s'est tout à fait rétractée" [the sensitivity of the author is completely different]. This remark may be a veiled allusion to the real author, an attempt to show that Poulet was aware of the origin of the manuscript in case anyone queried the difference in style. He also commented on the discernible influence of Kafka, enumerating many similar techniques, such as the mixture of realistic detail and poetry: "All the elements are there: the indeterminate subject and circumstances, linked to a constant pressure exerted on the plot; the diffuse symbolism (man looking for God, the spirit dreaming of its freedom, the white world tending to mix with the black world); the mixture of realism in detail and poetry in the whole; the impression of fate, founded on magic; the disturbing, vague conversations among speakers, each of whom follows his own line of thought without listening to the others; the heavy atmosphere that is lightened here by an underlying kindness and affability."

Poulet also mentioned, however, that unlike Kafka's work this novel had the "charme instinctif" and the "finesse souriante" that characterize Laye. He found that the conversations recalled those of *Alice in Wonderland*. Poulet also commented on the contrast "entre technique compliquée et l'ingénuité de l'inspiration" [between the complicated technique and the ingenuousness of the inspiration].Poulet criticized the lack of vigor and rhythm and lack of episodes that hold the reader in suspense. There was too much of a feeling of turning in circles, too much inconsistency in the character of Clarence. Poulet also commented that "Critics cannot fail to see that this second book has something too willed, too arbitrary, too bookish; that it does not have the necessary force; that it is simply a pale imitation . . . of a fashionable literary formula." In addition to this rather harsh judgment, Poulet found small faults that it would be easy to correct. Finally, he judged that the literary value of the work was considerable, but he was was less sure of its commercial value. Perhaps he was less happy with Soulié's work than with the collaborative effort that produced *L'Enfant noir*.

I have quoted this report at some length to show how clearly Poulet analyzed the novel (more accurately than he did *L'Enfant noir*) and how he commented about it in a way that Laye never did in any of his interviews, as well as to establish that Poulet was a literary critic of considerable intelligence and sensitivity.

While Poulet's reader's report was lukewarm, the second reader of the manuscript, Jacques Tournier, was more enthusiastic, calling the work marvelous: "I can't say how charmed I was." He noted passages that were too long and dialogues that could be shortened. He also noted that it was "extremely difficult to believe that Clarence is a white man," which seems rather amusing, now that we know the novel was primarily the work of a white European.

The manuscript that Tournier read had, he noted, many corrections, not all good ones in his opinion. This is an intriguing comment. Perhaps Laye read the manuscript and made changes before submitting it or perhaps someone else did. Unfortunately, we will never know. When I contacted Tournier in 1995, he had no memory of this particular manuscript among the hundreds he had read in the 1950s.

Someone at Plon noted at the top of Tournier's reader's report that it was urgent to have a third reader, Henri Hell. Hell was the head of Plon's office of readers, and his report was not in the files I obtained from Plon in 1978. One can only assume that it was favorable enough to outweigh Poulet's criticisms, in the judgment of the directors of Plon.

Poulet's review of *Le Regard du roi* in *Rivarol* can readily be seen as a veiled admission that Laye had a great deal of help in the composition of the novel.[10] Poulet began by saying that he was the first reader of the manuscript for *L'Enfant noir* and that he had wondered how the author could repeat his first success. (Laye said that one of the reasons he wrote the second novel was to prove that he could repeat his success.) Poulet then asserted that the author was "capable of assimilating the most recent and difficult European techniques without losing what gave his work its value, its ingenuousness and warmth, which are not at all 'primitive' but rather very decadent . . . like that found in the writing and the art of the last centuries of Carthage or Byzantium." Suddenly Laye, who was "primitive" in Poulet's comments on *L'Enfant noir*, is "decadent." Perhaps Poulet was really talking about Soulié. The theme of the novel, Poulet wrote, comes from Kafka and from *Alice in Wonderland*, between metaphysical anguish and humor. So, said Poulet, we have "the black child promoted to the status of avant-garde writer." Poulet assumed that the novel was primarily a dream and criticized the episode of the fish-women as going against "one of the most rigorous principles of magic realism" by having a dream within a dream. Laye in later years denied that the whole story was a dream, but many critics would agree with Poulet's reading.

Two of Poulet's comments clearly suggest that someone other than Laye was at least partly responsible for the novel. "I am not certain that the escapade of Clarence, a white man without money or ties, who finally sinks into the depths of equatorial witchcraft, did not stop in a library before taking on in an authentic way the breath of the savanna and the odors of the forest," Poulet commented. More pointedly, he considered that, at the moment of the tenderness toward the end of the novel, "c'est là que nous retrouvons, un peu exalté par *des pensées qui ne sont pas toutes issues de son propre fonds*, le gentil conteur de *l'Enfant noir*" [it is there that we encounter, a bit inspired by *ideas which did not all come from his own resources*, the good storyteller of *L'Enfant noir*] (my emphasis). When I found this review I thought that Poulet was signaling Soulié's presence to me.

Poulet had a long friendship with Céline. As a more established author published by Denoël, Poulet had read in 1932 the proofs of *Voyage au bout de la nuit*, which he admitted later to have underestimated. After the Second World War and his release from Belgian prison, Poulet visited Céline. In 1958 he published *Entretiens familiers avec L-F Céline*, a defense of Céline and an apology for Céline's anti-Semitism: "Because Céline had had an attack of extreme anti-Semitism before the war, he was considered a 'collaborator' with an enemy that, during the war, persecuted the Semites." Poulet said that even Céline's mediocre books (such as *Féerie pour une autre fois*) were of ten times more value than "all the Camus and all the Sartre books combined."[11] Among other authors whom Poulet praised was Drieu La Rochelle, the right-wing author who committed suicide after the defeat of Germany.

Interestingly, considering Laye's statement to several persons about the instruction Poulet gave him in the use of the subjunctive, Poulet quoted with delight Céline's use of the imperfect subjunctive: "Il fallut que moi, médecin romancier, je cachasse bien mon jeu" [It was necessary that I, a doctor novelist, had hidden my game]; "Sauf qu'il n'y avait aucune raison pour que je fusse là" [Except that there had been no reason for my having been there].[12] After this last quote Poulet added: "Again the imperfect subjunctive. Salute. Used with perfect ease. The language of Céline, apparently disordered, lies on a solid base" (140).

Céline's last work, *Rigodon*, written in 1960–61 and published posthumously by Gallimard in 1969, is a chronicle of his adventures at the end of the war when he escaped to Denmark. Céline begins with comments about Poulet that obviously date from well after the war. He describes conversations with Poulet in which he attacks Poulet's Christianity and specifically his acceptance of racially mixed marriages:

> I can see that Poulet is down on me . . . Robert Poulet with his death sentence . . . he doesn't talk about me any more in his column . . . he finally got on my nerves with his way of beating about the bush . . . "Are you sure your convictions won't bring you back to God?" [This is followed by several paragraphs of tirades against all "little Jesus" religions, in typical Céline style] their only real job . . . perfect agreement . . . is to besot and destroy the white race. [. . .] the children of your lovely mixed marriages will always be yellow, black, red, never white, never again white! [. . .] "You're too much given to paradoxes, Céline! the Chinese are antiracist! . . . and so are the blacks!" "That's rich! wait till they get here, won't take them a year to fuck everybody! that'll be the end of it, not a white man left!"[13]

I have been unable to find any reference to such marriages in Poulet's own work; indeed, the idea of miscegenation seems odd in the context of most of his writing. In *J'accuse la bourgeoisie* (1978), for example, he said that the idea of a universal miscegenation was against the general movement of life. Céline's tirade, typical of his irrational behavior in his later years, may be based on purely imaginary conversations with Poulet. Poulet himself said in *Mon ami Bardamu*, "there is not a word of truth in this bickering" (14). Poulet also said later, in *Ce n'est pas une vie* (1976), that Céline lied a lot. He repeated, in 1982, that the statements Céline made in these pages were absurd.[14]

Marc Laudelout, editor of *Le Bulletin Céline*, said that Céline often commented about how Catholic religion favored *métissage*. Because he considered Poulet to be very Catholic, Céline would have seen him as favoring miscegenation. Céline's comment might, however, have been a criticism of the mulatto babies produced in the naba's harem in *Le Regard du roi*. One can only guess, now, at how Poulet might have presented this episode to his friend, in praising Laye's novel. Poulet often visited Céline in Meudon in the 1950s, and Céline was reading some contemporary fiction at the time. A recent critic of Céline told me that his references in the novels are almost always accurate and that if he mentioned miscegenation in the context of Poulet, he probably meant it.[15] It is at least an intriguing possibility.

Poulet helped promote the works attributed to Laye through his reviews and his contacts with Belgian critics, particularly Hellens. He contributed to *L'Enfant noir* primarily by giving stylistic advice, probably before the manuscript was submitted to Plon. His contribution to *Le Regard du roi* is harder to judge. Comments in his reviews indicate indirectly that he was aware of the origin of the manuscript. He may have made suggestions to Soulié during the composition of the manuscript of the novel. As his own work often contains themes similar to those of *Le Regard du roi*—the creation of a fantasy life, the search for salvation through mystical experience, and encounters between European and non-Western cultures—his books were undoubtedly an influence on Soulié, who had praised Poulet's work in reviews written during the war years in Belgium.

Conclusion

Because Kesteloot's report of her interview with Laye was so often disbelieved and because all the principal players in this drama are dead, with the possible exception of Joncourt, my research has not been easy. Sometimes I thought I was more a detective than a scholar. Sometimes I became perhaps unduly suspicious. When I found that Kaké had spoken with Blancard about my interview with him in 1992, I wondered why it had seemed to him worth mentioning to another friend of Laye's, particularly one who did not believe Kesteloot, that someone was investigating the question of authorship of Laye's works.

For several years I followed many leads, some fruitful, some not. I spent hours searching in archives and through the Minitel (a French on-line telephone directory), trying unsuccessfully to locate a family named Barboteur who would have been in Africa, since Laye had told Leiner and me that a woman named Madame Baraboteur had helped him. I spent time trying to find a German named Teuscheur who supposedly worked for Deutsche Welle, without success, although several German friends helped me. Similarly, many letters to persons in Belgium named Falla (the maiden name of Soulié's wife) brought no response.

Some parts of the story, particularly the role of Joncourt (whose name, if that really was her name, I was given only in the summer of 1999), will probably remain a mystery. In 1999 I contacted over eighty persons with the name of Joncourt in France, without finding anyone who knew of an Aude Joncourt. Nor were there any Joncourts listed in Paris phone books for the years 1946– 55. Indeed, the search for Joncourt showed me some of the problems of getting information from a government bureaucracy. Aude Joncourt's father, Edouard, I was told, had been a high civil servant.

I found several possible leads. By checking in the *Bottin administratif*, a directory of government services, from 1948 to 1953, I found one administrator named Joncour, listed only in 1949 and 1950. This Joncour (no first name given) was an "administrateur de première classe" [administrator first class] and président du conseil d'administration de la coopérative de consommation du personnel du Ministère de la France d'Outre-Mer [president of the administrative committee of the cooperative for providing supplies to the personnel of the Ministry of France Overseas], working at 20 rue Monsieur, in the seventh arrondissement of Paris.

Through the archivist of the Secrétariat of France Overseas, I was put in touch with the Association of Former Students of the National School for France Overseas. The secretary of the association found an Edouard Joncour who received his diploma in 1932 and gave me his last address in Le Cannet in southern France and his birth date of 1901. Through the Minitel I found two listings under the name Joncour in Le Cannet. One was a daughter of Edouard, the other a daughter-in-law. Edouard had two daughters, Marie-Lucienne, born in 1932, and Renée-Vincente, born in 1935. The family had lived in Guinea until 1955, where Edouard worked in finance. Edouard had retired in 1960 and died in 1989. No one in the family was named Aude, nor had any of them studied anthropology. The two daughters seem too young to have been friends with Laye, and also they were in Guinea when he was in Paris. Marie-

Lucienne, to whom I spoke, knew of no other family named Joncour or Joncourt in Guinea when she was there.

Through the archives of the Ministry of France Overseas I found more information about this family. Edouard André Joncour served for many years in the ministry. He was in Guinea from 1928 to 1930, later in Côte d'Ivoire and Senegal, and again in Guinea several times before leaving in 1955 to go to Mauritania. He could be the Joncour who was listed in the *Bottin*, as he was on administrative leave with the ministry from 1946 to 1950, when he presumably worked in Paris.

At the Archives de Paris, I looked through the electoral rolls for the seventh arrondissement, where the Joncourt family supposedly lived. In 1960 an Edouard Joncourt was listed who was born April 21, 1925, in Les Côtes d'Armor, in a village named Le Moustoir in Brittany—the name Joncourt, many persons told me, was of Breton origin. He was living in 1960 at 17 rue Auguste Comte. For his profession the number eighty-nine, or perhaps eighty-four (it was written by hand), was listed. How was I to find the meaning of the code eighty-nine? Archivists in Paris did not know the code. The Mairie de Paris (city hall) did not know. I was told to try the Ministère de l'Emploi (Ministry of Labor), which had no information. Finally, the INSEE (Bureau of National Statistics) directed me to the one person who would know. When I reached him by phone, he told me that there was no code eighty-nine. Other codes in the eighties were students, retired, and so on. This Edouard was thirty-five when the list was made. He could have been a student or perhaps unemployed. He did seem the right age to be a brother to Aude. Le Moustoir, where he was born, now has five hundred inhabitants. When I contacted the town hall, they replied with some records. (An archivist in Paris had told me they should not provide records as I was not part of the family. She added, however, that I should try, since the little villages might not follow the rules.) Their records showed an Edouard Joncour (without a t) born April 22, 1925, one day later than the person listed in the electoral roles. His father was Jean Louis Joncour, born July 19, 1867, which seemed too old to make him Aude's father, if Aude's father had worked for the government in Guinea.

None of these Joncour(t) families was the right one. I wondered if I had been given a false name or if the right family was not listed in any documents to which I could gain access, but I could go no further. (There are, I learned, some persons with the name Joncourt in the Paris region who have unlisted phone numbers.) Attempts to find an Aude Joncourt among students of anthropology in the 1940s and 1950s also produced no results. Finally, in the summer of 2000, I found an Aude Joncourt listed in the Minitel. She turned out to be a young woman who knew of no one in her family named Aude. My story about French civil servants in Africa had no meaning for her.

Sometimes I wondered why files were missing. Although this may well have been bad luck, it was easy to feel suspicious. There were no manuscripts of *L'Enfant noir* or *Le Regard du roi* to be found. Plon files for the period when the first two novels were published were incomplete; readers' reports existed but not manuscripts, said to have been destroyed in a flood. Soulié's papers were in disorder and unavailable. Kelefa Keita, the adopted son of Soulié, never replied to letters or to inquiries from Guineans I know. After giving me some useful information, his sister Malon would say no more. The Ministry of Youth had no record of Laye's employment. Deutsche Welle could not find any trace of a person named Teuscheur in their files. The files of *La Table ronde* had nothing about the story submitted under the name of Camara Laye. Even the archives of Léopold III had been destroyed, making it difficult to ascertain the truth about Poulet's assertions that he had followed the king's wishes in his journalism during the occupation.

While important written records were almost nonexistent and many of the persons who knew the true story had died, detective work gradually produced results. Letters to scholars of African literature in many countries produced opinions but no proof. Reactions of critics to the rumors about the authorship of *Le Regard du roi* often reflected either a desire to defend the canon of established authors or a recognition of the aesthetic differences among Laye's works.

The most important of my contacts in the early 1990s was my interview on August 8, 1992, with Kaké, with whom Laye had stayed briefly during the period after his exile from Guinea. Kaké was the first person to mention to me the name of Soulié, a name that became increasingly important. Through conversations with Wauthier, I learned more about the efforts of the French government to encourage writing by Africans not radically opposed to French colonial policy after the Second World War. Wauthier also gave me his unpublished interview with Laye from 1956.

Gradually I traced persons who had known Laye. I had met one family, the Postel-Vinays, on Laye's recommendation in 1978. They had given me Laye's unpublished manuscript in which he advocated an exchange of children between France and Africa as a way of strengthening the French Union. Only in 1995, however, did I learn about André Postel-Vinay's sister, Lefaucheux, who played an important role in the publication of Laye's work. I found biographical notices and her contributions to the Constituent Assembly and the Assembly of the French Union and was able to consult the files of the National Council of French Women.

Poulet, whom I tried to contact through his last publisher, had died, at the age of ninety-three, only a few years before I wrote to him. In 1991 Jean-Luc Pidoux-Payot, then director at Plon, found nothing in the files concerning Laye to indicate that he did or did not write *Le Regard du roi*. Pidoux-Payot added that Laye undoubtedly received help with his manuscripts from readers or editors at Plon but nothing more. I contacted Jacques Tournier, the second reader of *Le Regard du roi*, through one of his publishers. Unfortunately, after over forty years, he had no clear memory of the novel or of Poulet. Sorel, who had met and recorded Laye in 1976, helped me to contact others who knew Laye in the 1960s and 1970s.

I met a few persons who had known Laye in Guinea in the 1960s, especially Lalande, who had worked in an office next to Laye's in Conakry, and Blancard, who had worked on radio scripts with Laye for Radio Guinée. Although these two Frenchwomen were sympathetic to African literature and had stayed in Guinea after independence, when almost all of their compatriots had left, they had different opinions of Laye's abilities.

It was only after meeting Simon Njami, a young Cameroonian writer and editor of *La Revue noire*, in Paris, December 20, 1994, that I became convinced that Laye was not the main author of *Le Regard du roi*. Much information, but always tantalizingly incomplete, came from Njami, who gave me some details at our first meeting, a meeting that was initially an interview with him as one of the young African writers living in France.

Njami told me about the four persons, all Europeans, involved in the writing of *L'Enfant noir*, a story that Laye had told Njami's father. Njami would not give names initially. Obviously, however, Soulié was involved and perhaps also Poulet. I felt that Njami volunteered some information because I already knew the name Soulié. Njami spoke to his father after our first interview, and in a second interview, on April 3, 1995, he told me that his father would not answer me beyond asserting, for political reasons, that the books are Laye's.

In a third interview, July 11, 1995, Njami said that two persons, Poulet and Soulié, acted as "conseillers littéraires," helping Laye get beyond the local and personal in *L'Enfant noir*. They both had a considerable knowledge of African history, both pre- and post-colonial. There were two others, and at least one was a woman. In a later conversation, on August 5, 1995, Njami spoke of a woman who was highly educated, very rich, and with experience in Africa (perhaps, I then thought, the Madame Baraboteur Laye had mentioned in my interview with him). At some point after 1955, she went to Lausanne with Laye and met Dr. Njami, the father. At the time of Laye's arrival in France, there was a great deal of interest in Africa. Intellectuals were, said the younger Njami, looking for a "good nigger."

Njami said that almost everyone of his father's generation would be anxious to do nothing to undermine the validity of African literature, as there had been too many attributions of African work to Europeans. Njami mentioned the case of Yambo Ouologuem and said that *Le Devoir de violence* is an important novel, despite the plagiarism. But the Prix Renaudot was taken away from Ouologuem, who is now in Mali and has written nothing for some years.[1]

A Cameroonian friend of mine and professor of African literature, Jeanne Dingomé, interviewed Dr. Njami, the father, for me on July 19, 1995, and wrote to me on July 24 from Douala to say that Njami told her that he didn't work particularly on Laye, though he had studied Laye's works in his school days and even used them in his teaching career. He said that he intended to reply to my letter to him. He felt, however, that whites always try to prove that blacks do not achieve anything; even if he had any proof that Laye had a co-author for *Le Regard du roi*, he would never give it to anyone. Njami even wondered why Laye's next-of-kin, his daughter who is an academic, was reluctant to shed light on the matter to the point where strangers had to be solicited.

I have met one of Laye's children, his oldest daughter, Aïcha, who is not an academic. I first met her in 1978, when she was twenty-two, and I met her again in Paris in 1993. She has been very gracious in her hospitality. She remembers helping her father by typing and retyping his later manuscripts. I have also spoken to a son, Mady Camara, who is in the army in France. I do not know of a daughter who is an academic. In any case, one would not expect the family to investigate this question. Dr. Njami's suggestion that he studied Laye's work in school is obviously incorrect, as he was a professor in Switzerland within a year of the publication of *Le Regard du roi*. This mistake is of little importance, except perhaps to suggest that he found the interview in some way tense.

In a second letter, dated October 17, 1995, Dingomé wrote that she doubted whether Dr. Njami would ever change his mind. She added that France in particular has a very curious manner of using the Africans to sell a certain image of Africa. Dingomé, an African scholar of a younger generation than that of Njami, rather than seeing this research as an attack on the validity of African literature, considers it a way of showing how the French may have used a writer for their own purposes.

A bit later, another Cameroonian scholar and friend, Ambroise Kom, offered to approach Dr. Njami for me. Kom wrote me on March 7, 1996, stating that Njami had told Dingomé all he had to say and would add nothing.

Having learned the importance of Poulet and particularly Soulié, I began to investigate the world of right-wing Belgian authors during the Second World War, the world of collaborators, many of whom were condemned to death and escaped to France. My work was greatly aided by a British historian of modern Belgium, Martin Conway, whose advice on consulting archives was especially valuable. Poulet was easy to trace, as there are a number of journalists who remember him, and scholars still work on his writings. Soulié seemed unknown until I mentioned his pen name, Gille Anthelme. An e-mail contact with the Hoover Institution at Stanford University brought me copies of Soulié's writings in newspapers during the war. More recently I was given permission to consult the files on Soulié in the archives of the Military Court in Brussels, which contain clippings from several publications, organized as documents for the prosecution in his trial. I was also fortunate to get help from the Archives of the Préfecture de Police in Paris concerning Soulié and Poulet.

Just as many Africans did not want to talk about any influence from Europeans, many Europeans who had known Poulet and Soulié were either reluctant to talk about the fascist past of these two or wanted especially to defend the reputation of Poulet. I contacted literary figures who knew Poulet or, more rarely, Soulié, in Belgium and interviewed Galic, the editor of *Rivarol*, the right-wing journal for which Poulet wrote until almost the end of his life. The office of *Rivarol* has a large photo of Jean-Marie Le Pen on the wall of its reception area, and Galic began by telling me of Poulet's last articles denying the Holocaust. She was, however, helpful. Through her lead I was fortunate to meet Liliane Elsen, the widow of a good friend of Poulet, Claude Elsen, who had worked on the same right-wing journals in Belgium and for Plon. Liliane Elsen also knew Soulié. All of these contacts led, gradually, to a picture of the milieu in which *Le Regard du roi* was created.

The next avenue of investigation was other Guineans who had known Laye in France. Through the Guinean ambassador to France in the mid-1990s, I made contact with the sister of the family that had helped Laye come to France, whose brother had been adopted by Soulié. Still later, through contacts with the widow of Kaké, I finally reached Kaba, who knew Laye later in his life and knew Soulié in the 1960s. At this point, I was as close as I could come to hard evidence of a cooperation between Laye and Soulié.

I thought I had followed every lead and there was nothing more to add, but the story is not over. In June 2001, while I was preparing the final manuscript of this book, I attended a conference in Paris on the work of the Congolese writer Emmanuel Dongala. Thierry Sinda, a scholar of African cinema who was born in France of Congolese parents, heard me say that I was working on Laye. He told me he had learned through a Guinean journalist, Vanfing Koné, of a Swiss man, whose name he thought was Saussère or Saussure, who had finished the manuscript of *L'Enfant noir*. In a telephone conversation on June 18 Sinda added that it was possible to find some Swiss expressions in the language of *L'Enfant noir*. He thought that this Swiss person had a hand in all Laye's work until *Dramouss*. He added that Christiane Diop of Présence Africaine knew the story but would not tell anyone. Sinda suggested that I might find Koné through *Amina*, a magazine for African women for which he sometimes wrote. At first I was disturbed that there might be another person, previously unknown to me, involved in the works signed Camara Laye. However, my first telephone call to Koné, on June 18, 2001, confirmed that the writer he had mentioned to Sinda was indeed Soulié.

When I conducted my second telephone interview with Sinda a few days later, he strangely tried to convince me that there was nothing to the story of a ghostwriter and that I should quit my investigations. Laye spoke French, as is evident in the interviews he gave at Radio France Internationale, Sinda

pointed out. An editor would merely have made a few corrections. This explanation was obviously in contrast to what Sinda had said initially. Sinda added
that there was much jealousy of Laye because he was successful, which might
explain rumors I had been told. Beti, for example, was not as well known in
France as Laye and therefore criticized him. Sinda's arguments were similar to
those I had heard for many years. Why, if he were the author, did Soulié not
write under a pseudonym if he did not want to publish under his own name?
The style of *Le Regard du roi* was not that different from that of *L'Enfant noir*.
I would surely be strongly criticized if I published anything. Sinda changed his
attitude, I believe, because he had spoken to his father, Martial Sinda, a historian who wrote several books about the Congo, knew Laye, and wanted to defend his reputation. Martial Sinda refused to speak to me. As his books concern
liberationist politics, I can understand why my book would be upsetting to
him.[2]

Koné, with whom I spoke several times by telephone and whom I interviewed in person, was, however, quite willing to talk about his experiences in
the 1950s and 1960s in Paris and in Guinea. Although he said he knew nothing
of a study of the Belgian (or Swiss) expressions in work signed Camara Laye,
he gave me new information about the life of Soulié in Paris in the 1950s.

Born in 1940, Koné has lived in France since 1957, working as a journalist
for various publications about Africa and returning occasionally to Guinea.
Before he came to Paris to study in a lycée at the age of seventeen, he had already read *L'Enfant noir*. Impressed with the first major literary work of his
country, he traveled to Kouroussa to meet Laye's parents. Koné, who is from
Beyla in the Malinké region, knows all the Guineans connected to the story,
who are often related to his friend Kelefa Keita: Kaké, whose first wife was a
member of the Keita family; Malon, Kelefa's sister; and Kaba, also a Malinké,
who came to Paris later.

Koné saw Kelefa Keita often after his arrival in Paris. In 1957, Keita had,
Koné thought, already been adopted by Soulié, with whom he lived in an apartment on the rue des Francs-Bourgeois. Koné and other Guinean friends,
among them Sidibé Bana, later a minister in the Guinean government, were invited to Soulié's apartment to have a drink. Soulié didn't talk to them much. He
lay in a hammock and looked on with an ironic smile. He was always calm and
friendly to his guests but discreet about his own life. He had a great interest in

Africa, particularly Guinea. If he was most interested in the Belgian Congo before he came to France, Soulié became fascinated by Guinea after he met Laye.
Koné could not remember any Africans from other countries at Soulié's apartment. There were never any women in the apartment. Koné learned that Soulié's wife lived in Belgium. Soulié lived modestly, and Koné did not know the
extent of his wealth until after his death, when Keita spoke about the buildings
he owned in Paris and in Belgium. (Koné supposed the money came from Soulié's writing.)

The description of Soulié lying in a hammock reminded me of a passage in
Le Regard du roi that has always seemed to me a European's imagined Africa
rather than a real place:

> Ah! c'est fameux le Sud quand on habite les pays du Nord! . . . Et ce qu'on
> voit? Un hamac accroché à deux cocotiers, en bordure du lagon! (95)
>
> [*Oh, the South, it's marvelous, the South, when you live in the North! . . .
> And what do you see? A hammock hanging between a pair of coconut palms
> at the edge of a lagoon!*] *(106)*

Koné had no idea that Soulié had been condemned by the Belgian government in 1944 nor that he was homosexual. He knew that young Africans who
needed money were sometimes approached by French homosexuals. He also
felt certain that both Kelefa Keita and Laye were not homosexuals. Keita continued to see Soulié regularly between 1958 and 1976, when Soulié died. Koné
knew that Keita told Soulié some Malinké tales. (This is presumably the basis
of the book to which Malon Keita Kouyaté referred, which was perhaps submitted to L'Harmattan). According to Koné, Keita returned to Guinea and began
drinking heavily after Soulié's death. By 1989, when Koné saw him, he had lost
all his inheritance from Soulié.

Koné thinks that Soulié wrote the final draft of all Laye's work—novels,
stories, and articles—that was published when he was in Paris. He claims that
the first idea for *L'Enfant noir* was Laye's and that this makes him the author.
He added that he believes the first idea for *Le Regard du roi* was also Laye's. He
had not seen copies of any manuscripts, however, nor had he spoken to Soulié
about Laye. He based his opinions partly on the fact that Laye did not have a
literary education. Koné met Laye in Guinea in 1962 when Laye was working

for Radio Guinée. From his strongly anticolonial perspective, Koné considered that Laye did not have any political consciousness.[3]

Laye was but one of the Africans in Paris whom the French had groomed to return to their native lands as leaders with pro-French views. He was Lefaucheux's African, whom she helped to find employment, briefly in a car factory and, more importantly, later with the French government in her brother's funding agency, and whom she piloted into a position as an acclaimed author with the help of another, still unknown, woman. It is clear from Mitterrand's schemes to woo Houphouët-Boigny away from the French Communist Party, Césaire's break with the Communist Party, the denunciation of Madeleine Rousseau by the Communists, and the long debate over the constitution for the Fourth Republic that for some time the French government and the Communist Party had been fighting for the soul and control of the African independence movement. In a better world people would not have had to choose between neocolonialism and Stalinism. Laye wanted a union or cooperation between France and its colonies. What the woman I have called Aude Joncourt wanted we will probably never know. Perhaps she was an innocent or a pawn, perhaps she was in love with Laye, or perhaps she too saw herself as helping France and Africa.

Laye was one of many from the colonies who came to Europe after the war with a sense of adventure and a desire to improve himself. He was unwilling to return to Guinea after his year of studies and, like many others who hoped to find ways to further their education and stay on in Europe, he eventually drifted into another life. How he survived is not clear, but after he met Soulié and came under the sponsorship of Lefaucheux he became an African author who would return to a high administrative position in West Africa and represent French interests. Having landed on his feet in Paris and been carefully "formed" to express pro-French views, he may not even have been aware of how he was being used. Africans with formal qualifications and administrative experience were still a rarity, and Laye would have soon expected a place among the elite to replace or work along with the French.

He was an oddity, however, in that he was not trained in the classics, not a candidate for a doctorate in the humanities, and not an intellectual. He was unlike Senghor, Alioune Diop, Houphouët-Boigny, and Césaire. French diplomats and leading politicians were usually intellectuals, writers, products of a rigorous system of selection and examinations that produced a brilliant elite at ease in the humanities, philosophy, and letters. Such people who reached the top expected to rule, and those from the colonies who replaced them had a similar formation. Laye did not. Perhaps it was by chance that Laye came under the wings of Lefaucheux or perhaps there was no other suitable candidate from Guinea, but a conscious effort was made to transform Laye into a writer-intellectual-leader.

Somehow, Laye never really fit. His books needed to be written for him. There were always promises of more books on the way, but they were not written, and there is no evidence that they were started. He was given a job with Postel-Vinay's agency to train him for high responsibilities that he could not fulfill. Charming, personable, he was not a Senghor or Césaire. Once he returned to Guinea he was the odd man out. He was appointed to represent Guinea in Ghana but did not speak much English.

The French Union Laye believed in was abandoned as impractical. Unlike most of West Africa, Guinea would soon refuse the new status offered by France and move rapidly toward a horrible tyranny. Laye undiplomatically opposed Sékou Touré and was soon in exile. While Laye the student trying to survive and being tempted into passing himself off as an author is understandable, it is as an opponent to Sékou Touré and an exile that Laye becomes a much more sympathetic figure. He was no longer a voice of French interests but part of an exiled opposition, and as such he was an embarrassment to the French, who had cut their losses and were trying to mend their fences with Sékou Touré. The French and their allies did not rush to Laye's aid. Senghor advised against publishing an attack on Sékou Touré. Toward the end of Laye's life it was a group of European admirers of "Camara Laye" the writer who raised money for the treatment he needed in France. Laye himself had become a literary figure whose survival depended on his being "Camara Laye," author of two famous novels published in the early 1950s. He was obviously troubled by the situation and in Africa mentioned to several people that others had written those books.

We will never know how high up were Laye's contacts in the French government. It is likely that he was brought to the attention of Mendès-France and Mitterrand, and it is possible that he spoke with them once or twice. He was for a time useful to the French, but he was not a major investment and could be forgotten. There were other African writers who headed governments or had important positions in the newly independent countries, such as Senghor, Cheick Hamidou Kane, Dadié, and Oyono, among others. There were artists who could be displayed internationally and intellectuals who could form ties between France and its former colonies. From the perspective of the French government, the creation of Camara Laye became a dead end. In exile from Guinea, Laye was more trouble than he was worth. It is unfortunate that he never told someone the details of his real life, as it would have made a fascinating story.

Koné's comment at the end of my interview with him confirmed what I had discovered about the influence of French colonial policy. Laye was, he felt, formed to be a good servant of the colonial regime without questioning it. Because of the Guinean rejection of de Gaulle in 1958, Laye could not fulfill his ambitions.

CONSIDERING LAYE NOW

In the introduction to *Le Maître de la parole* Laye continued the praise of French culture and what it brought to Africa that can be found throughout his work. He also made an unsatisfactory attempt to explain how Africans' reactions to art might differ from Europeans'. Africans, he said, because they are closer to nature, are more aware of a divine presence in the world. To show that some Europeans are also conscious of a divine presence, he chose a rather odd group of artists: Leonardo de Vinci, James (presumably William, though no first name is given), Kafka, Bernanos, and Lautréamont. Lautréamont in particular seems out of place; it is perhaps a reflection of the interest of Soulié and other Surrealists in Lautréamont's work, which Laye picked up secondhand.

Laye also mentioned vaguely the work of René Grousset, without showing any real knowledge of it. He referred to Grousset's noting how technological progress is only complementary to civilization. The reference is rather vague. Grousset is known for his studies of the civilizations of the East and a history, *The Empire of the Steppes*. Laye mentioned him, I thought originally, because he was the grandfather of Reine Carducci, whose financial and moral support during Laye's long illness kept him alive. Grousset, however, was quoted in

"Et demain?," the *Présence africaine* article of 1957 that speaks of justice for those who lost the Second World War: "material progress does not necessarily lead to improvement in customs, morals, or spiritual values."[4] Undoubtedly Soulié, who wrote an early poem about the steppes and was interested in Eastern civilizations, knew Grousset's work.[5] After sorting through so much evidence, I found it amusing that Soulié had read the work of the grandfather of the last person to help Laye.

The story I have uncovered can have many different conclusions. Some readers will remain unconvinced. While I, too, would like something unquestionable like a written "confession," I suspect that nothing, not even a manuscript, would convince the unconvinced. Some will feel disillusioned that another African writer has been found not to be the principal author of his best work. They might, however, consider whether the desire for African literature, especially in the 1940s and 1950s, was not a cause of such fraudulent production. Where there is a demand it will be met. In the case of Laye there was the desire not only for an African literature but also for one that spoke of a common humanity, that ignored the real history of colonialism, and that was useful to French interests. There is enough excellent writing by Achebe, Soyinka, Senghor, Beti, Ben Okri, Nuruddin Farah, Tierno Monénembo, and others that African literature is not seriously harmed by the revelation of a few ghostwriters or shared authorships.

I certainly do not want to excuse Soulié's and Poulet's anti-Semitism and collaboration with the fascists, nor do I want to take away from Laye's courage and glory, but this story does show that actual lives are different from the assumptions we often make about them. Here are two Belgians, condemned for collaboration, writing classics of African literature. Being a collaborator did not stop Soulié from being a homosexual attracted to African men and wanting to be accepted by them. Yes, if you wish, Soulié is another European sentimentalizing the "Other," hoping "they" will replace the society that had rejected him, but his story is more interesting than that, just as *Le Regard du roi* is much more than such a psychological explanation. Somehow, being in hiding and knowing Laye turned Soulié into a real writer for this one book. And then there is Poulet, a real writer if a minor one, living as a hack in Paris, editing others, writing self-justifications of his politics, still a racist, yet showing Laye how to use tenses, helping shape and then editing two of the books published as

Laye's, and adding to their richness. Poulet had to earn a living, but he was also a "pro," a writer who cared about writing, so by one of those weird twists of fate this collaborator with the Germans became part of an "African" writer.

Many interpretations of Laye's first two novels based on Laye's biography or historical and cultural contexts may now seem embarrassing, but other interpretations still are true. *Le Regard du roi*, for example, remains a quest for spiritual salvation and an example of interracial communion, although now interpretation will need to give more attention to the homosexual motifs in the text. The knowledge that *L'Enfant noir* is not solely Laye's helps to explain its various styles and uneven quality. This *L'Enfant noir* is perhaps even more suitable for an era when art is seen as overlapping and contradictory discourses that lack organic unity. The immense difference in kind between *L'Enfant noir* and *Le Regard du roi* can now be understood, as can the drop in quality and woodenness of most of the writing in *Dramouss* and *Le Maître de la parole*. There were different people in different combinations writing under the name of Camara Laye. If teachers are going to have problems fitting *L'Enfant noir* and *Le Regard du roi* into their courses, it is additional evidence that we now need some way to structure the study of literature other than by nations or "race."

As I was ready to send this manuscript to the publisher, I learned that *The Radiance of the King* has been republished with an introduction by Toni Morrison. She sees the novel as in many ways a reply to earlier European descriptions of Africa, exploiting and reworking images used by white writers and reinventing "storybook Africa" from a new perspective. While the Europeans she mentions, all writing in English—Joyce Cary, Elspeth Huxley, and H. Rider Haggard—are not those Soulié presumably would have known, Morrison's claim that Laye reworked images from European writers describes what Soulié actually did. Although she sees the novel as a reply to European discourse, her reading suggests that the author knew European culture well, better than a young Guinean who had spent seven years in France could have. Morrison also notes that the novel differs from other work by Laye—"the autobiographical groove Camara Laye settled into was violently disrupted just once"—without speculating on the reasons for this violent disruption.[6]

L'Enfant noir is still Laye Camara's story, and we are unlikely ever to know how much he might have contributed to its final form or to *Le Regard du roi*.

That Soulié had a manuscript handy, as Laye told Kesteloot, does not mean that Laye might not have given him suggestions. The books published under the name Camara Laye are no different from what they were previously. The words and form have not changed; the themes and subject matter remain the same. If *L'Enfant noir* and *Le Regard du roi* were classics before, they should be classics now.

NOTES

Unless otherwise cited, all statements from individuals are taken from correspondence with and interviews conducted by the author, all of which are listed in the bibliography.

INTRODUCTION

1 See Mouralis, *République et colonies*, 42–46.
2 Brochure from the Quinzaine des Réalisateurs, Cannes, 1995; copy in author's possession.
3 Kesteloot, *Anthologie négro-africaine*, 536.
4 Soyinka to author, December 18, 1991.
5 Laye is a first name, a shortened form of Abdoulaye, and Camara is a common surname in Malinké, Guinea. Laye Camara used this inversion because in schools in France or in the colonies, pupils from elementary grades onward were called by their last name followed by their first name. This reversal of first and last names for authors was used several times for books written by Africans. Another well-known example is Sembène Ousmane, where Sembène is the family name.
6 For references to letters, conversations, and interviews mentioned in the text, consult the bibliography. Citations in English are to the published translations of works by Camara Laye, in the editions marked with an asterisk (*) in the bibliography. Where there are no published translations, of Laye's work or others', I have provided the translations.
7 I found other discrepancies in what Laye had told me and others about his life in Paris when he was writing his early novels. He did not mention Soulié. He also told me in 1978, when I asked about his reader at Plon, that the reader had died in 1960, whereas the reader, Robert Poulet, died only in 1989.

1. A HISTORICAL CONTEXT FOR *L'ENFANT NOIR*

1 Jack, *Francophone Literatures*, 223, citing *Outre-mer* 1 (1929): 3–5. "Mission civilisatrice" is often translated as "the white man's burden." The French, however, stress the culture they are giving to those they colonize rather than the difficulties of the enterprise.

2 Jack, *Francophone Literatures*, 224, citing Roland Lebel, *Histoire de la littérature coloniale en France* (Paris: Librairie Larose, 1931), 85.

3 Blair, *African Literature in French*, 77.

4 For a full account of Diagne's activities, see Mouralis, *République et colonies*, 194ff.

5 I am indebted to Cornevin's *Histoire de l'Afrique contemporaine* for information on the period of the war and the Brazzaville conference.

6 Mouralis, *République et colonies*, 226.

7 Wauthier, *Quatre présidents*, 27.

8 Wright, *Reshaping of French Democracy*, 142. For information on the constitutional assemblies and the politics of the period after the war, I am also indebted to Chapsal, *La Vie politique*, and Rioux, *La France de la Quatrième République*.

9 Wright, *Reshaping of French Democracy*, 150.

10 Wauthier, *Quatre présidents*, 31.

11 Quoted in Mouralis, *République et colonies*, 44.

12 Quoted in Mouralis, *République et colonies*, 230. Mouralis comments that nationalist movements in West Africa between 1945 and 1960 were often favorable to some form of assimilation.

13 Makward, *Mayotte Capécia*, 57.

14 Quoted from review in *Echo de Nice*, May 4, 1950, in Makward, *Mayotte Capécia*, 34. After extensive investigations, Makward has not been able to discover who wrote the work attributed to Capécia and to what extent Capécia herself contributed to the novels.

15 When I taught French in Nigeria in the 1960s and 1970s, I found that BELC had been influential in supporting French teachers at Nigerian universities but was less happy with British and American staff.

16 Luc, *La Belle Histoire*, 79.

17 Protocol dated June 21, 1963, Archives Nationales du Ministère de la Coopèration. While this would have been close to the time that Laye worked with Radio Guinée, no names are mentioned in the documents at the archives.

18 Northcutt, *Mitterrand*, 51.

19 Northcutt, *Mitterrand*, 35, quoting *Ma Part de vérité* (Paris: Fayard, 1969), 35.

20 Mitterrand, *Aux Frontières de l'Union Française*, 29, 34, my translations.

21 Quoted in Rioux, *La France de la Quatrième République*, 67, 35. (By 1956, however, the right-wing activists pressing for Algérie Française felt that Mitterrand was not militant enough and that he had shown unfortunate tendencies when in the Ministry of France Overseas in the past.)

22 Senghor cited in Mudimbe, *Surreptitious Speech*, xi; my italics.

23 Dupré sees this conservatism as a reason why the Académie Française and many critics now favor the work of the Cameroonian novelist Calixthe Beyala. Interestingly, Beti made the same comparison between Laye and Beyala in "L'Affaire Calixthe Beyala." Decraene, in "In Memoriam," suggests that Parisian publishers were looking for those who criticized the colonial regime. I can find no evidence to support this suggestion.

2. THE LIFE OF LAYE CAMARA

1 Ten years after Laye's arrival, there were over twenty-five hundred Africans studying in Europe (Pageard, *Littérature négro-africaine*, 19). Discrepancies in dates are frequent in Laye's comments. In the introduction to *Le Maître de la parole*, Laye wrote that he lived in Paris from 1946 to 1956. I and most critics have assumed he arrived in 1947. In *Dramouss* Fatoman speaks of returning to Guinea after six years; Laye returned for a visit in February 1954.

2 F. Lavinal, for the firm Peugeot, to author, September 22, 1997. In an early biographical introduction to *Camara Laye: Écrivain guinéen*, ed. Roger Mercier, Monique Battestini, and Simon Battestini, the editors state that Laye worked at Simca for eight months (4). Laye also told Alain Fresco in 1977 that he worked at Simca for eight months (Fresco, "Tradition and Modernity," 23). Perhaps he had forgotten how long he worked at various jobs. The term "ouvrier spécialisé" denoted a class of manual workers with no training prior to their employment. Many of these workers were immigrants, mostly from Europe, especially Italy.

3 Autra, "Principales Étapes," 58. Laye told a Nigerian student of my husband's at Ahmadu Bello University, who was studying French in Dakar in 1974, that a white woman had written *L'Enfant noir*.

4 Telephone interview with Simon Njami, August 5, 1995. The relationship between Laye and Joncourt may have been purely literary. At some point he probably had a French girlfriend, and Joncourt is the most likely person, as *Dramouss* would indicate. According to Jacqueline Sorel, who interviewed Laye for Radio France in 1976, Camara Laye was a man who needed to be taken care of, pampered (interview with Sorel, May 8, 1978). My husband remembers Laye alluding to the ease with which he could pick up women on the Left Bank in the 1950s.

5 After having praised *L'Enfant noir* for its "style d'une extraordinaire limpidité" ("extraordinarily clear style"), Autra comments that "If Camara Laye received praise in literary circles, he did not fail to attract the attention of the Ministry for the Colonies, looking for collaborators still unaware of the harmful effects of colonialism" ("Principales Étapes," 58). Autra perhaps did not realize how much attention Laye had received from the government even before the publication of *L'Enfant noir*.

6 "Interview avec Camara Laye," 162.

7 Elisabeth Rabut, Archives de la France d'Outre-Mer, to author, July 24, 1995.

8 Diallo interview, April 20, 1978.

9 There were 157 candidates for the Prix Veillon in 1954. According to the editors of *Camara Laye: Écrivain guinéen*, *L'Enfant noir* was also a candidate for the major French literary prizes that year (Mercier, Battestini, and Battestini, 5).

10 Mercier, Battestini, and Battestini, *Camara Laye*, 5.

11 Diop, *Le Temps de Tamango*, 50.

1 2   Radio France broadcast, No. LO2102.

1 3   "Camara Laye nous parle."

1 4   See Irele, "Camara Laye," 617.

1 5   Quoted in *Mongo Beti parle*, 89.

1 6   Orengo to Laye, June 7, 1955; Maurice Bourdel, Plon, to Mr. Rosetti, "Films d'A-riel", June 7, 1955; Orengo to Rosetti, June 20, 1955, all in Plon files.

1 7   "Camara Laye nous parle."

1 8   Fresco, "Tradition and Modernity," 75.

1 9   Bernard, "Camara Laye," 310.

2 0   Fresco, interview with Camara Laye, March 25, 1977, in "Tradition and Modernity," 28–29.

2 1   Laye, "Premiers contacts." Alain Fresco believes that this article to some extent contradicts Laye's later conference paper in which he complains of loneliness. (Fresco, "Tradition and Modernity," 25–27) Fresco also quotes Laye in an interview saying that he lived in various milieus (interview of April 6, 1977, in Fresco, "Tradition and Modernity," 27).

2 2   Undated readers' reports in Plon files include two unfavorable comments on "Les Yeux de la statue," one stating that it was inferior to "Le Prince" (which was published in *La Table ronde* in 1954), the other saying that it seemed the work of a very young author. These reports suggest that "Les Yeux de la statue" was written around 1954 or 1955.

2 3   Sellin, "Pretender to the Throne."

2 4   Laye, "Le Prince", 87.

2 5   Laye, "Et demain?" 291.

2 6   In my interview with him, Paulin Joachim claimed that Laye attended the first Congrès des Écrivains et Artistes Noirs in Paris in September 1956 but was obviously not at ease. Laye's name is not mentioned among those who spoke or participated in the discussions at the congress. Joachim may be mistaken, as Laye was in Cotonou, Dahomey (now Bénin), at that time, although he could have returned for the conference. Katharina Städtler, who has done extensive research on the Présence Africaine group in the 1940s and 1950s, encountered a great number of names of Africans as well as of Europeans who were the Afrophile intellectuals of the time, but Laye's name was never mentioned (Städtler to author, February 9, 1998). Bennetta Jules-Rosette has studied the Présence Africaine group in *Black Paris*.

2 7   Anise Postel-Vinay has several letters that Laye wrote to her. One, from Cotonou, October 2, 1956, speaks of his family (his first daughter, Aïcha, was born in Cotonou). He adds that he now realizes he was most happy in childhood.

2 8   Wauthier to author, January 24, 1992.

2 9   Denis Castaing, Caisse Française de Développement, to author, July 24, 1995.

3 0   Blancard saw Laye writing the material that they collected and preparing it for broadcast. She mentioned in a letter to me that he knew how to use the subjunctive. (It

is surprising how often Laye's ability to use the subjunctive was somewhat patronizingly cited to me by French persons as a proof of the authenticity of work signed Camara Laye.)

3 1 Regarding Laye's claims that he was setting out to rehabilitate African civilization, Dorothy Blair comments that his arguments are "not those of orthodox Negritude, or of a specifically African civilization, but of an universal aspiration to spirituality and a transcendence of rationalism and positive values with a certain Rousseauesque rejection of the appurtenances of a mechanized age" (*African Literature in French*, 196).

3 2 Kaké was one of the leaders of the Organization for the Liberation of Guinea as well as a professor, writer, and journalist. In 1982, when Sékou Touré came to Paris, officials from the Guinean Embassy tried to kidnap Kaké. (See Wauthier, *Quatre présidents*, 446.)

3 3 Fresco, interview of April 19, 1977, in "Tradition and Modernity," 55, and discussion of the date of composition in "Tradition and Modernity," 55–58. Fresco states that Emile Snyder saw the early version of *Dramouss* with annotations by Sékou Touré.

3 4 Reviews in *La Tribune de Lausanne*, September 18, 1966; *La Vie des Métiers*, October 1966; and *Culture Française* 1 (1967), from press cuttings in the Plon files.

3 5 Kesteloot makes a similar criticism in her *Anthologie négro-africaine*, 537. Why, she asks, should Laye write an adaptation of the epic of Soundiata instead of a direct translation from the Manding?

3 6 Quotation from documents in Plon files.

3 7 Fresco states that Marie left Dakar in 1970 but that Laye married Ramatoulaye in 1969 (Fresco, "Tradition and Modernity," 62, 341). If this is true, it contradicts Laye's claim that he took his second wife to care for the children when Marie was imprisoned in Guinea. If Laye's story is not true, it shows the contradictions often evident in Laye's recollection of dates.

3 8 There were no records of Teuscheur's work at Deutsche Welle. I have been unsuccessful in attempts to find out if he was in Paris around 1950. I am uncertain whether there was such a person.

3 9 Deduck, "Kafka's Influence," 239.

4 0 "Entretien avec Camara Laye," 56.

4 1 Kafka was widely discussed in the 1940s, in both English and French. The French edition of *The Trial* appeared in 1933, but *The Castle*, from which there are more echoes in *Le Regard du roi*, appeared only in 1947. The aphorisms were published in France in 1946 as *Description d'un combat*. They are much less well known to readers of Kafka than his other works.

4 2 Rubin, "Laye's Commitment," 24.

4 3 Lawson, "Radiance of Camara Laye," 80.

4 4 Lawson, "Radiance of Camara Laye," 81. "I read of his life" is, of course, of little importance for the use of Kafka in *Le Regard du roi*.

4 5 "Interview avec Camara Laye," 156.

46 Where two sets of page numbers are given, the first refers to the French publication and the second to the English.

47 Nor is there any indication that the author is treating his narrator's statements with irony.

48 *Cadres* would be better translated as *management*, instead of *regiments*.

49 Carducci said that Laye had no sense of money. She gave him a checkbook, with funds from the appeal, but he couldn't keep track of the checks he wrote.

3. CRITICAL REACTIONS

1 Beti, "Afrique noire, littérature rose"; Diop, *Le Temps de Tamango*, 55.

2 Quoted in Lequeret, *La Revue*.

3 King, *Writings of Camara Laye*, 23.

4 King, *Writings of Camara Laye*, 34.

5 King, *Writings of Camara Laye*, 125

6 According to Eloïse Brière, who knew Mohamadou K. Kane in Dakar, Kane assumed that *Le Regard du roi* was not written by Camara Laye. Brière interview, April 1999.

7 Kakou, "Camara Laye."

8 Soyinka, *Myth*, *Literature*, 121–26. More recently, Ada Uzoamaka Azodo wrote, "We believe that only an African, originating in black culture, could, finally, feel deeply in his or her flesh, the profound significance of the symbols." Most of her discussion, however, is based on European studies of the imaginary by such scholars as Gilbert Durand, Gaston Bachelard, and Mircea Eliade. Azodo, *L'Imaginaire*, 1. (Although she writes in French, Azodo is from Anglophone West Africa.)

9 Lawson, *Western Scar*, 48.

10 Harrow, "A Sufi Interpretation," 135.

11 Harrow speculates vaguely about such possibilities: "it is not inconceivable that Shadhiliyya practices, which were once well-known in the Futa Jalon, might have survived and influenced [Laye] or that he learned of it elsewhere." He continues, "Noaga and Nagoa's spinning bears no real obvious resemblance to any other tradition or mysticism, be it African or any other that I am aware of" (148). I thought the spinning might be derived from whirling dervishes, of Middle Eastern origin.

12 Julien, "Narrative Model," 798.

13 Julien, *African Novels*, 125.

14 Bertrand, "Gender and Spirituality."

15 Sellin, "Alienation," 464.

16 Ungar, "Blinded by the Light," 126.

17 Hollier, *Le Collège de sociologie*, 24.

18 Jahn, *Muntu*, 213; Beier to author, August 30, 1997.

19 Wauthier, *Literature and Thought of Modern Africa*, 70.

20 Laye, unpublished paper in defense of the French Union, Postel-Vinay files, and "Interview avec Camara Laye," 156.

21 Sorel considers *L'Enfant noir* Laye's story, with much help in writing. She mentioned other African writers, who had much more education than Laye but needed help writing in French, especially with verbs.

22 Chemain, *L'Imaginaire*, 377.

23 King, *Writings of Camara Laye*, 38.

24 King, *Writings of Camara Laye*, 48.

25 King, *Writings of Camara Laye*, 106.

26 Wauthier, *Afrique des Africains*, 73.

27 See Irele, "Camara Laye."

28 Beti, Review of *Le Regard du roi*, 143.

29 Autra, "Principales Étapes," 58.

30 Kesteloot, "Camara Laye," 58.

31 Kesteloot, *Anthologie négro-africaine*, 536n.

32 Dorsey, Review of *The Western Scar*, 436.

33 Lawson, letter in reply, 476–77.

34 Dorsey, "Reply to William Lawson."

35 Chemain and Chemain, "Pour une lecture," 155–56.

36 *Dictionnaire Universel Francophone*, 724.

37 Robert Poulet worked in Africa, but there is no evidence that he visited Ouagadougou.

38 Krzywicki, *"Le Regard du roi,"* 64.

39 Krzywicki, e-mail message to author, January 25, 1999.

40 Alter, "Arbeit Macht Fraud."

41 Blair, *African Literature in French*, 15.

42 Halen, paper presented at the conference on Africanists.

43 Beier cited in Obafemi, *Forty Years in African Art*, 26–27.

44 Gates, "'Authenticity' of the Lesson of Little Tree," 27.

45 Stavans, review of *Rigoberta Menchú*. Several persons who knew Laye in Africa after 1956 have spoken of his loneliness and insecurity. I have tried to make Laye a sympathetic human being, not a target of attack.

46 Riesz, "Audible Gasps," 89.

47 In "L'Acculturation à rebours," Riesz cites other examples of reverse acculturation, including Alejo Carpentier's *Los Pasos perdidos* (1953) and Michel Tournier's *Vendredi ou les limbes de Pacifique* (1967).

48 King, *Writings of Camara Laye*, 67.

49 King, *Writings of Camara Laye*, 123.

50 See Krzywicki, *Wielosc Kultur i tekst*, appendix C.

51 Kesteloot, *Anthologie négro-africaine*, 537: "pourquoi adapter et non pas *traduire*" [why adapt rather than translate?].

4. STYLISTIC EVIDENCE IN *LE REGARD DU ROI*

1 The published English translations cannot, of course, reflect the tone or the level of the vocabulary, so I have included them only as needed for clarity.

2 Interview with Anne Trevarthen, maître de conférence at the University of Paris VII, June 29, 1997.

3 Senghor, "Laye Camara et Lamine Niang," 173.

4 King, *Writings of Camara Laye*, 44; Larson, *Emergence of African Fiction*, 179.

5 Fresco, "Tradition and Modernity," 245, from notes taken after a conversation with Professor Roy Sieber, Bloomington, Indiana, June 20, 1980.

6 Messages to me from Claire Dehon and Karen Keim have confirmed the geographical inconsistency about the use of cloth. Messages from Irene d'Almeida, Claire Dehon, and Liliane Schraüwen mentioned the filing of teeth occasionally in West Africa but particularly in the Congo. Jean-François Duclos says in Senegal and Mali the custom was particularly for women of noble birth. Abdoulaye Keita, a Guinean born in 1956, also remembered from his childhood only women with filed teeth. As for going naked except for a covering on the genitalia, he thought this existed only among the Tanda ethnie in Koundara, in the northwest of Guinea. When I taught in Nigeria in the 1960s a student told me that my miniskirts were shocking to him.

7 Mouralis, *L'Europe, l'Afrique*, 184.

8 Mouralis, "Le Cri de Sarzan," 344.

9 Quaghebeur, "Eléments pour une étude," 260. Africans, speaking a learned second language, almost always tried to use correct French. Not until the mid-1960s, with Ahmadou Kourouma's *Les Soleils de l'indépendance*, was there an equivalent in Francophone African writing to the use of a local form of a European language, such as that found much earlier among Nigerian writers.

10 The last two of these pluperfect subjunctives use this verb form to replace a past conditional, grammatically the "conditionnels passés deuxième forme" mentioned in Léopold, Review of *L'Enfant noir*.

11 Poulet, *Ce n'est pas une vie*, 245.

5. JONCOURT AND LEFAUCHEUX

1 André Postel-Vinay describes his life during the war in *Un Fou s'évade*.

2 A biography by Henry Solus included in the volume of the *Académie des Sciences d'Outre-Mer* in 1975 notes, however, that "she understood feminism as essentially feminine" (448). For information on Marie-Hélène Lefaucheux, I am also indebted to Richecour, "Marie-Hélène Lefaucheux," and *Marie-Hélène Lefaucheux*, the memorial brochure published by the Conseil National des Femmes Françaises.

3 Lefaucheux, foreword, 10.

4 Griaule had been in charge of the Dakar-Djibouti Mission in the 1930s. Michel Leiris's *Afrique fantôme*, a journal of his experience with the mission, describes incidents in which he was unable to find his way in the tropics and describes sexuality in relation to the sacred. Leiris's journal may have been one source of inspiration for *Le Regard du roi*. Griaule had, according to Bernard Mouralis, an essentialist and traditional view of African societies (*République et colonies*, 38). *L'Enfant noir* might be said to express a similar view.

5 Assemblée de l'Union Française, proceedings, 1951, 148–49, in Archives de l'Assemblée de l'Union Française.

6 Assemblée de l'Union Française, proceedings, 1953, quote on 31, in Archives de l'Assemblée de l'Union Française.

7 *Les Femmes de l'Union Française*, no. 22 (February–March 1954): 5.

8 Lefaucheux, "Impressions d'Indochine," 3.

6. INTRODUCING FRANCIS SOULIÉ

1 In one letter in 1929 to Robert Guiette, a poet and literary critic in Antwerp who contributed to some of the same journals as Soulié, Soulié mentions that he hasn't been in Antwerp for almost twenty years (since his childhood, presumably), and in another letter to Guiette he says he must accept being a citizen of Liege.

2 *Sélection* lasted until 1933 but changed to a magazine strictly devoted to painting and sculpture in 1928, at which point there was no longer an editorial board listed. It was financed by art galleries.

3 Aron and Soucy, *Les Revues littéraires Belges*, 30–40. Magazines Hellens edited included *Signaux de France et de Belgique* (1921), *Le Disque vert* (1922), and *Nord* (1929). Poulet and Soulié contributed to *Le Disque vert* and *Nord*. Among the more prominent writers who wrote for Hellens were Blaise Cendrars, Jean Cocteau, and Henri Michaux.

4 Soulié, "Cécile," 72.

5 Soulié, "Contre André Breton," 377.

6 Soulié, "Le Roman," 492.

7 Soulié, "Caligula," 230.

8 Conway, *Collaboration in Belgium*, 23.

9 "Présentation," in Aron et al., *Leurs occupations*, 13.

10 Conway, *Collaboration in Belgium*,173.

11 Aubenas, "1942."

12 Fincoeur, "Le Monde."

13 After the war, testifying for an investigation on collaboration, a photographer spoke of a meeting between thirty *La Meuse* staff members and German officers on about May 22, 1940: "We agreed to cooperate because we felt that against force there was no possible resistance." *La Légia* file, L'Auditorat Général près la Cour Militaire, Brussels.

14 In spite of his predictions of victory, Soulié seems to have felt that the Germans

might lose the war. An undated letter in his file at the Auditorat Général près la Cour Militaire, Brussels, contains a strange sentence: "We could go . . . to Burma, to Tunisia, depending on what happens."

15 Thys, "La Collaboration intellectuelle," 14–15.

16 Marc Carghese, a director of Radio Bruxelles, to Soulié, July 27, 1942, Soulié file, L'Auditorat Général près la Cour Militaire, Brussels.

17 This interest in architecture, mentioned in a paper broadcast October 13, 1942, might be compared to comments on architecture in Laye's article "Et demain?" (1957).

18 Soulié's distrust of financiers is perhaps echoed in Clarence's dislike of those who take his money from him in *Le regard du roi*.

19 De Jonghe, *Tempête sur la brousse*, 41.

20 Quoted in Nabil, "Notre Terre wallonne," 119.

21 Soulié, "Ebauche d'un Charlot," 120.

22 Conway to author, February 18, 1994.

23 Martin, "Cassandre," 262.

24 Soulié, "Ebauche d'un Charlot," 113.

7. FRANCIS SOULIÉ AFTER THE WAR

1 Conway, *Collaboration in Belgium*, 277.

2 His mother owned a number of valuable buildings in prime locations in Liege, on the rue Léopold, the boulevard Frère-Orban, and the quai St Léonard, to mention only a few.

3 Conway, *Collaboration in Belgium*, 277, 344.

4 "Le Portrait," 117, and "Le Char de feu," 112, in Hellens, *Réalités fantastiques*.

5 Gauguin, *Noa Noa*, 17.

6 Hesse, *Siddhartha*, 6.

7 Céline, *Voyage*, 188.

8 Kirkup, preface to *Guardian of the Word*, 10–11.

9 Kunze, "L'Européen déraciné." See also Chevrier, "La Vision."

8. THE LIFE OF ROBERT POULET

1 Stengers to author, June 3, 1998. See Poulet, *Ce n'est pas une vie*, 229, for a reference to his work in Africa.

2 Letter in the Poulet file, Musée de la Littérature, Bibliothèque Royale, Brussels.

3 See Hubin, "Les Débuts."

4 Poulet, "Avis au lecteur," *La Revue réactionnaire*, no. 1 (April 1933): 4.

5 Aron and Soucy, *Les Revues littéraires*, 40.

6 Quaghebeur, "Eléments pour une étude," 236.

7 See Siné, "L'Épuration," 14, and Delcord, "A propos de quelques 'chapelles' politico-littéraires," 177–78.

8 Willequet, *La Belgique*, 72. There was no mention of who sent the message. Poulet's activities during the war are well documented in various studies and explained by some commentators trying to exonerate him from the charges of collaboration with the enemy. Willequet's work is one of many examples I found that exaggerate Poulet's importance. Willequet felt no need to explain why Poulet would be particularly needed in Belgium in 1940.

9 Conway, *Collaboration in Belgium*, 85.

1 0 Poulet, *L'Enfer-ciel*, 28.

1 1 Conway, *Collaboration in Belgium*, 86.

1 2 When Streel was executed after the war, Poulet helped Streel's widow. Conway interview, May 18, 1999.

1 3 In a letter in his own defense written while in prison, Pierre Hubermont cites Poulet's assurance that he learned through Capelle that the king liked what Hubermont wrote in *Le Nouveau Journal*. Poulet files, Centre de Recherche et d'Études Historiques de la Seconde Guerre Mondiale, Brussels.

1 4 Lacour interview, July 3, 1997; Fabrice Schurmans, "Lecture," in Lacour, *Panique*.

1 5 I have not been able to locate any confirmation of this.

1 6 Quaghebeur, "Eléments," 267.

1 7 Conway, *Collaboration in Belgium*, 128.

1 8 Willequet, *La Belgique*, 84, 89, 318.

1 9 *Le Soir*, July 24, 1945, 2. Poulet's career continues to interest Belgians. André Sempoux's novel *Le Dévoreur* (1995) uses Poulet and some of his wartime writings as a model for one of his characters.

2 0 This is the rumor that Poulet spread, but, according to Martin Conway it was untrue (Conway to author, October 11, 1995). In any case, it does not fit well with Poulet's claim to be a royalist.

2 1 According to Guy Dupré, Poulet was not allowed to publish under his real name in Belgium. He used the pseudonym Walter Orlando, for example, in his first review of *L'Enfant noir* in the Brussels paper *Le Phare* (September 20, 1953).

2 2 Poulet, *Ce n'est pas une vie*, 242–43.

2 3 Assouline, *Hergé*, 213, 254.

2 4 Poulet, *Ce n'est pas une vie*, 233.

2 5 Neal to author, July 18, 1995.

2 6 Guy Dupré praised Poulet's talent and showed me Georges Bernanos's article on Poulet's *Les Ténèbres* (1934), in which Bernanos calls it a work of "génie" and speaks of "this almost imperceptible shift from life to death" (Dupré interview, July 6, 1998). Bernanos's review was published in *Le Jour*, April 9, 1934.

2 7 Poulet, "Les Conditions du roman," 136–37.

2 8 Poulet, *Handji*, 340–41.

2 9 Poulet, *L'Enfer-ciel*, 205.

3 0 Poulet, *Nuptial*, 248, 249.

31 Poulet, *La Hutte de cochenille*, 242.

32 Poulet, *Le Livre de quelques-uns*, 29, 168.

33 Celine's preface was not published with the novel. It can an be found in Godard, *Céline*, 15.

34 Poulet, "Robert Poulet," 19.

35 Krzywicki, "*Le Regard du roi,*," 71.

36 Poulet, *La Conjecture*, 124.

9. ROBERT POULET AT PLON

1 Information on the history of Plon from a mimeographed brochure, "Historique Plon," provided by the Librairie Plon.

2 Elsen interview, July 10, 1997. Elsen also said that Orengo, although married with two children, was gay. This might have been a link with Soulié. Orengo was, according to Camille Galic, part of the old guard at Plon. When he left, Plon changed for the worse from her perspective; that is, it moved toward the center.

3 Mammeri, *La Colline oubliée*, 92.

4 Cited in Jack, *Francophone Literatures*, 170.

5 See Yeager, *Vietnamese Novel in French*, 78–81, 176–78.

6 Marc Quaghebeur, however, suggests that Poulet may have played a role in helping to have published several novels by the Brazilian writer Lucien Marchal in the 1950s. Marchal, born in 1893, was one of the dominant Brazilian novelists at the time. "Eléments," 267.

7 Poulet, Review of *La Mort*.

8 Poulet, Review of *L'Enfant noir*.

9 See Blair, *African Literature in French*, 17–18.

10 Poulet, Review of *Le Regard du roi*.

11 Poulet, *Mon ami Bardamu*, 35. After Céline's death in 1961, Poulet wrote a preface and edited the text of *Le Pont de Londres*, which was published by Gallimard in 1964. Three versions of the manuscript were found, dating perhaps from 1944. Poulet chose the best of the three, adding the conclusion from the first version.

12 Poulet, *Mon ami Bardamu*, 80, 140.

13 Céline, *Rigodon*, 1–2. I have left Céline's famous three dots in the text. My own elisions are marked by dots within brackets.

14 Poulet, "Robert Poulet," 21.

15 Hewitt to author, May 15, 1999.

CONCLUSION

1 From some of his later comments, I realized that Njami had been very disturbed that the Prix Renaudot was taken away from Ouologuem on the basis of plagiarism. He was not, however, adverse to suggesting possible ghostwriting for other recent African novelists.

Njami, who was born in Switzerland and has spent most of his life in France, wrote a novel, *Cercueil et cie*, based on the work of Chester Himes and Himes's life in Europe. He is interested in questions of the relationships among people from Africa and the African diaspora and the problems of black identity. He was obviously initially unhappy at disturbing the canon of African authors, although he volunteered his information.

2 Martial Sinda's publications include *André Matsoua: Fondateur du mouvement de libération du Congo* (Dakar: Nouvelles Editions Africaines, 1978); *Le Messianisme congolais et ses incidences politiques* (Paris: Payot, 1972); and *Simon Kimbangui: Prophète et martyr zaïrois* (Dakar: Nouvelles Editions Africaines, 1977).

3 Koné holds strong opinions about the French as colonizers, very different from those of Laye. He thinks the French are more egotistical, petty, and Negrophobic than other European colonizers.

4 Laye, "Et demain?" 294.

5 Soulié might also have known Dino Buzzati's *Le Désert des Tartares*, the novel published in France in 1949 that James Kirkup found similar to *Le Regard du roi*.

6 Morrison, "On 'The Radiance of the King.' "

BIBLIOGRAPHY

WORKS BY AND INTERVIEWS WITH CAMARA LAYE

PUBLISHED SOURCES

UNPUBLISHED SOURCES

Archival Collections

Selected Letters to the Author

Interviews Conducted by the Author

•

WORKS BY AND INTERVIEWS WITH CAMARA LAYE

"L'Ame de l'Afrique dans sa partie guinéenne." Paper presented at Colloque sur la littérature africaine d'expression française. Dakar, Senegal, 1963.

"L'Afrique et l'appel de profondeurs." Paper presented at Fourah Bay Conference, Sierra Leone, 1963.

"The Black Man and Art." *African Arts*, autumn 1970, 58–59.

"Et demain?" *Présence africaine*, nos. 14–15 (1957): 290–95.

Dramouss. *Paris: Plon, 1966; Paris: Presses Pocket, 1976. Translated as *A Dream of Africa*, trans. James Kirkup (London: Collins, 1970); American edition, with an introduction by Emile Snyder (New York: Macmillan-Collier, 1971).

L'Enfant noir. Paris: Plon, 1953; *Paris: Presses Pocket, 1976. Edited with notes in English by Joyce Hutchinson (Cambridge: Cambridge University Press, 1966); translated as *The African Child*, trans. James Kirkup (London: Collins, 1955); *The Dark Child*, *American edition, with an introduction by Philippe Thoby-Marcelin (New York: Farrar, Straus and Giroux, 1955).

Le Maître de la parole. *Paris: Plon, 1976; paperback edition, Paris: Plon, 1980. Translated as *The Guardian of the Word*, trans. James Kirkup (London: Fontana/Collins, 1980).

"Prélude et fin d'un cauchemar." *Fraternité-Matin* (Abidjan, Côte d'Ivoire), December 17, 1976.

"Premiers contacts avec Paris." *Bingo* (Dakar, Senegal), no. 14 (1954): 21–22.

"Le Prince." *La Table ronde*, no. 74 (February 1954): 72–87.

Le Regard du roi. Paris: Plon, 1954; *Paris: Presses Pocket, 1975. Translated as *The Radiance of the King*, trans. James Kirkup (London: Collins, 1956); (*London: Fontana, 1965); American edition, with an introduction by Albert Gérard (New York: Macmillan-Collier, 1971); new edition, with an introduction by Toni Morrison (New York: New York Review of Books, 2001).

"Le Rêve dans la société traditionnelle malinké." Paper presented at the Conference on Manding Studies, School of Oriental and African Studies, University of London, 1972. Cyclostyled papers are available in the library of the University of California, Los Angeles.

"Tradition orale: Répondre à l'appel des profondeurs." *Fraternité-Matin* (Abidjan, Côte d'Ivoire), March 12, 1976.

"Les Yeux de la statue." *Présence africaine*, no. 13 (1957): 102–10. Translated as "The Eyes of the Statue," trans. Una Maclean, *Black Orpheus*, no. 5 (1959): 19–27; republished in *More Modern African Stories*, ed. Charles Larson (London: Fontana-Collins, 1975).

"Camara Laye, l'écrivain est obligé de se taire ou de tordre sa plume." Interview by Gaoussou Kamissoko. *Fraternité-Matin* (Abidjan, Côte d'Ivoire), April 6, 1976.

"Camara Laye nous parle de son voyage en Guinée et de ses projets." *Paris-Dakar*, February 6, 1954, 2.

"'Dramouss,' c'est l'aventure intellectuelle d'un Malinké porté vers le surréalisme." *Fraternité-Matin* (Abidjan, Côte d'Ivoire), September 22, 1966, 7.

"Entretien avec Camara Laye." Interview by Irmelin Hossman. *Afrique*, no. 26 (July 1963): 54–57.

"Gros Plan sur la cora." *Eburnea* (Abidjan, Côte d'Ivoire), no. 67 (January 1973): 36–37, 48.

"Interview avec Camara Laye." By Jacqueline Leiner. *Présence francophone*, no. 10 (spring 1975): 153–67.

Interview by Guy-Roger N'Da for Télévision Ivoirienne. September 27, 1972. Published in *Fraternité-Matin* (Abidjan, Côte d'Ivoire), October 3 and October 10, 1972.

Interview by Jacqueline Sorel. "Camara Laye." In the series *Archives sonores de la littérature noire*. ARCL, Radio France International, 1977.

"Laye: Commitment to timeless values." Interview by J. Steven Rubin. *Africa Report* 17, no. 5 (May 1972): 20–24.

PUBLISHED SOURCES

Alter, Robert. "Arbeit Macht Fraud." Review of *The Wilkomirski Affair: A Study in Biographical Truth*, by Stefan Maechler. *New Republic*, April 30, 2001, 35–38.

Aron, Paul, Dirk De Geest, Pierre Halen, and Antoon Vanden Braembussche. *Leurs occupations: L'Impact de la Seconde Guerre mondiale sur la littérature en Belgique.* Actes de la section "Littérature" du colloque Société, culture et mentalités. L'Impact de la Seconde Guerre mondiale en Belgique, Brussels, October 1995. Brussels: Textyles Editions, 1997.

Aron, Paul, and Pierre-Yves Soucy. *Les Revues littéraires belges de langue française de 1830 à nos jours.* Édition augmentée. Brussels: Labor, 1998.

Assouline, Pierre. *L'Épuration des intellectuels.* Brussels: Editions Complexe, 1990.

———. *Hergé.* Paris: Plon, 1996.

Aubenas, Florence. "1942: Les Réticences illusoires de l'administration belge." *Libération*, December 10, 1997, 14–15.

Autra, Mamadou Traoré Ray. "Principales Étapes de la vie de Camara Laye." *Notes africaines*, no. 175 (July 1982): 57–58.

Azodo, Ada Uzoamaka. *L'Imaginaire dans les romans de Camara Laye.* New York: Peter Lang, 1993.

Becker, Jean-Jacques. *Histoire politique de la France depuis 1945.* Paris: Armand Colin, 1994.

Bernard, Paul R. "Camara Laye: A Bio-bibliography." *Africana Journal* 9, no. 4 (1978): 307–21.

Bertrand, Brenda. "Gender and Spirituality: Initiation into the Korè in Camara Laye's *Le Regard du roi*." *French Review* 67, no.4 (March 1994): 648–61.

Beti, Mongo (Alexandre Biyidi). "L'Affaire Calixthe Beyala, ou comment sortir du néo-colonialisme en littérature." *Palabres* 1, nos. 3 & 4 (1997): 39–48.

———. "Afrique noire, littérature rose." *Présence africaine* 1, no.5 (1955): 133–40.

———. Review of *L'Enfant Noir*. Special issue, "Trois Ecrivains noirs." *Présence africaine*, no. 16 (1954): 419–20.

———. Review of *Le Regard du roi*. *Présence africaine*, 1–2 (1955): 143–45.

Blair, Dorothy. *African Literature in French.* Cambridge: Cambridge University Press, 1976.

Bottin Administratif, 1948–53.

Burke, Séan. *The Death and Return of the Author.* Edinburgh: Edinburgh University Press, 1992.

Céline, Louis-Ferdinand. *Rigodon.* Paris: Gallimard, 1969; Paris: Folio, 1996.

———. *Voyage au bout de la nuit.* Paris: Gallimard, 1952.

Chapsal, Jacques. *La Vie politique en France de 1940 à 1958.* Paris: Presses Universitaires de France, 1984.

Chemain, Roger. *L'Imaginaire dans le roman africain.* Paris: Harmattan, 1986.

Chemain, Roger, and Arlette Chemain. "Pour une lecture politique de 'Le regard du roi' de Camara Laye." *Présence africaine* 131 (1984): 155–68.

Chevallier, Laurent. *L'Enfant noir.* Un film adapté du roman de Camara Laye. Paris: Rhéa Productions; Guinea: OONACIG; France: Films du Paradoxe, 1995.

Chevrier, Jacques. "La Vision de l'autre monde dans *L'Afrique fantôme* de Michel Leiris, ou l'impossible sacralité." In *Africa, America, Asia, Australia* (Rome), no. 19 (1997): 99–105.

Conway, Martin. *Collaboration in Belgium: Léon Degrelle and the Rexist Movement, 1940–1944.* New Haven: Yale University Press, 1993.

Cornevin, Marianne. *Histoire de l'Afrique contemporaine: De La Deuxième Guerre mondiale à nos jours.* Paris: Payot, 1972.

Dantoing, Alain. "Du Fascisme occidental à la politique de présence: Robert Poulet." In *1940: Belgique: Une Société en crise, un pays en guerre.* Actes du colloque à Bruxelles, du 22–26 octobre 1990. 337–43. Brussels: Centre de Recherches et d'Etudes Historiques de la Seconde Guerre Mondiale.

De Becker, Raymond. "La Collaboration en Belgique (1940–1944) ou une révolution avortée." (Manuscript attributed to De Becker.) *Courrier hebdomadaire du C. R. I.S. P.,* no. 497–98 (October 1970): 2–70.

Decraene, Philippe. "In Memoriam." *Présence africaine,* 114 (1980): 229–30.

Deduck, Patricia A. "Kafka's Influence on Camara Laye's *Le Regard du roi.*" *Studies in Twentieth-Century Literature* 4, no. 2 (1980): 239–55.

De Jonghe, Sylva. *Tempête sur la brousse: Roman nègre.* Translated from the Flemish by Jo Linten. Brussels: Editions du Carrefour, 1943.

Delcord, Bernard. "A propos de quelques 'chapelles' politico-littéraires en Belgique 1919–1945." *Cahier-Budragen,* no. 10 (November 1986): 183–205.

Dictionnaire Universel Francophone. Paris: Hachette, 1997.

Diop, Boubacar Boris. *Le Temps de Tamango.* Paris: Editions de l'Harmattan, 1981.

Dorsey, David. "Reply to William Lawson." *Research in African Literatures* 16, no. 3 (1985): 477–8.

———. Review of *The Western Scar,* by William Lawson. *Research in African Literatures* 15, no. 3 (1984): 436–38.

Duffy, Patricia D. "To Paris and Back: Seeking a Balance." *Research in African Literatures* 31, no. 1 (spring 2000): 12–31.

Faure, Christian. *Le Projet culturel de Vichy: Folklore et révolution nationale, 1940–1944.* Lyon: Presses Universitaires de Lyon, 1989.

Fincoeur, Michel B. "Le Monde de l'édition en Belgique durant la Seconde Guerre mondiale: L'Exemple des éditions de la Toison d'Or." In Aron et al., *Leurs occupations,* 21–60.

Fresco, Alain David. "Tradition and Modernity in the Fiction of Laye Camara." Ph.D. diss., Indiana University, May 1981.

Garnier, Christine. [Doéllé, pseud.] *Va-t'en avec les tiens.* Paris: Grasset, 1951.

Gates, Henry Louis, Jr. "'Authenticity' of the Lesson of Little Tree." *New York Times Book Review,* November 24, 1991, 1, 26–28.

Gauguin, Paul. *Noa Noa.* Trans. O. F. Theis. New York: Dover, 1985.

Gérard-Libois, Jules. *L'An 40: La Belgique occupée.* Brussels: Crisp, 1971.

Gide, André. *Voyage au Congo*. Paris: Gallimard, 1929. Translated as *Travels in the Congo*, trans. Dorothy Bussy. (Berkeley: University of California Press, 1962).

Godard, Henri, ed. *Céline: Préfaces et dédicaces*. Tusson, Charente: Du Lérot, 1987.

Gordon, Bertram M. *Collaborationism in France during the Second World War*. Ithaca, NY: Cornell University Press, 1980.

Gouzi, Nabila Berrada. "Les Mercenaires de la plume sortent du maquis." *Jeune Afrique* no. 1622 (February 6–12, 1992): 48–51.

Grillot, Alphonse, et d'autres. *Pierre Lefaucheux*. Paris: Imprimerie Georges Lang, 1955.

Halen, Pierre. Paper on Belgians writing as Africans, presented at the conference of Africanists, University of Cergy-Pontoise, France, May 10, 1995.

———. "Le Champ littéraire comme espace des conflits de l'identité coloniale." In Aron et al., *Leurs occupations*, 171–82.

Harrow, Kenneth. "A Sufi Interpretation of *Le Regard du roi*." *Research in African Literatures* 14, no. 2 (1983): 135–64.

Hellens, Franz. *Réalités fantastiques*. Paris: Gallimard, 1966. (Includes the original book, published in 1923.)

Hesse, Hermann. *Siddhartha*. Trans. Hilda Rosner. New York: Bantam Books, 1971.

———. *Steppenwolf*. Trans. Joseph Mileck. New York: Henry Holt, 1990.

Hewitt, Nicholas. *The Life of Céline*. Oxford: Blackwell, 1999.

———. *Literature and the Right in Post-war France*. Oxford: Berg, 1996.

Hollier, Denis. *Le Collège de sociologie*. Paris: Gallimard, 1979.

Hubin, Christian. "Les Débuts de Cassandre." Dissertation, Université Catholique de Louvain, 1980.

Huyse, Luc, and Steven Dhondt. *La Répression des collaborations 1942–1952: Un Passé toujours présent*. Brussels: Crisp, 1993.

Irele, Abiola. "Camara Laye: An Imagination Attuned to the Spiritual." *West Africa*, April 7, 1980, 617–18.

Jack, Belinda. *Francophone Literatures*. New York: Oxford University Press, 1996.

Jacobson, Howard. "Black Swan of Trespass: Great Hoaxes and the Perils of Authenticity." *Times Literary Supplement*, October 3, 1997, 14–15.

Jahn, Janheinz. *Muntu*. Trans. Marjorie Greene. New York: Grove, 1961.

Jules-Rosette, Bennetta. *Black Paris: The African Writers' Landscape*. Urbana: University of Illinois Press, 1998.

Julien, Eileen. *African Novels and the Question of Orality*. Bloomington: Indiana University Press, 1992.

———. "A Narrative Model for Camara Laye's *Le Regard du roi*." *French Review* 60, no. 4 (1982): 798–803.

Kaba, Lansiné. "The Cultural Revolution, Artistic Creativity, and Freedom of Expression in Guinea." *Journal of Modern African Studies* 14, no. 2 (1976): 201–18.

Kafka, Franz. *Le Procès*. Trans. Alexandre Vialette. Paris: Gallimard, 1933.

———. *Description d'un combat*. (Translation of "Aphorisms," by Clara Malraux and Rainer Dorland.) Paris: Maeght, 1946.

———. *Le Château*. Trans. Alexandre Vialette. Paris: Gallimard, 1947. English translation, *The Castle*, trans. Willa and Edwin Muir (New York: Alfred A. Knopf, 1968).

Kakou, Hyacinthe. "Camara Laye: Le Dur Appel du passé." *Ivoir Soir*, January 27, 1993.

Kane, Mohamadou. *Roman africain et traditions*. Dakar, Senegal: NEA, 1982.

Keita, Mohamed Salif. "Camara Laye 12 ans après." *L'Evénement de Guinée* no. 014 (janvier–février 1992): 22–23.

Keita, Mohamed Salif, ed. PPP (*Plume Papier Parole*) (Conakry, Guinea), no. 1 (April–May 1995): 1–3.

Kesteloot, Lilyan. *Anthologie négro-africaine*. Nouvelle édition. 1981; Vanves, France: EDICEF, 1992.

———. "Camara Laye ou le départ d'un ami." *Notes africaines*, no. 175 (July 1982): 58–59.

King, Adele. *The Writings of Camara Laye*. London: Heinemann, 1980.

Krzywicki, Janusz. *"Le Regard du roi," signé par Camara Laye: Possibilités d'interprétation*. Studies of the Department of African Languages and Cultures, no. 23. Warsaw: Warsaw University, Institute of Oriental Studies, Department of African Languages and Cultures, 1998.

———. "Les Symboles, les corrélations et les références dans *Le Regard du roi* de Camara Laye." Studies of the Department of African Languages and Cultures, no. 20. 5–40. Warsaw: Warsaw University, Institute of Oriental Studies, Department of African Languages and Cultures, 1996.

———. *Wielosc Kultur i tekst. Lektury "Spojrzenia krola" Camary Laye*. Warsaw: Instytut Orientalistyczny Uniwersytetu Warszawskiego, 1992. (Esp. appendix C, pp. 215–21, "Choix de citations dissimulées et de phrases transposées du *Regard du roi* dans *Le Maître de la parole* de Camara Laye.")

Kunze, Cornélie. "L'Européen déraciné et l'Afrique guérisseuse: Une Relecture du roman *Le Regard du roi* de Camara Laye." In *Littérature et maladie en Afrique*, Actes du Congrès de l'A. P. E. L. A., sous la direction de Jacqueline Bardolph, 75–93. Paris: L'Harmattan, 1994.

Lacour, José-André. *Panique en Occident*. 1943. Reprint, Tournai: Belgium, 1994.

Larson, Charles. *The Emergence of African Fiction*. Bloomington: Indiana University Press, 1972.

Launay, Jacques de, and Jacques Offergeld. *La Vie quotidienne des Belges sous l'occupation*. Brussels: Paul Legrain, 1982.

Lawson, William. Letter in reply to a review of *The Western Scar*. *Research in African Literatures* 16, no. 3 (1985): 476–77.

———. "The Radiance of Camara Laye." *Yardbird Reader* 4 (1975): 78–89.

———. *The Western Scar*. Athens: Ohio University Press, 1982.

Lee, Sonia. *Camara Laye*. Boston: Twayne, 1984.

Lefaucheux, Marie-Hélène. "Dans le domaine de l'enseignement le Maroc nous donne un bel exemple." *Femmes de l'Union Française*, no. 2 (January–February 1947).

———. "L'Évolution féminine aux Nations-Unies." *Femmes de l'Union Française*, no. 14 (September–October 1951): 1.

———. Foreword to *Women in a Changing World: The Dynamic Story of the International Council of Women since 1888*. London: Routledge & Kegan Paul, 1966.

———. "Impressions d'Indochine." *Femmes de l'Union Française*, nos. 16–17 (May–June 1952): 2–3.

Leiris, Michel. *L'Afrique fantôme*. 1934. Reprint, Paris: Gallimard, 1988.

Léopold, Christiane. Review of *L'Enfant noir*, by Camara Laye. *Les Femmes de l'Union Française*, no. 22 (February–March 1954): 7.

Lequeret, Elisabeth. "La Revue de presse de RFI." Press Review of Radio France Internationale. www.rfi.fr. October 21, 1998.

Luc, Marc. *La Belle Histoire de l'Union Française*. Paris: IMA, 1954[?].

Makward, Christiane. *Mayotte Capécia ou l'aliénation selon Fanon*. Paris: Karthala, 1999.

Mammeri, Mouloud. *La Colline oubliée*. 1952. Reprint, Paris: Gallimard, 1992.

Marceau, Félicien. *Les Années courtes*. Paris: Gallimard, 1968.

Marie-Hélène Lefaucheux: 26 février 1904–25 février 1964. Memorial pamphlet. Sponsored by Conseil National des Femmes Françaises. Paris: Cedias, 1964.

Martin, Pascal. "*Cassandre*, hebdomadaire belge de la vie politique, littéraire et artistique, 1937–1938." Dissertation, Université Catholique de Louvain, Belgium, 1986.

Mercier, Roger, Monique Battestini, and Simon Battestini, eds. *Camara Laye: Écrivain guinéen*. Littérature africaine, no. 2. Paris: Fernand Nathan, 1964.

Mitterrand, François. *Aux Frontières de l'Union Française*. Paris: Julliard, 1953.

Mongo Beti parle (interviews with Ambroise Kom). Bayreuth African Studies Series, no. 54. Bayreuth, Germany: Bayreuth African Studies, 2001.

Morrison, Toni. "On 'The Radiance of the King.'" *New York Review of Books*, August 9, 2001, 18–20.

Mouralis, Bernard. "Le Cri de Sarzan et le sommeil de Clarence." In *Littérature et maladie en Afrique*, Actes du Congrès de l'A. P. E. L. A., sous la direction de Jacqueline Bardolph, 337–48. Paris: L'Harmattan, 1994.

———. *L'Europe, l'Afrique et la folie*. Paris: Présence Africaine, 1993.

———. *République et colonies: Entre histoire et mémoire*. Paris: Présence Africaine, 1999.

Mudimbe, V. Y., ed. *The Surreptitious Speech: Présence Africaine and the Politics of Otherness, 1947–1987*. Chicago: University of Chicago Press, 1992.

Nabil, Jijakli Mohamed. "*Notre Terre wallonne*: Un Hebdomadaire wallon pendant la Seconde Guerre mondiale." Dissertation, Université Libre de Bruxelles, 1986–87.

Northcutt, Wayne. *Mitterrand: A Political Biography*. New York: Holmes & Meier, 1992.

Obafemi, Olu. *Forty Years in African Art and Life: Reflections on Ulli Beier*. Bayreuth, Germany: Iwalewa-Haus, University of Bayreuth, 1993.

Obumselu, Ben. "The French and Moslem Backgrounds of *The Radiance of the King*." *Research in African Literatures* 11, no. 1 (1980): 1–25.

Ogude, S. E. "Facts into Fiction: Equiano's Narrative Reconsidered." *Research in African Literatures* 13, no. 1 (1982): 31–42.

Pageard, Robert, *Littérature négro-africaine d'expression française* Paris: L'Ecole, 1979.

Postel-Vinay, André, *Un Fou s'évade: Souvenirs de 1941–42* Paris: Transfaire, 1996.

Poulet, Robert. *L'Ange et les dieux*. Brussels: La Toison d'Or, 1942.

———. "A propos des 'Anges Noirs': François Mauriac." *Cassandre* 3, no. 6 (February 8, 1936): 9.

———. *Aveux spontanés*. Paris: Plon, 1963.

———. "Avis au lecteur." *La Revue réactionnaire*, no. 1 (April 1933).

———. *La Caléidoscope: Trente-neuf portraits d'écrivains*. Lausanne: L'Age d'Homme, 1982.

———. *Ce n'est pas une vie*. Paris: Denoël, 1976.

———. *Le Coeur antipodique*. Paris: Editions de France, 1932.

———. "Les Conditions du roman et la question du 'roman poétique.'" *Nord* 2 (July 1929): 121–39.

———. *La Conjecture*. Paris: La Table Ronde, 1981.

———. *Contre l'amour, la jeunesse, la plèbe*. Paris: Denoël, 1971.

———. *Dis-moi qui te hante*. Paris: Nouvelles Editions Latines, 1977.

———. *L'Enfer-ciel: Journal d'un condamné à mort*. Paris: La Jeune Parque, 1948; Paris: Plon, 1952.

———. *La Fleur de l'imagination*. Brussels: Toison d'Or, 1944.

———. *Les Gazomètres*. Liege, Belgium: Vaillant-Carmanne, 1939.

———. *Handji*. Paris: Denoël, 1931; Paris: Plon, 1955.

———. *L'Histoire de l'être*. Paris: Denoël, 1973.

———. *L'Homme qui n'avait pas compris*. Brussels: Didier Hatier, 1988.

———. *La Hutte de cochenille*. Paris: Plon, 1953.

———. *J'accuse la bourgeoisie*. Paris: Copernic, 1978.

———. *La Lanterne magique*. Paris: Debresse, 1956.

———. *Le Livre de quelques-uns*. Paris: Plon, 1957.

———. *Maximilien*. Antwerp: Ça Ira, 1936.

———. *Le Meilleur et le pire*. Paris: Denoël, 1932.

———. *Mon ami Bardamu*. Paris: Plon, 1971.

———. *Nuptial*. Paris: Deux-Rives, 1956.

———. "Un Pas de plus vers la vérité." (On Henri Roques's thesis questioning the Holocaust) *Rivarol*, October 25, 1985.

———. *Prélude à l'apocalypse*. Paris: Denoël, 1934; Lausanne: L'Age d'Homme, 1981.

———. Review of *L'Enfant noir*, by Camara Laye. *Rivarol*, no. 147 (November 6–12, 1953): 4.

————. Review of *La Mort dans ce jardin*, by José André Lacour. *Rivarol*, no. 195 (October 7, 1954): 6.

————. Review of *Le Regard du roi*, by Camara Laye. *Rivarol*, no. 202 (November 25, 1954): 6.

————. *La Révolution est à droite*. Paris: Denoël, 1934.

————. "Robert Poulet: Romancier de l'invisible et moraliste sans illusion." Interview by Marc Laudelout. *Le Nouvel Europe--Magazine*, no. 143 (May 1982): 19–21.

————. *Les Sources de la vie*. Paris: Plon, 1967.

————. *Les Ténèbres*. Paris: Denoël, 1934; Paris: Plon, 1958.

————. *Le Trottoir*. Paris: Denoël, 1931.

———— [as Walter Orlando]. Review of *L'Enfant noir*, by Camara Laye. *Le Phare* (Brussels), September 20, 1953.

Quaghebeur, Marc. "Eléments pour une étude du champ littéraire belge francophone de l'après-guerre." In Aron et al., *Leurs occupations*, 235–70.

Rémi, Georges Hergé. *Tintin au Congo*. 1946. Reprint, Tournai, Belgium: Casterman, 1974.

Richecour, Jeanne-Françoise de. "Marie-Hélène Lefaucheux: Résistante et apôtre de la promotion féminine." *Lunes*, no. 6 (January 1999): 46–53.

Riesz, János. "L'Acculturation à rebours: Un Thème littéraire." *Diogène*, no. 135 (July–September 1986): 50–64.

————. " 'Audible Gasps from the Audience': Accusations of Plagiarism against Several African Authors and Their Historical Context." *Yearbook of Comparative and General Literature*, no. 43 (1995): 84–97. Published in French as "Accusations de plagiat contre plusieurs auteurs africains et contextes historiques," *Palabres* 1, nos. 3 & 4 (1997): 105–23.

Rioux, Jean-Pierre. *La France de la Quatrième République*. Vol. 2, *L'Expansion et l'impuissance 1952–1958*. Paris: Seuil, 1983.

Rubin, J. Steven. "Laye's Commitment to Timeless Values." *Africa Report* 17, no. 5 (May 1972): 20, 22, 24.

Sante, Luc. *The Factory of Facts*. London: Granta, 1998.

Sellin, Eric. "Alienation in the Novels of Camara Laye." *Pan-African Journal* 4, no. 4 (fall 1971): 455–72.

————. "Pretender to the Throne: Camara Laye's 'Le Prince.'" *Africana Journal* 15, no. 4 (1981): 333–37.

Senghor, Léopold S. "Laye Camara et Lamine Diakhaté, ou l'art n'est pas d'un parti" and "Laye Camara et Lamine Niang, ou l'art doit être incarné." In *Liberté I*, 155–58, 173–74. Paris: Seuil, 1964.

Simenon, Georges. *Le Coup de lune*. Paris: Fayard, 1933.

Siné, Frédérique. "L'Épuration des journalistes collaborateurs belges francophones après la Seconde Guerre mondiale." Dissertation, Université Libre de Bruxelles, 1995–96.

Skattum, Ingse. "De Bakoroba Kané à Camara Laye. La Répétition comme trait d'oralité dans la littérature mandingue traditionnelle et moderne." Thesis, University of Oslo, 1992.

Solus, Henry. "Biography of Marie-Hélène Lefaucheux." In *Académie des Sciences d'Outre-Mer 1975–76*, 448–54. 7 vols. Paris: Académie, 1975–86.

Songolo, Aliko. "Surrealism and Black Literatures in French." *French Review* 60, no. 6 (1982): 724–31.

Soulié, Francis. "'Anvers' and 'Adoration.'" *Sélection: Atelier d'art contemporain* 3 (1923–24): 383–84.

———. "Caligula." *Nord* 3 (1930): 215–47.

———. "Cécile ou l'aventure en chemin de fer." *Sélection: Atelier d'art contemporain* 3, no. 1 (November 1923): 70–73.

———. "Contre André Breton." *Sélection: Atelier d'art contemporain* 4, no. 1 (October 1924): 369–81.

———. "Ebauche d'un Charlot." *Sélection: Atelier d'art contemporain* 3, no. 6 (April 1924): 113–30.

———. "Max Jacob, Poète." *Créer*, no. 2 (1922): 41–45.

———. "Poèmes: 'Foire' and 'Raspoutine.'" *Sélection: Atelier d'art contemporain* 3, no. 6 (April 1924): 492–94.

———. "Le Roman." *Sélection: Atelier d'art contemporain* 6, no. 1 (October 1926): 491–507.

———. "Sous le signe de la jeunesse." *Nord* 2 (July 1929): 140–51.

Soyinka, Wole. *Myth, Literature and the African World.* Cambridge: Cambridge University Press, 1976.

Stavans, Ilan. Review of *Rigoberta Menchú and the Story of All Poor Guatemalans*, by David Stoll. *Times Literary Supplement*, April 23, 1999, 10.

Thys, Pierre. "La Collaboration intellectuelle en Belgique francophone pendant la Seconde Guerre mondiale: Le Cas de Radio-Bruxelles." Dissertation, Université Libre de Bruxelles, 1993–94.

Ungar, Steven. "Blinded by the Light: Surreal and Sacred in Camara Laye's *Le Regard du roi.*" *Dada/Surrealism* 13 (1984): 123–28.

Wauthier, Claude. *Afrique des Africains.* Paris: Seuil, 1964; *second edition, Paris: Seul, 1973.

———. *The Literature and Thought of Modern Africa.* Second English-language edition. Washington DC: Three Continents Press, 1979.

———. *Quatre présidents et l'Afrique.* Paris: Seuil, 1995.

Willequet, Jacques. *La Belgique sous la botte: Résistances et collaborations 1940–1945.* Paris: Editions Universitaires, 1986.

Wright, Gordon. *The Reshaping of French Democracy.* New York: Reynal & Hitchcock, 1948.

Yeager, Jack A. *The Vietnamese Novel in French*. Hanover NH: University Press of New England, 1987.

Zahan, Dominique. *Sociétés d'initiation Bambara*. Paris: Mouton & Co., 1960.

UNPUBLISHED SOURCES

Archival Collections

Archives de la France d'Outre-Mer, Aix-en-Provence, France. Documents copied by archives staff from Edouard Joncourt, files EEII 6688, EEII 5429.

Archives de la Préfecture de Police de Paris, Paris. Documents copied by archives staff from Francis Soulié and Robert Poulet files.

Archives de l'Institut National de l'Audio-visuel, Maison de la Radio, Paris.
   Camara Laye files and tapes. (Consulted in 1978.)
   Radio broadcasts:
      "Le goût de livres: Comment j'ai fait *L'Enfant noir*." Radio France, LO 2102, 1954.
      Camara Laye. Interviewed by Yves le Gall. Radio France Internationale, EC 22, n.d. (1954?).
      Camara Laye. Interview. Radio France Internationale, EC 1917, September 6, 1966.
      "Un texte sur la sculpture africaine, lu par l'auteur." Radio France, LO 6464, November 8, 1954.

Archives du Ministère des Affaires Etrangères, Paris. Documents copied by archives staff from Edouard Joncourt files.

Archives Nationales du Ministère de la Coopération, Paris. Files for Guinea and Dahomey. DOM/TOM/62.

L'Auditorat Général près la Cour Militaire, Brussels.
   Joseph Jumeau (Pierre Hubermont) files.
   La Légia, files on condemnations of staff.
   Francis Soulié files.
   René Tonus files.

Bibliothèque Administrative de la Ville de Paris, Paris.
   Archives de l'Assemblée de l'Union Française, 1949–55. Marie-Hélène Lefaucheux files.
   Archives de l'Assemblée Nationale Constituante. Marie-Hélène Lefaucheux files.
   Archives Départementales de Paris. Marie-Hélène Lefaucheux files.

Bibliothèque Nationale, Paris. Archives de l'Academie d'Outre-Mer. Marie-Hélène Lefaucheux files.

Bibliothèque Royale, Brussels.
   Créer, 1922–23.
   Le Disque vert, 1925.
   Nord, 1929–30.
   La Revue réactionnaire, 1933.

Sélection: Atelier d'art contemporain, 1920–33.

Centre de Recherche et d'Études Historiques de la Seconde Guerre Mondiale, Brussels.

    Cassandre, December 1, 1934–July 18, 1936.

    Pierre Hubermont files, W3 70–72.

    Robert Poulet files, PP9 and PV57.

Conseil National des Femmes Françaises, Paris.

    Femmes de l'Union Française, December 1946–March 1954

    Marie-Hélène Lefaucheux files.

Hoover Institution Archives, Stanford University, Stanford, California. Documents copied by archives staff from newspaper files, *Terre wallonne* and *La Légia*, regarding Francis Soulié.

Musée de la Littérature, Bibliothèque Royale, Brussels.

    Gille Anthelme files (pseudonym of Soulié).

    Melot du Dy files.

    Robert Poulet files.

Plon offices, Paris. Camara Laye files. (Consulted in 1978.)

Selected Letters to the Author

Amigues, Louis, Archives du Ministère des Affaires Etrangères, Paris. June 16, 1999.

Assouline, Pierre. January 16, 1997.

Barish, Evelyn. November 11, 1993.

Battestini, Simon. December 1, 1991.

Beier, Ulli. August 30, 1997.

Beti, Mongo. January 4, 1998.

Blair, Dorothy. November 20, 1991.

Blancard, Anne. January 13, 1993.

Bourgeacq, Jacques. January 8, 1992.

Bouteiller, Françoise, Conseil National des Femmes Françaises, Paris. January 28, 1999.

Camara, Cheick Oumar. March 15, 1996.

Camara, Sory. March 13, 1978.

Castaing, Denis, Caisse Française de Développement. July 24, 1995.

Conway, Martin. February 18, 1994; October 11, 28, 1995; August 18, 1997.

Dehon, Claire. October 21, 1991.

Delaunois, Jean-Marc. September, 14, November 25, 1995.

Delcord, Bernard. December 14, 1995.

De Vidts, L., Auditorat Général près la Cour Militaire, Brussels. July 3, 1999.

Dingomé, Jeanne. July 24, October 17, 1995.

Dorsey, David. August 12, 1992.

Duffy, Patricia. August 11, 1988; January 28, April 2, 1992.

Durand-Evrard, F., Archives d'Outre-Mer, Aix-en-Provence. July 2, 1999.

Echeruo, Michael. December 20, 1991.

Gérard, Albert. November 17, 1991.

Halen, Pierre. May 29, 1995; August 25, 1997.

Hewitt, Nicholas. May 15, 1999.

Keita, Mohamed Salif. November 3, 1995.

Kesteloot, Lilyan. February 22, 1992; December 13, 1995; February 15, 1996.

Kirkup, James. December 30, 1991; August 18, 1997.

Klee, Hans Dieter, Deutsche Welle, Cologne, Germany. August 20, 1992.

Kom, Ambroise. March 7, 1996.

Kunze, Cornelie. January 3, 1992.

Larson, Charles. December 15, 1991.

Lavinal, F., Peugeot, Poissy, France. September 22, 1997.

Laye, Camara. January 18, February 15, September 17, 1978; April 1, 1979.

Lee, Sonia. January 19, 1992.

Moore, Gerald. February 16, 1992.

Mouralis, Bernard. March 3, 1992.

Neal, Michael. July 18, 1995.

Nourrit, Chantal. June 11, 1997.

Palmer, Eustace. February 11, 1992.

Pidoux-Payot, Jean-Luc. June 24, 1991.

Postel-Vinay, André. December 3, 1995.

Préfecture de Police, Paris. August 28 and 31, 1995; October 31, 1995.

Rabut, Elisabeth, Archives d'Outre-Mer, Aix-en-Provence. July 24, 1995.

Ricard, Alain. February 15, 1992.

Richard, René. March 11, 1993.

Sabatier, Robert. February 4, 1995.

Sellin, Eric. September 27, 1991.

Skattum, Ingse. July 10, 1992.

Soyinka, Wole. December 18, 1991.

Städtler, Katharina. February 9, 1998.

Stengers, Jean. June 3, 1998.

Tournier, Jacques. November 19, 1995.

Van Boelaere, Fernand Toussaint (Poulet's stepson). October 23, 1997.

Wake, Clive. December 13, 1991.

Wauthier, Claude. January 24, 1992.

Interviews Conducted by the Author

Beti, Mongo. Telephone interview, January 3, 1998.

Bouteiller, Françoise. July 9, 1999.

Brière, Eloïse. April 1999.

Buat, Nicolas. June 10, 1999.

Camara, Aïcha. July 1993.

Camara, Mady. Telephone interview, July 1995.

Carducci, Reine. June 16, 1997.

Chevrier, Jacques. August 4, 1992; June 27, 1997.

Colardelle, Marcelle. Telephone interview, June 26, 1997.

Conway, Martin. March 29, May 10, May 18, 1999.

Delaunois, Jean-Jacques. Telephone interviews, July 4, December 10, 1997.

Diallo, Tierno. April 20, 1978.

Dupré, Guy. July 6, 1998.

Elsen, Liliane. July 10, 1997.

Galic, Camille. June 19, 1997.

Joachim, Paulin. July 12, 1997.

Kaba, Lansiné. Telephone interview, September 25, 1997.

Kaké, Ibrahima. August 8 1992; telephone interview, August 11, 1992.

Kamara, Lamine. July 18, 1995.

Kesteloot, Lilyan. July 10, 1992.

Koné, Vanfing Nfaff Doré. June 25, 2001; telephone interviews, June 18, June 21, 2001.

Kouyaté, Malon Keita. Telephone interviews, July 31, 1995; June 28, December 2, 1997.

Kwahulé, Koffi. May 8, 2001.

Lacour, José-André. July 3, 1997.

Lalande, Fanny. July 16, 1992.

Laudelout, Marc. Telephone interview, July 1, 1997.

Laye, Camara. May 30; June 4, 11, 1978; telephone interviews, June 13, 17, and 22, 1978.

Leiner, Jacqueline. July 23, 1992.

Lewis, David. Telephone interview, August 14, 1997.

Lopes, Henri. July 12, 1995.

Lorifo, Marie. Telephone interview, July 19, 1993.

Marceau, Félicien. Telephone interview, June 3, 1999.

Monceau, Comte Ivan. Telephone interview, July 4, 1997 .

N'Djehoya, Blaise. November 2, 1994.

Neal, Michael. July 10, 1995.

Njami, Simon. December 20, 1994; April 3, July 11, 1995, telephone interviews, August 1,
    August 5, 1995; June 6, 1997; June 16, 1998; June 19, July 9, 1999.

Person, Yves. June 21, 1978.

Postel-Vinay, André. July 24, 1992; July 13, 1995; July 1, 1997.

Postel-Vinay, André and Anise. June 19, 1978.

Pryen, Denis. June 2, 1997.

Silvain, Pierre. June 22, 1998.

Sinda, Thierry. Telephone interviews, June 18 and 21, 2001.

Sorel, Jacqueline. May 8, 1978; telephone interviews, July 28, 1992; June 23 and 29, 1997.

Tchak, Sami. May 3, 2001.

Trevarthen, Anne, maître de conférence, University of Paris VII. June 29, 1997.

Vandrome, Pol. Telephone interview, July 4, 1997.

Wauthier, Claude. August 11, 1992; telephone interviews, July 9, August 7, 1997.

INDEX